THE EMOTIONALLY DISTURBED CHILD

A Book of Readings

Second Printing

The Emotionally Disturbed Child

A Book of Readings

Compiled and Edited by

LARRY A. FAAS

Associate Professor of Special Education
Arizona State University
Tempe, Arizona

CHARLES C THOMAS • PUBLISHER
Springfield • Illinois • U.S.A.

Published and Distributed Throughout the World by

CHARLES C THOMAS • PUBLISHER

Bannerstone House

301-327 East Lawrence Avenue, Springfield, Illinois, U.S.A.

First Printing, 1970
Second Printing, 1975

With THOMAS BOOKS *careful attention is given to all details of
manufacturing and design. It is the Publisher's desire to present books that are
satisfactory as to their physical qualities and artistic possibilities and
appropriate for their particular use.* THOMAS BOOKS *will be true to those
laws of quality that assure a good name and good will.*

Printed in the United States of America

R

Contributors

WALTER B. BARBE
Editor, Highlights for Children
Honesdale, Pennsylvania

WESLEY C. BECKER
Professor of Psychology
University of Illinois
Urbana, Illinois

GASTON F. BLOM
Director, Day Care Center
Professor of Psychiatry and Education
University of Colorado Medical Center
Denver, Colorado

ELI M. BOWER
Professor of Education
University of California
Berkeley, California

L. K. BRENDTRO
President, Starr Commonwealth for
Boys
Albion, Michigan

PAUL BRUCE
Chairman, Department of Counselor
Education
San Diego State College
San Diego, California

TED CHRISTIANSEN
Chairman, Department of Special
Education Services
Madison College
Harrisonburg, Virginia

NAOMI COHEN
Assistant Professor of Education
Arizona State University
Tempe, Arizona

SHIRLEY COHEN
Education Department
Brooklyn College
Brooklyn, New York

EILEEN M. CONNOR
Program Director
United Cerebral Palsy Association
Pittsburgh, Pennsylvania

GEORGE T. DONAHUE
Manager, Washington Office
E. F. Shelley and Company, Inc.
Washington, D.C.

VENITA DYER
Special Education Teacher
Scottsdale High School
Scottsdale, Arizona

LOUISE S. EMERY
Director, The Forum School
Ridgewood, New Jersey

LARRY A. FAAS
Assistant Professor of Education
Arizona State University
Tempe, Arizona

CHRISTOPHER FAEGRE
Assistant Program Director
American Institutes for Research
Silver Spring, Maryland

RALPH A. GARCEA
Guidance Services Associate
Syracuse City School District
Syracuse, New York

STEPHEN E. GOLDSTON
Special Assistant to the Director
National Institute of Mental Health

NORRIS G. HARING
Director, Experimental Education Unit
Child Development and Mental
Retardation Center
University of Washington
Seattle, Washington

LOUIS HAY
Assistant Director, Junior Guidance
Classes Program
Board of Education—City of New York
Brooklyn, New York

FRANK M. HEWETT
Associate Professor of Education and
Psychiatry
University of California at Los Angeles
Los Angeles, California

WILLIAM G. HOLLISTER
Director, Community Psychiatry
University of North Carolina Medical
School
Chapel Hill, North Carolina

STANLEY JACOBSON
Educational Specialist, Child Research
Branch
National Institutes of Health
Bethesda, Maryland

ORVAL G. JOHNSON
Chairman, Special Education
Department
Southern Illinois University
Edwardsville, Illinois

LEO KANNER
Professor of Child Psychiatry
Johns Hopkins University
Baltimore, Maryland

PETER KNOBLOCK
Associate Professor of Special Education
Division of Special Education and
Rehabilitation
Syracuse University
Syracuse, New York

LEVI LATHEN
Education Specialist, Elgin Public
Schools and Psychology Instructor,
Elgin Community College
Elgin, Illinois

BEATRICE LEVISON
Remedial Therapist
Northside Center for Child
Development
New York City, New York

WAYNE R. MAES
Associate Professor of Education
Arizona State University
Tempe, Arizona

GARRY L. MARTIN
Assistant Professor of Psychology
St. Pauls College
University of Manitoba
Winnepeg, Canada

GORDON MCCLURE
School Counselor
Ottawa Public School Board
Ottawa, Ontario, Canada

MARJORIE MCQUEEN
Research Social Worker
Childrens Research Center
University of Illinois
Urbana, Illinois

WILLIAM C. MORSE
Professor of Education and Psychology
University of Michigan
Ann Arbor, Michigan

JOHN F. MULDOON
Executive Director, Craig House—
Technoma Workshop
Pittsburgh, Pennsylvania

RUTH G. NEWMAN
Director, Institute of Educational
Services
Washington School of Psychiatry
Washington, D.C.

DANIEL K. O'LEARY
Assistant Professor of Psychology
State University of New York
Stony Brook, New York

JUNE B. PIMM
Consulting Psychologist
Pimm Consultants Limited
Ottawa, Ontario, Canada

RICHARD B. POWERS
Assistant Professor of Psychology
Eastern Washington State College
Cheney, Washington

HERBERT C. QUAY
Chairman, Division of Educational
Psychology
Temple University
Philadelphia, Pennsylvania

VICTOR A. REING
Coordinator of Special Education
Board of Education
New Rochelle, New York

MARVIN I. SHAPIRO
Clinical Associate Professor, Child
Psychiatry
University of Pittsburgh Medical
School
Pittsburgh, Pennsylvania

ROBERT L. SPRAGUE
Research Psychologist
Childrens Research Center
University of Illinois
Urbana, Illinois

PHYLLIS R. STERN
Psychology Instructor
Centennial High School
Champaign, Illinois

JOHN S. WERRY
Director, Institute for Juvenile Research
Chicago, Illinois

RICHARD WHEELAN
Chairman, Department of Special
Education and Associate Professor of
Education and Pediatrics
University of Kansas Medical Center,
Kansas City, Kansas and University of
Kansas, Lawrence, Kansas

MARY ALICE WHITE
Professor of Psychology and Education
Teachers College, Columbia University
New York, New York

BEATRICE A. WRIGHT
Professor of Psychology
University of Kansas
Lawrence, Kansas

Preface

The rapid growth of today's universities and their programs for the preparation of teachers of disturbed children has made assigned library readings impractical if not totally impossible on many campuses. When the large number of students enrolled in a preparation program all attempt to gain access to a single reading, the futility of their efforts becomes obvious. These class assignments often tie up large amounts of significant literature making it difficult for individual students who wish to conduct research.

The readings in this book are selected to provide the reader with an overview of educational services provided for school children who are emotionally disturbed. This book will be useful to the university student preparing to teach the disturbed child, to the school administrator, school psychologist, school social worker, elementary school counselor, and the teacher of disturbed children.

General considerations discussed in Sections A, B, and C include a review of man's approach to defining emotional disturbance, the identification of children with emotional problems, and the dynamics of disturbance.

Sections D, E, and F focus upon curricular and facility adaptations involved in the creation of a therapeutic program for disturbed children in an educational setting. Included is a survey of several experimental projects and techniques which are being suggested for use with disturbed students.

The book's concluding sections concentrate upon management and discipline, behavior modification, the teacher of the disturbed child, and prevention of emotional disturbance. Following these sections is a bibliography listing some of the many other fine articles and books dealing with the emotionally disturbed child.

I would like to extend my thanks to the authors, editors, and publishers who granted permission to reprint their work in this volume. I am especially appreciative of the efforts of Gloria Esquerria, Kathy France, Irma Letson, and Alma Vega, who assisted me in the preparation of the final manuscript. Particular gratitude is expressed to my wife Patricia, for her critical evaluation and assistance.

Tempe, Arizona   L.A.F.

Contents

SECTION A
Introduction and History

SECTION B
Identification

SECTION C

SECTION D

Curricular and Facility Adaptations

SECTION E

Experimental Projects and Approaches

SECTION G
Management and Discipline

SECTION H
Behavior Modification

SECTION I
Teachers of Disturbed Children

SECTION J
Prevention

THE EMOTIONALLY DISTURBED CHILD

A Book of Readings

SECTION A

INTRODUCTION AND HISTORY

Chapter 1

Introduction To The Education Of Disturbed Children

LARRY A. FAAS

Services and educational programs for disturbed children in the schools have greatly increased in the last ten years. Prior to that time, the only social work, counseling, and psychological services available in most communities were obtained through non-school child guidance or social service agencies. Until recently most existing educational programs for disturbed children were located in large city schools and mental hospitals. Much of the growth currently being observed can be attributed to changes in training programs, psychological theory, and public receptivity of mental health programs.

Before World War II most training programs for mental health personnel focused upon the problems of children. Following the war the emphasis of many training programs shifted from children to adults, due to financial support of training programs provided by the Veterans Administration (Kirk, 1969). In the last ten years PL 85-926 and the National Defense Education Act have been instrumental in reversing this trend through support of training programs for school counselors and teachers of disturbed children.

Until a few years ago psychoanalytic theory was the dominant force in psychotherapy. Accompanying this domination were strict restrictions regarding who could perform therapy and where it could occur. The analytic therapist's tendency to focus upon a student's past experiences in search of solutions to his present problems has often included exploration of taboo areas regarded by school administrators as too volatile to be safely included in school services. As a result school administrators

5

traditionally have been reluctant to support the establishment
of school programs for disturbed children. Instead the schools
have followed the practice of referring problem children to non-
school agencies. This shifting of responsibility has often resulted
in the school's loss of contact with the child's therapist and a
failure to involve the student's teacher in the therapeutic process.

The resurgence of behaviorism and the emergence of humanistic psychology as major forces in psychology (Bruce, 1966) has
opened the door for development of special programs for disturbed children in the schools. The behaviorist's emphasis upon
using current behavior as a baseline from which future behavior
might develop through the process of systematic modification,
and the humanistic psychologist's emphasis upon what the person may become (Maslow, 1943) are currently having a profound effect on psychodiagnosis, psychotherapy, and education.
This new emphasis upon *what the person may become* is contributing much to the school's entry into the therapeutic community.

Accompanying these changes in attitude and philosophy have
been changes in the role of the psychologist, social worker, and
counselor who, until recently, seldom entered the schools or
attempted to communicate with teachers of disturbed students.
Today we find an increasing number of mental health team
members on school payrolls where they are working closely with
the teachers in a consultive role. This has increased the effectiveness by enabling them to serve the increasing numbers of disturbed students.

Despite these trends there remain many problems of attitude
and philosophy which must be dealt with in providing therapeutic services for the school child. Among these problems are
the series of questions associated with defining disturbance, its
incidence, identifying the disturbed child, and determination of
appropriate teaching and therapeutic techniques.

The term "emotional disturbance" is defined in many ways
and is used somewhat loosely by both professionals and members
of the lay public. Various terms such as maladjusted, deviant,
delinquent, and behavior disorder appear frequently in the lit-

erature. The reader often faces the problem of deciding whether two authors who use the same term are describing the same type and severity of behavior problem. Cohen, in her 1968 study of terminology, substantiated Kirk's suggestion (1962) that the way a behavioral situation is described is largely a function of the observer's orientation. Kirk suggested that while a boy's parents might regard their son as being a "bad boy," his teacher would regard him as "incorrigible," and a social worker might call him "socially maladjusted." At the same time the psychologist would refer to the boy as "emotionally disturbed" while a judge would refer to him as "delinquent."

Traditionally, emotional disturbance has been regarded in terms of labels denoting types of psychopathology. This procedure, although useful in communication between certain homogeneous groups of diagnosticians, has been of limited use to the educators who, as Frierson and Barbe described in 1967, are much more concerned with effect than cause. This concern among educators about what to do with the disturbed student has prompted the development of educationally-oriented definitions which stress the effect of the student's behavior upon his own achievement and adjustment as well as upon the lives of his classmates.

Attempts to determine the incidence of emotional disturbance according to Barlow (1966) have been greatly complicated by the lack of a commonly accepted definition. As a result incidence figures vary according to the definition and identification criteria employed. Glavin and Quay suggested in 1969 that greater significance should be attached to patterns of maladjustment than to studies of the incidence of emotional disturbance.

Earlier findings which suggested that twice as many boys as girls are identified as emotionally disturbed were supported by McCaffrey and Cumming's 1967 study. Their findings indicate that 78 percent of the boys and 66 percent of the girls identified as being emotionally disturbed also had learning problems. This strongly suggests that in many cases observed behavior problems may be secondary to other basic problems.

The articles in the following sections have been selected because of their application to the various accepted and suggested procedures for identifying, understanding, and working with disturbed children.

References

Barlow, Bruce: The emotionally and socially handicapped. *Rev Educ Res, 36:* 120-133, 1966.

Bruce, Paul: Three forces in psychology and their ethical and educational implications. *Educ Forum, 30:* 277-285, 1966.

Cohen, Naomi W.: *Emotionally Disturbed: A Terminological Inquiry.* Unpublished Doctoral Dissertation. Tempe, Ariz. State Univ., 1968.

Frierson, Edward C., and Barbe, Walter B.: *Educating Children With Learning Disabilities.* New York, Appleton, 1967.

Glavin, John P., and Quay, Herbert C.: Behavior disorders. *Rev Educ Res, 39:* 83-102, 1969.

Kirk, Samuel A.: *Educating Exceptional Children.* Boston, Houghton, 1962.

Kirk, Samuel A.: What is unique about the doctorate in special education? In *Doctoral Preparation in the Field of Special Education,* Gene Hensley and Dorothy Buck, Ed., Boulder, Colorado, Western Interstate Commission for Higher Education, 1969, pp. 1-8.

Maslow, Abraham H.: A theory of human motivation. *Psychol Rev, 50:* 370-396, 1943.

McCaffrey, Isabel, and Cumming, John: *Behavior Patterns Associated with Persistent Emotional Disturbances of School Children in Regular Classes of Elementary Grades.* Onondaga County: Mental Health Research Unit, N. Y. State Depart. of Mental Hygiene, 1967, 23 pp.

Chapter 2

Emotionally Disturbed Children: A Historical Review

LEO KANNER

IT IS CUSTOMARY to begin a historical account with the search for the earliest observations, ideas, and practices pertaining to the topic under consideration. Ancient and medieval sources are consulted; discovered references are interpreted in the light of the overall culture of the times and locale; eventually, an evolutionary pattern emerges which links the gradual steps from primitive origins to the facts and theories available when the quest is undertaken.

Similar efforts concerned with emotional disorders of children lead to the amazing disclosure of the total absence of an illusion, however casual, before the eighteenth century. Folklore, which seizes upon every conceivable aspect of human life, is peculiarly silent. Theologic, medical, and fictional writings have nothing to say. This does not warrant the assumption that infantile emotions always ran a smooth course in the past and that the occurrence of their disturbances is a relatively recent phenomenon. The truth is that, aside from occasional pious pleas for nondescript philanthropy, our ancestral lawgivers, physicians, and philosophers seem to have been indifferent toward the afflicted among many categories of the young and, for that matter, of the grown-ups as well. It was not until the decades immediately

Presented in a symposium, "Research on Emotionally Disturbed Children," at the biennial meeting of the Society for Research in Child Development, Pennsylvania State University, March 1961. Reprinted from *Child Development*, Vol. 32 (1962), pp. 97-102. By permission of the author and publisher. Published by Child Development Publications of the Society for Research in Child Development.

before and after the French and American revolutions that the new doctrine of the rights of the individual engendered an unprecedented spurt of humanitarian reforms. Vigorous spokesmen arose for the active alleviation of the plight of the slaves, the prison inmates, the insane, the blind, the deaf, and the mental defectives. For the first time, handicapped children were seen and heard. Young enthusiasts, mostly men in their twenties, undeterred by the skepticism of their renowned mentors, began to experiment with remedial and educational methods.

There was still no comprehension of the kind of children's difficulties which manifested themselves in disorganized feeling, thinking, and acting. Here and there sporadic sketches made their appearance, mostly with the implication of inherent evil. A few examples may suffice to give the flavor of these reports from the pens of outstanding alienists. I should like to precede them with the story of little Emerentia, as chronicled in a clergyman's diary which is cited in the masterful autobiographic novel, *Der grüne Heinrich* by Gottfried Keller (1921), in whose native village the incident had taken place in 1713:

> This 7-year-old girl, the offspring of an aristocratic family, whose father remarried after an unhappy first matrimony, offended her "noble and godfearing" stepmother by her peculiar behavior. Worst of all, she would not join in the prayers and was panic-stricken when taken to the black-robed preacher in the dark and gloomy chapel. She avoided contact with people by hiding in closets or running away from home. The local physician had nothing to offer beyond declaring that she might be insane. She was placed in the custody of a minister known for his rigid orthodoxy. The minister, who saw in her ways the machinations of a "baneful and infernal" power, used a number of would-be therapeutic devices. He laid her on a bench and beat her with a cat-o'nine-tails. He locked her in a dark pantry. He subjected her to a period of starvation. He clothed her in a frock of burlap. Under these circumstances, the child did not last long. She died after a few months, and everybody felt relieved. The minister was amply rewarded for his efforts by Emerentia's parents.

Such was the general milieu in which the alienists of those days came upon specimens of childhood psychosis. The great Esquirol (pp. 384-385) reported in 1838 the cases of three "little

homicidal monomaniacs." Of an 11-year-old girl who pushed
two infants into a well he had nothing more to say than that she
"was known for her evil habits." An 8-year-old girl who threatened to kill her stepmother and her brother was returned to her
grandparents who had violently disapproved of her father's re-
marriage. A 7½-year-old girl who had been tossed about among
relatives refused to play, had temper tantrums, masturbated excessively, and expressed regret that her mother did not die; the
neighbors, to teach her a lesson, put flour into a glass of wine,
told her it was arsenic, and forced her to swallow it. On psychiatric advice, she was sent to a convent, where she promptly
developed pediculosis. Eventually, she was apprenticed to a
jewel cutter and was said to be submissive and to attend church
services on Sundays.

In 1841, Descuret told of a boy who lived with a nurse during
the first two years of his life. When he was taken to his home,
he grew pale, sad, and morose, refused to eat, and did not respond to his parents. The usual toys and diversions had no effect.
On medical advice, the nurse was called back and, in the father's
words, "from that moment on he began to live again." Eventually, he was separated from the nurse, first for a few hours,
then for a whole day, then for a week, until finally the child was
accustomed to her absence.

This last example indicates an emerging desire to look for possible explanations of deviant child behavior on other than pseu-
dotheologic and pseudomoralistic grounds.

Around the middle of the nineteenth century, a growing number of such anecdotal bits was published, and a few psychiatrists
were no longer satisfied with the mere mechanical recording of
observed or quoted instances. In 1867, Maudsley included in his
Physiology and Pathology of Mind a thirty-four-page chapter on
"Insanity of Early Life." In it, he tried to correlate symptomatology with the developmental status at the time of onset and
suggested a classification of infantile psychoses. There was ob-
jection on the part of those who persisted in denying the existence of mental illness in children. In the 1880 revision of his
book, Maudsley felt compelled to counter such criticism with
an introductory paragraph, which said, somewhat apologetically:

How unnatural! is an excalamation of pained surprise which some
of the more striking instances of insanity in young children are apt
to provoke. However, to call a thing unnatural is not to take it out
of the domain of natural law, notwithstanding that, when it has been
so designated, it is sometimes thought that no more needs to be
said. Anomalies, when rightly studied, yield rare instruction; they
witness and attract attention to the operation of hidden laws or of
known laws under new and unknown conditions; and so set the
inquirer on new and fruitful paths of research. For this reason it
will not be amiss to occupy a separate chapter with a consideration
of the abnormal phenomena of mental derangement in children
(p. 259).

In the last two decades of the nineteenth century, courageous
attempts were made to collect and organize the existing material
in monographs on "psychic disorders," "mental diseases," or "insanity" of children. These were the texts by Emminghaus
(1887) in Germany, Moreau de Tours (1888) and Manheimer
(1899) in France, and Ireland (1898) in Great Britain. There
was a tendency toward fatalism which saw in the disorders the
irreversible results of heredity, degeneracy, masturbation, over-
work, religious preoccupation, intestinal parasites, or sudden
changes of temperature.

Thus, around 1900, there was an assortment of publications,
ranging all the way from single case reports to elaborate texts and
announcing to an astonished world that children were known to
display psychotic phenomena.

It was the year 1900 in which Ellen Key, the famous Swedish
sociologist, made her much-quoted prophetic announcement that
the twentieth century was destined to be "the century of the
child." It is indeed remarkable that in the next few years many
efforts converged on the interest in the doings and experiences
of infants and children. The diaries of Preyer, Darwin, Pesta-
lozzi, Tiedemann, and other writers, expanded by Stanley Hall's
questionnaires, had paved the way for the new science of developmental psychology and the monumental work of Binet,
whose first draft of the psychometric scale was made public in
1905. This was the year in which Freud, on the basis of elicited
adult patients' reminiscences, gave literary form to his theory of
infantile sexuality. Three years later, Clifford Beers introduced

the idea of the prevention of mental illness, focusing on the need to intercept behavioral deviations at the time of their earliest appearance. The establishment of juvenile courts, inaugurated in 1899 in Denver and in Chicago, led eventually to Healy's contributions in the teens of this century. Educators joined in by building into the school systems special instructional facilities for pupils with visual, auditory, neuro-orthopedic, and intellectual handicaps.

Yet it was not until the 1930's that consistent attempts were made to study children with severe emotional disturbances from the point of view of diagnosis, etiology, therapy, and prognosis. When the change did occur, it was centered around the concept of childhood schizophrenia. By that time, general agreement had been reached that children were not altogether immune against the illness described by Kraepelin as dementia praecox and referred to by Bleuler as the group of the schizophrenias. Ziehen and Homburger had given in their textbooks (both in 1926) ample space to a discussion of its incidence in preadolescence and adolescence. De Sanctis (1925), at about the same time, had suggested the term "dementia praecocissima" for an assortment of marked disturbances appearing in preschool age. Increasing awareness of the looseness with which childhood schizophrenia was diagnosed or failed to be diagnosed caused Potter in 1933 to delineate the concept so that there might be a consensus with regard to the nosologic assignment of any individual child. In the framework of this and similar definitions, the next step consisted of the search for a clear demarcation of existing variations in onset, symptoms, and course. Ssucharewa (1932) in Russia, Lutz (1937) in Switzerland, and Despert (1938) in this country distinguished between cases with acute and insidious onset, with the implication that the peculiarities of the beginning determined the phenomenology and the progress of the illness.

In the 1940's, a period of controversy and confusion was inaugurated because of the parallel advocacy of two antithetical trends. On the one hand, there was a tendency to revert to pre-Kraepelinian indefiniteness. Beata Rank (1949) introduced the notion of the "atypical child," with intended disregard of any distinctions between childhood psychosis, mental defect, and any other form of "severe disturbances of early development." Problems of mother-child relationship were declared to be a common causative denominator. Szurek proclaimed categorically: "We are beginning to consider it clinically fruitless, and even unnecessary, to draw any sharp dividing lines between a condition that one could consider psychoneurotic and another that one could call psychosis, autism, atypical development, or schizophrenia" (Szurek, p. 522).

On the other hand, there was a decided disinclination to house an assortment of heterogeneous clinical entities under one supposedly common etiologic roof. Kanner, in 1943, outlined the syndrome of early infantile autism. Mahler, in 1949, described a form which she named symbiotic infantile psychosis. In the same year, Bergman and Escalona called attention to what they called children with unusual sensitivity to sensory stimulation. In 1954, Robinson and Vitale added the group of children with circumscribed interest patterns. Bender, seeing the origin of childhood schizophrenia in a maturation lag at the embryonic level, subdivided the condition into three clinical types: (a) the pseudodefective or autistic type; (b) the pseudoneurotic or phobic, obsessive, compulsive, hypochondriac type; (c) the pseudopsychopathic or paranoid, acting-out, aggressive, antisocial type.

It is strange, indeed, that a historical review of emotional disturbances of children should occupy itself predominantly, or almost exclusively, with psychoses and, more specifically, with schizophrenia. It is equally strange that, seek as one may, it is impossible to find anywhere a definition of the term "emotionally disturbed children" which had somehow crept into the literature some thirty years ago and has since then been used widely, sometimes as a generality with no terminologic boundaries whatever and sometimes with reference to certain psychotic and near-psychotic conditions. This is extremely important in the consideration and evaluation of past, ongoing, and planned research. It can be said that these studies do exclude such emotional disorders as occasional temper tantrums or night terrors of otherwise well-adjusted children; chronicity is apparently a paramount requirement. Also left out are emotional problems associated with, or secondary to, inherent mental deficiency or demonstrable organ pathology. But this still leaves a wide variety of heterogeneous conditions which, if thrown together indiscriminately, impart no greater meaning to a study than did the sixteenth century treatises on the fevers or the nineteenth century studies of the blood pressure of "the insane" or of the heredity of "feeblemindedness." It may perhaps be legitimate to link them together from the standpoint of practical epidemiology and the improvement of public health facilities but, beyond this, it would hardly do to claim scientific validity for any research which sets out to look for unitary features in disparate conditions.

A historical survey teaches us that progress has always consisted of a breaking down of diffuse generic concepts into specific categories. We no longer speculate about fevers generically; bacteriology knows of totally different varieties of febrile illness. We no longer speak about insanity generically; we recognize a variety of psychotic reaction types. We no longer speak about feeblemindedness generically; we know that there is a vast difference between mongolism, microcephaly, and phenylketonuria; it would not occur to anyone to lump them together in any meaningful investigation. I believe that the time has come to acknowledge the heterogeneity of the many conditions comprised under the generic term, "emotionally disturbed children." We shall then be in a position to study each of these varieties with true precision. A symposium on the use of the term in scientific publications would, at this juncture, be a major contribution to clarity and mutual understanding.

References

Bender, L. Current research in childhood schizophrenia. *Amer J Psychiat, 110:* 855-856, 1954.

Bergman, P., and Escalona, S.: Unusual sensitivities in very young children. *Psychoanal Stud Child, 3-4:* 333-352, 1949.

DeSanctis, S.: *Neuropsichiatria infantile.* Rome, Stock, 1925.

Descuret, J. B. F.: *Médecine de passions.* Paris, Béchet et Labé. 1841.

Despert, J. L.: Schizophrenia in children. *Psychiat Quart, 12:* 366-371, 1938.

Emminghaus, H.: *Die psychischen Störungen des Kindesalters.* Tübingen, Laupp, 1887.

Esquirol, J. E. D.: *Maladies mentales.* Pari:, Baillère, 1838, vol. I.

Homburger, A.: *Vorlesungen über die Psychopathologie des Kindesalters.* Berlin, Springer, 1926.

Ireland, W. W.: *The Mental Affections of Children.* Blakiston, 1898.

Kanner, L.: Problems of nosology and psychodynamics of early infantile autism. *Amer J Orthopsychiat, 19:* 416-426, 1949.

Keller, G.: *Der grüne Heinrich.* Munich, Deutsch-Meister-Verlag, 1921, vol. I.

Key, E.: *The Century Of The Child.* (English Rev.) New York, Putnam, 1909.

Lutz, J.: *Über die Schizophrenie im Kindesalter.* Zurich, Füssli, 1937.

Mahler, M. S.: On child psychosis and schizophrenia. *Psychoanal. Stud Child, 7:* 286-305, 1952.

Manheimer, M.: *Les troubles mentaux de l'enfance.* Paris, Société d'Editions Scientifiques, 1899.

Maudsley, H.: *The pathology of the mind.* New York, Appleton, 1880.

Moreau de Tours, P.: *La folie chez les enfants.* Paris, Baillère, 1888.

Potter, H. W.: Schizophrenia in children. *Amer J Psychiat, 89:* 1253-1270, 1933.

Rank, B.: Adaptation of the psychoanalytic techniques for the treatment of young children with atypical development. *Amer J Orthopsychiat, 19:* 130-139, 1949.

Robinson, F. J., and Vitale, L. J.: Children with circumscribed interest patterns. *Amer J Orthopsychiat, 24:* 755-766, 1954.

Ssucharewa, G.: Über den Verlauf der Schizophrenien im Kindesalter. *Z Ges Neurol Psychiat, 142:* 309-321, 1932.

Szurek, S. A.: Psychotic episodes and psychic maldevelopment. *Amer J Orthopsychiat, 26:* 519-543, 1956.

Ziehen, T.: *Die Geisteskrankheiten des Kindesalters.* Berlin, Reuther and Reinhard, 1926.

SECTION B

IDENTIFICATION

Chapter 3

Locating Children With Emotional Problems

WALTER B. BARBE

CLASSROOM TEACHERS ARE CONSTANTLY being told that they must be aware of the emotional problems of their pupils, but how can the teacher know which children have emotional problems? If every child who misbehaves is labeled maladjusted, there will probably be few children who do not carry such a label. Many of the children who never misbehave are probably the very ones for whom the label would properly apply.

Just as a child has curly hair, blue eyes, and a fair complexion, so also may the child's emotional make-up be described. The emotional make-up is certainly not as obvious, but it is present, nevertheless, and perhaps far more important.

Various terms are used to describe a child's adjustments. The two terms, "personality" and "emotional adjustment," are synonymous. Generally speaking, the emotional make-up of the child is concerned with how well he has adjusted to life situations both at home and at school. It must be recognized that every child will have different situations to which he must adjust. When the child is unable to adjust to any particular one of these situations, and reacts to it by either becoming aggressive or withdrawn in other situations, he is then said to have an emotional problem.

The teacher is in the best position to identify children with emotional problems. He is not only with the child a large part of each day, but he also is able to observe the child more objectively than the parent. Also, the teacher has a group of children

Reprinted from *Childhood Education*, Vol. 30 (1953), pp. 127-130. By permission of the author and publisher.

19

of approximately the same age with whom he can compare each child. This is, in a sense, a norm by which he may judge normal behavior and normal adjustment.

If the teacher is to locate emotional problems by means of observation, he should know specifically what problems for which to look. Any type of observed behavior, to be considered important, should be consistent. Merely the occurrence of one outburst from Johnny is not sufficient reason to label him socially maladjusted. The children in the classroom quickly forget the isolated instances of misbehavior, for they accept the fact that an occasional outlet for our emotions is essential to good mental health. The most important aspect, therefore, is that the behavior be consistent, and that it is not merely a child's way of learning to adjust by trial and error.

There are two distinct types of behavior which may be indicative of emotional maladjustments in children. Neither is more or less important than the other. For very obvious reasons, the outward type of behavior, aggressiveness, will attract more attention than the retiring type of behavior. In the classroom where thirty-five to forty children must be taken care of, the child who sits back and is no trouble may be considered a model child. Teachers are coming to realize that this child, just as the aggressive child, also may be having emotional problems. While rebellion is not to be encouraged, it is only a natural stage in the development of all children to either try their ability at being important or to defy authority at least occasionally. When too many children have such natural urges at one time, the teacher feels that he has had a most trying day. But if the children were not to express their freedom occasionally, it would be a very dull existence, much more difficult than the way things are at present.

What Is Aggressive Behavior?

In attempting to determine the extent of aggressive behavior which should be considered serious, a teacher can ask the following questions about a child:

1. Does he consistently lie, even when the truth would sometimes do just as well?

2. Does he cheat even when he doesn't need to merely for the sake of cheating?

3. Does he steal, or report things of his own to be stolen when they are not?

4. Is he intentionally destructive?

5. Is he cruel?

6. Does he consistently bully younger children?

7. In his relations with adults, is he arrogant and defiant?

8. Does he frequently have temper tantrums?

An affirmative answer to one of these does not necessarily imply that the child has an emotional problem, but it is indication that he is not satisfactorily adjusting to the group. An affirmative answer to several of these indicates a child who needs help.

All lying is not an indication of emotional maladjustment. But it may be a symptom if the child believes that it is better not to tell the truth than to face reality. Cheating and stealing may be attempts to compensate for inability or inequality in other ways. Recognized early, these are not major problems and the classroom teacher can adequately provide for this child. If it is a pattern which is once started and persists throughout school, it becomes a serious problem. Destructiveness is not a natural trait in children. They may be careless, but intentionally destroying property, whether it belongs to them or not, is an indication of aggressiveness which needs to be recognized. Merely telling the child to stop or punishing him will do nothing to correct a basically serious problem.

Even though it is sometimes said that children are cruel, they are not unless we, as adults, make them believe that this is an acceptable method of adjustment. Sometimes a child may be cruel merely because he does not understand. When told that his actions are unkind and cruel, he will not persist in them. Bullying, another form of cruelty directed at another child, may be the insecure child's way of attempting to gain status in the eyes of others, or it may be the child's way of getting even for treatment which he receives from his parents or from other older brothers and sisters.

Arrogance and defiance are the child's ways of saying that he has had too much freedom to give it up now. The spoiled, pampered child may use such actions when he suddenly realizes that the teacher is not going to allow him to have his way all of the time. As disagreeable as this child may appear to be, it is not his fault that he cannot adjust. He needs understanding in order to realize that the rights of others must be respected. The parents must cooperate in any attempt to help this child. All of the good intentions behind pampering can result in only one thing—an unhappy child, unable to understand why he is not always given what he has come to believe are his rights.

Temper tantrums, if they occur frequently, are serious indications of emotional maladjustment. Punishment should not be used to stop them. The teacher should be firm with the child, but allow him a position in the classroom in which he can feel secure.

Retiring Behavior Is Dangerous

The child who is aggressive is more likely to be recognized as a problem by the teacher than the child who is retiring. More and more teachers realize that the retiring child, while he certainly is not a problem in the sense that he causes trouble in the class, may be a very serious emotional problem. In attempting to determine the extent of retiring behavior which indicates maladjustment, a teacher may ask the following questions about a child:

1. Is he overly sensitive, so that he cries frequently?
2. Does he daydream a great deal and seem to prefer his daydreams to activities with other children?
3. Does he try extremely hard to please, even at the expense of losing friends?
4. Is he easily frightened and does he have unusual fears?
5. Is he overly selfish?
6. Does he make up stories to enhance his own position?

Of course, children frequently cry in the first few weeks of school. This must be recognized as normal, for having to leave the protection of a mother is quite a difficult adjustment for some children to make. If the crying persists, however, steps should be taken to remedy whatever is causing it. It may be that the child is too immature to be away from his mother and before he decides that he completely hates school, it would be better to send him home for another year. Next year he would be better adapted emotionally to cope with the trials of every-day school problems. It is more important to observe how easily the child gets over his crying than the fact that the child cries occasionally. While it should certainly not be encouraged, cry-ing is an emotional release which some children, particularly girls, may have adopted.

The child who daydreams a great deal and prefers his day-dreams to activities with other children is trying to escape from a situation which he finds unpleasant. While such children are certainly no problem in the sense that they disrupt the class, they are serious problems within themselves. Merely forcing the child to participate is no solution and may make the situation worse.

While it is extremely difficult not to like the child who works hard to gain the favor of the teacher, if he does so even at the expense of losing friends, it is a behavior problem. Complete rejection by the teacher is not the answer, but neither is encour-agement of the behavior. Providing the child satisfaction in ways more acceptable to the group is one way to divert this desire to please into normal channels.

The child who is easily frightened is insecure. He knows that he fears something, but doesn't know what. Making up fears of unusual things is a way of giving form to his fears. The teacher should not encourage these fears, but neither should he punish the child because of them. As unreasonable as they may sound, they are very real to the child.

Making up stories to enhance one's own position is a natural reaction for an insecure child.

Physical Factors to be Noted

Along with these less tangible factors which the teacher may look for in identifying emotional problems, there are definite physical factors which may be observed. Only one of these might not be an indication of an emotional problem, but it should lead the teacher to ask some of the questions previously listed.

1. Does the child bite his nails?
2. Does the child have any face twitching (known as tics)?
3. Does the child constantly pull or twist his hair, chew on his clothing, or pick or scratch his body?
4. Does he have a weak, high-pitched, or strained voice or is he constantly clearing his throat?
5. Is he conscious of excessive overweight or underweight?
6. Is he conscious of extreme tallness or shortness?

While certainly not all nail biting is an indication of an emotional maladjustment, it is nevertheless a very important indication. Frequently, it is only a habit, even though there may have been some emotional stress which originally caused it.

Facial twitchings are important symptoms of emotional maladjustment. The teacher is in no position to try to correct this difficulty and should not hesitate to refer the child for psychiatric help.

Pulling or twisting hair, chewing on clothing, and picking and scratching are all signs of nervousness. It is not natural for a young child to be nervous. An effort should be made to remove the child from situations in which he is nervous.

The child's voice is frequently a better indication of his emotional adjustment than any other outward sign. The strained, high-pitched voice reflects extreme tension. Constantly clearing one's throat is also a sign of this tension.

Excessive overweight or underweight, as well as extreme tallness or shortness, necessitate emotional adjustments quite different from those of the average pupil. If the child is unable to make these adjustments, the teacher should help him make them.

What Can The Teacher Do?

It is not likely that the teacher will find a child who is a serious emotional problem if only one affirmative answer is given to the questions which have been asked. In most instances, there will be a number of indications. It is the teacher's responsibility to locate emotional problems early in order that steps may be taken to help the child. Following these steps may aid the teacher in doing this. The next logical question which will be asked is, "What can I do about a child who has been identified as having emotional problems?"

Actually, there is a great deal that the teacher can do for this child. Understanding the child is of the greatest importance. Providing the child with a happy school situation in which he can feel secure and in which he can meet success frequently is of the greatest importance. Home visitations and conferences with parents and former teachers frequently will shed much light on the child's problem. The teacher must realize, however, that treatment of serious emotional problems does not lie within his realm. If the school has a psychologist, the child should be referred to him. If not, the parents should be encouraged to take the child to a child guidance center. If the services of these are not available, the child should visit a private psychologist or psychiatrist. If the parents are unable to afford this, almost any of the charitable organizations will give financial assistance.

Recognizing that the child has an emotional problem is a major first step. Determining the reason for the problem is a beneficial next step. Referral in those cases which seem to be of a serious nature is the logical third step.

Chapter 4

A Process For Identifying Disturbed Children

Eli M. Bower

In a world where the flick of a switch can turn darkness into light, where a spin of a dial can transport a person from the South Pole to an Iowa football field, where one can drive about in a pushbutton car with the assurance that the stove at home will turn the oven off when the meat is done—in such a world it would not be surprising for a kind of faith in magic to be prevalent. Attitudes which result from technology's amazing simplification of everyday time-space problems through easily operated gadgets may be displaced onto problems in the social-personal areas of living. This search for the magical solution is perhaps most evident in the approach to complex problems about which little scientific knowledge is available and which directly involve the human personality. It is especially so in regard to the problem of mental illness.

The search for a kind of psychological penicillin by which mental illness and its associated disabilities could be prevented has been particularly intriguing. Such a search often leads to the discovery or rediscovery that the public school is an institution whose services are available to all the children in the community, which employs professional personnel trained in the understanding of personality development in children, and which can and often does establish ancillary services to help teachers and parents. It is not surprising, then, for agencies dealing with problems created by poor mental health to look to the school as

Reprinted from *Children*, Vol. 4, No. 4 (1957), pp. 143-147. By permission of the author and publisher.

an avenue for reducing the rate of psychological morbidity in our population.

Often the specific request made of the school is: "Identify and help emotionally disturbed children early." The possible effectiveness of early identification in preventing unwholesome personality development rests on at least two assumptions which need scientific clarification. The first is that emotional disturbance is the result of a progressively developing condition visible and susceptible to evaluation early in a person's life. Its corollary is that the school, as now constituted, can recognize this condition economically and within the present framework of daily activities.

The second assumption is that the child who is identified early in life as emotionally disturbed can be helped with less trouble to himself and the community than would be the case at a later period in his life. Although the assumption that the earlier the identification the easier the cure seems both logically and psychologically sound, it is still a proposition based on faith and conviction.

The Study Design

Acknowledging these gaps in knowledge, and in spite of them, the California State Department of Education initiated in September 1955 a study concerned with early identification of emotionally disturbed children. Specifically, the study was aimed at discovering to what extent a teacher-centered procedure might be employed for identifying disturbed children in a class and to what extent information ordinarily obtained by the classroom teacher about children might be used for this purpose, "Identification" was conceived of as a process rather than an act—a process which might favorably affect the teacher's perception of behavior and help point the way to remedial measures. The study plan was based on the assumption that to be effective this process had to be carried out by the teacher as the person in the school most closely involved with the children, the one who had more day-to-day contacts with each child than anyone else on the school staff, and the one who was in the most advantageous position to observe the children's relationships and behavioral patterns.

Before involving the teacher in the study, the study staff asked the psychiatrist, psychologist, or counselor in each participating school to identify some children who were being seen or who had been seen by the clinical staff and who in their opinion were "emotionally disturbed." Classes in which one or more of these children were enrolled were then selected for participation in the study without revealing to the teacher the criterion for selection.

The purpose of the study, as explained to the teachers, was to study all the children in the class. Some of the teachers knew that some of the children in their classes had been seen by the school psychologist or clinic; others did not. In any case, the only knowledge the study staff wished to keep from the teacher was the reason for the selection of her class. This, the staff felt, would be necessary to prevent the research itself from biasing the teacher's perception of her children.

Several conditions were agreed upon by the study staff and the schools in regard to the information the teachers would be asked to collect. These were as follows:

1. It could be obtained by teachers in their everyday, routine interaction with the class.

2. Gathering and recording it would not involve a disproportionate amount of teacher time.

3. The type of data expected could be so defined as to have the same operational meaning to each teacher.

4. It would tap as many sources as economically possible for indication of the child's behavior.

5. The information-gathering procedure would allow the part of "suspectician" to fit harmoniously and acceptably into the teacher's perception of her role and responsibilities.

The categories of information finally selected for the teachers to collect about each child were

1. Individual scores from group intelligence test.

2. Individual scores from group achievement test in arithmetic and reading.

3. Individual responses to a group administered personality inventory, "Thinking About Yourself" (California, 1957).

4. Results of a sociogram, "The Class Play" (California, 1957).
5. Age-grade relationship.
6. Rate of absence.
7. Rating of socioeconomic index based on father's occupation.
8. Teacher's rating of the child's physical status.
9. Teacher's rating of the child's emotional status.

Information in all these categories was collected on approximately 4,400 children by approximately 200 teachers of fourth, fifth, and sixth grades in about 75 school districts. Among the children were 207 clinically designated emotionally disturbed children—162 boys, 45 girls.

In the instructions to the clinicians no sex ratio for selection was indicated. It is interesting to note that the resultant random selection resulted in a ratio of emotionally disturbed boys and girls very close to the ratio of referrals.

The information was collected by each teacher for all the children in her class on a special form devised by the State Department of Education and returned to the department for processing.

The first analysis of the data was to determine to what extent, if any, this information could help a teacher to differentiate the emotionally disturbed child from the rest of the children in the class, how many emotionally disturbed children there were in the school population, how they were perceived by other children, and how they perceived themselves. It was proposed that as part of this study the data which significantly differentiated the emotionally disturbed child from the others be analyzed to discover the degree of differentiation. Then each item of the differentiating data would be weighted in proportion to the size of its ability to differentiate. For example, if "The Class Play" technique and group I.Q. scores both turned out to be significant but one turned out to be twice as discriminating as the other, they would be weighted accordingly. After the weights were assigned, the data and the weights would be tried out by a variety of teachers and classes to learn what corrections, additions, or subtractions needed to be made in the process.

The Findings

A detailed report of the results of this study will soon be published by the California State Department of Education. Following is a brief summary of the aspects of the information collected by each teacher which differentiate the emotionally disturbed children (those selected by the clinicians) from others of their classroom. (In all these statements the word "significantly" refers to the 0.01 level of confidence, meaning that there would be one chance in a hundred that a difference as large as the obtained difference would occur by chance. "They" refers to the selected emotionally disturbed group):

1. The emotionally disturbed children scored significantly lower on group I.Q. tests. On psychological tests given individually, they approached the mean of the group.

2. They scored significantly lower on reading and arithmetic achievement tests. The differences were greater and more significant on arithmetic achievement. The higher the school grade, the greater the differences between the emotionally disturbed child and the rest of the class.

3. They differed significantly from the other children in the class in their self-perception as revealed in some of the items in the Personality Inventory. Emotionally disturbed boys exhibited greater dissatisfaction with self and their school behavior than the other boys. Emotionally disturbed girls showed less dissatisfaction with self than the rest of the girls in the class.

4. On the sociogram, "The Class Play," the other children in the class tended to select emotionally disturbed children for hostile, inadequate, or negative roles and failed to select them for the positive, good roles. Hostile children particularly were selected for roles consistent with their behavior.

5. The emotionally disturbed children came from homes which were not significantly different in socioeconomic level from those of other children generally. (This fact was revealed by a chi-square test comparing the distribution of the occupations of the fathers of the emotionally disturbed children and the occupations of the fathers of the rest of the children in the class.)

6. Altogether 87 percent of the clinically known emotionally

disturbed children were rated by their classroom teachers as among the most poorly adjusted children in the class (Table I). Nearly 61 percent of these were described by the teachers as being overly aggressive or defiant often or most of the time (Table II), while 25 percent were designated as being overly withdrawn or timid quite often or most of the time (Table III). As perceived by teachers, 4.4 percent of all the children in the class were overly aggressive or defiant most of the time (Table II), while 6.1 percent were overly withdrawn or timid most of the time (Table III).

Some of the implications of the study might have been expected. Others may be more surprising. Here are a few:

1. Children's judgments of other children's personality are surprisingly accurate and predictive.

2. Teacher's judgments of emotional disturbance are very much like the judgment of clinicians.

TABLE I.

TEACHER RATING OF EACH CHILD IN RESPONSE TO: HOW WOULD YOU RATE THIS CHILD'S ADJUSTMENT WITH RESPECT TO HIS PRESENT GROUP?

Rating	Males		Females		Total	
	Number	Percent	Number	Percent	Number	Percent
TOTAL GROUP						
Among the best........	673	23.0	893	33.5	1,566	28.0
Among the average....	1,368	46.9	1,314	49.3	2,682	48.0
Among the poorest....	879	30.1	460	17.2	1,339	24.0
Total.................	2,920	52.3	2,667	47.7	5,587	100.0
EMOTIONALLY DISTURBED GROUP						
Among the best........	3	1.9	2	4.5	5	2.4
Among the average....	17	10.4	5	11.4	22	10.7
Among the poorest....	142	87.7	37	84.1	179	86.9
Total.................	162	78.6	44	21.4	206	100.0

TABLE II.

TEACHER RATING OF EACH CHILD IN RESPONSE TO: IS THIS CHILD OVERLY AGGRESSIVE OR DEFIANT?

	Males		Females		Total	
Rating	Number	Percent	Number	Percent	Number	Percent
TOTAL GROUP						
Seldom or never........	1,579	54.0	1,945	73.0	3,524	63.0
Not very often..........	709	24.2	404	15.1	1,113	19.9
Quite often................	469	16.0	239	9.0	708	12.7
Most of the time........	169	5.8	78	2.9	247	4.4
Total..................	2,926	52.3	2,666	47.7	5,592	100.0
EMOTIONALLY DISTURBED GROUP						
Seldom or never........	31	19.1	17	37.8	48	23,2
Not very often..........	27	16.7	6	13.3	33	15.9
Quite often..............	57	35.2	15	33.3	72	34.8
Most of the time......	47	29.0	7	15.6	54	26.1
Total..................	162	78.2	45	21.8	207	100.0

3. Teachers in this study selected a greater number of children as being overly withdrawn or timid most of the time than as overly aggressive or defiant most of the time.

4. At least three children in each average classroom can be regarded as having emotional problems of sufficient strength to warrant the appellation "emotionally disturbed child."

5. The differences between emotionally disturbed children and the others seem to increase with each grade level. In essence, the rich get richer while the poor get poorer.

A Psychological Thermometer

It should be reemphasized that this study was aimed at securing a "psychological thermometer" about schoolchildren for persons in a favorable position to use such a device, and at nothing more. Like the medicine-chest thermometer which may add little information to the obvious fact that a person has a high

TABLE III.

TEACHER RATING OF EACH CHILD IN RESPONSE TO: IS THIS CHILD
OVERLY WITHDRAWN OR TIMID?

Rating	Males Number	Percent	Females Number	Percent	Total Number	Percent
TOTAL GROUP						
Seldom or never........	1,700	58.1	1,367	51.2	3,067	54.8
Not very often..........	732	25.0	699	26.2	1,431	25.6
Quite often...............	351	12.0	406	15.2	757	13.5
Most of the time......	144	4.9	197	7.4	341	6.1
Total.................	2,927	52.3	2,669	47.7	5,596	100.0
EMOTIONALLY DISTURBED GROUP						
Seldom or never........	87	53.7	15	33.3	102	49.3
Not very often..........	40	24.7	14	31.1	54	26.1
Quite often...............	20	12.3	9	20.0	29	14.0
Most of the time........	15	9.3	7	15.6	22	10.6
Total.................	162	78.3	45	21.7	207	100.0

temperature, such a psychological thermometer may confirm a suspicion, reject a suspicion, or raise a suspicion. It may provide teachers with a more accurate base than personal supposition for communicating with specialists, as well as a possible gage from which individual change can be assessed. It may provide the teacher with a method for evaluating her own processes. It may also raise pertinent questions in a teacher's mind, particularly when it does not confirm her judgment about a specific child or when it indicates that a formerly unnoticed child might be having difficulties.

For example, a teacher reported that the sociogram, "The Class Play" (a device in which children select roles for themselves and other members of the class for a hypothetical play), did not seem to be a very reliable method for learning about the children since some of the results in her class did not coincide with her observations. She noted that a child whom she saw as a leader of the class was not chosen as such by the other children. When asked whether both perceptions might not be correct, she answered: "Well, he always seems to be a leader when I'm around." But a few weeks later she reported that the other children did feel differently about the child than she had supposed.

"You know," this teacher observed, "it's interesting really to find out that your idea about a child isn't the only one. I think I see him a little differently now because I am also able to accept how others see him."

One part of "The Class Play" provides for a comparison of the role each child selected for himself and the roles selected for him by his classmates. Thus it serves as a device for studying the reality-testing aspects of a child's personality and for making some inferences about how a child sees himself and how others see him.

A highly intelligent fifth-grade girl who was chosen for many negative and hostile roles by her classmates chose negative roles for herself when asked which parts she thought her classmates would choose her to play and which parts her teacher would ask her to play. But in answer to the question, "Which part would you like to play?" she chose the heroine role. Later this girl told her teacher that she realized how her classmates felt about her but that she felt she was gaining greater understanding of herself, "that she knew what she was up against and was working on it."

A boy received eight positive and eight negative choices by the class. His teacher found that his nickname among the children, "Little Nuisance," was an honest reflection of the mixture of affection and irritation his classmates felt in regard to him. The boy saw himself as the class did, choosing himself for an equal number of appropriate positive and negative roles, and accepted the appellation with good grace. Other parts of the data gathered on this child by the teacher led her to a more meaningful understanding of how this child perceived himself and how other children reacted to him.

Possibilities of Process

This process for helping the teacher identify the emotionally disturbed children in her class might be regarded as a kind of action research with two major purposes: (1) to help the teacher understand the relativity of her perception of the children; (2) to provide teachers with a systematic, meaningful procedure for using available information about children in verifying or rejecting hypotheses about their adjustment status.

As Coladarci (1956) points out, "the teacher must be an active, continuous inquirer into the validity of his own procedures." This process may very well help the teacher become a more effective inquirer.

It is also possible that this process might be helpful to the teacher-clinical staff relationships.

An emotionally disturbed child whose behavior is erratic or disrupting can and often does induce anxiety and despair in a teacher: Often the relationship of the class and teacher to the emotionally disturbed child is such that no solution but separation of the child from the group is acceptable. When this point is reached, the teacher often seeks the help of the clinician as a "waver of the magic wand"—that is, as a person who can solve the problem quickly either by changing the child's personality or by changing his room. It is sometimes difficult for the teacher to accept the fact that her expectations cannot be met and that she must participate in the slow process of "understanding" the child.

Intellectually the teacher may recognize the limitations of the clinical service; emotionally, however, she may be disappointed that nothing happens and that she is still plagued with the problem. In time, therefore, she may come to feel that the clinical service offers little to help her. The psychologist or guidance worker on the other hand may be so overwhelmed by the numbers and seriousness of problems brought to them that he becomes immersed solely in the clinical nature of his task. As Krugman (1954) points out, "Because there is almost never sufficient staff in a school-guidance program to do what needs to be done, the tendency is usually to focus on emergencies or immediately annoying problems. . . . We still have too great a tendency to throw our full armamentarium of personality appraisal methods into efforts to salvage the problem child."

The anxiety induced in a teacher by one or more emotionally disturbed children is often visited upon all the children in the class. As a result those children with situational or incipient problems who can be helped by the teacher may be overlooked or over-evaluated. However, a teacher who "knows" the children and the class may be more comfortable about seeking help and more aware of her own personal anxieties and biases in appraising children. It may be necessary at times for a teacher to accept the fact that some children are seriously disturbed and need psychiatric treatment. The number and urgency of serious problems may be greatly reduced, however, if the teacher-clinical team can be helped to make the most of the school's potential for preventing personality distortions in children.

This preliminary investigation has approached the problem of identification by backing into it—ascertaining certain relationships between the emotionally disturbed child and his school environment. In order to test the on-the-job validity of the process of identifying such children by comparing the factors in these relationships, the teachers in a number of schools of various types will be given the opportunity to use it. The focus of research may then be shifted to seek answers to such questions as

1. What, if anything, happens to the teacher as she uses this procedure?

2. What happens to her relationships to the children and to the clinician?

3. What kinds of children are referred or discussed?

4. Are there changes in the quality and levels of relationships?

5. Which children, who should have been identified, were not?

For the most part we have been attempting to promote mental health in our society by trying to deal with the consequences of mental illness and its allied manifestations. This is about as effective as trying to turn back the Mississippi at New Orleans. Not that we don't need dikes and erosion prevention up and down the line. But, as Daniel Blain (1956) has asked, "Is it not possible to build dams higher up the stream and to plant more trees on the slopes and hold the water in?"

Certainly there are at present no magic buttons which we can push to insure increased amounts of emotional maturity for our future citizens. It would seem most profitable, however, to attack the problem of enhancing personality growth at definite points with specific programs of action and evaluation. For if there is a potential for magic, it lies in the resiliency of the child. Perhaps through this and similar projects it will be possible to learn more of the exact nature of this resiliency and how we can make the most of it in promoting mental health.

References

Blain, Daniel: In a speech at the Western Interstate Commission on Mental Health, Salt Lake City, June 2, 1956.

California State Department of Education: *Thinking About Yourself.* Sacramento, 1957.

California State Department of Education: *The Class Play.* Sacramento, 1957.

Coladarci, Arthur: The relevancy of educational psychology. *Educational Leadership,* May 1956, p. 490.

Krugman, M.: Appraisal and treatment of personality problems in a guidance program. In *Education In A Free World.* Washington, A. C. E., 1954, p. 114-121.

Chapter 5

Evaluating Psychological Problems Of School Children

MARY ALICE WHITE

Recently I was trout fishing on the Battenkill River in Vermont. When friends of mine came to visit I noticed how differently they looked at the same scenery that I had been studying. They thought the Battenkill a lovely stream, but they didn't comment on its gravel bottom which trout love. They thought the overhanging willows and birch were picturesque, while to me they meant ideal cover for brown trout. They found the water a little chilly for swimming, but they didn't seem to realize that those cool temperatures meant the trout would still be there. The waterfall, scenic to them, meant oxygenated water to me. The difference between what they saw, and what I saw, made an old saying come back to me: "We find what we seek."

As psychologists, I am afraid we often find what we seek. Those of us who are clinically trained or oriented, and who study the problems of school children, so often find evidence in these children to fit our particular clinical point of view. I would like to suggest that we make our evaluations a little more objective, a little closer to the evidence that does exist. In leaping to conclusions about intrafamilial dynamics, we can be leaping to a misdiagnosis.

I will start with a postulate. My postulate is that a child (or any person) should be considered innocent of psychological problems until proven guilty. I would define a psychological prob-

Reprinted from *Exceptional Children*, Vol. 28 (1961), pp. 75-78. By permission of the author and publisher.

lem to mean that a person's difficulties with life stem primarily from his own personality structure, acting and reacting upon his environment so as to cause internal discontent or loss of productivity. Excluded from this definition, by implication, are reactions to an unusual stress, those which stem from physiological causes, those bred by cultural conflict, and those which are a common part of human development or decline. Of course, psychological problems will appear in many of these circumstances, reactive to the basic cause. Psychological problems then, by the definition I propose, must come primarily from the individual himself, due to whatever misconceptions or twists of personality that lie within him. To correct such problems would require change within the individual. Changing his environment, his physiology, his stage in the developmental cycle, or his culture, would not solve this problem.

With this definition, I think the burden of proof lies upon us, as psychologists, when we say a pupil has psychological problems. There are several questions to be answered before we can feel that a proper diagnosis has been reached.

Necessary Questions

What Is The Evidence To Indicate That Any Problem Exists?

Most of us are familiar with the misdiagnoses made at this point. You have encountered a teacher whose chemistry reacted badly to a particular pupil, even as ours does, but the pupil did not have a psychological problem. Because a teacher or a parent refers a child is not proof enough. The problem may lie in their own perception of the child, and not in the child.

We must ask, What behavioral evidence exists? What do others say of this youngster? How often has the so-called problem occurred? How long has it been going on? How acute is it? Is it periodic or chronic? What has been tried? Who else acknowledges the problem? What do the pupil's peers think? What does the child think?

There is no substitute for a thorough history. It is here that the evidence is sifted and many so-called problems turn out to be passing situations or misconceptions.

What Is The Child's Learning Ability?

You may think me old-fashioned because I put such early emphasis on what we call intelligence. Thirty years ago, I.Q.'s were the rage among psychologists. Now they are the rage among parents and admission officers, while some psychologists seem to find them old hat. We all know what's wrong with I.Q.'s and how we measure them. But perhaps we forget what's right about them.

If we are evaluating a pupil, we must remember that school is primarily a learning situation. How well that child learns and performs makes a great deal of difference to his parents, to his peers, and let me stress, to himself. A child's ability to learn in a school situation, whether we like it or not, determines to a large extent his place in school society. And intelligence, regardless of whether we like it and the manner in which it is measured, seems to have a great deal to do with that school performance. We all should remember that I.Q. is positively correlated with the amount of education completed; that it is one of the best single predictors for educational success; and that I.Q., socioeconomic status, and peer popularity in school have some rather high intercorrelations. Therefore, if a pupil has been referred to a school psychologist, one obvious question to be answered is, What is this child's learning ability? Has it been adequately measured? What could be influencing his scores? What can we expect scholastically from this child?

Let me add a word of caution about how we psychologists interpret I.Q.'s. So many times we hear ourselves say that this child has no real learning difficulty because his I.Q. is 110. But how many of us have made a distribution of the actual I.Q.'s in our school system to see where this places our pupil? You may be surprised to find, particularly if you are in a privileged school community, that 110 I.Q. is only the 44th percentile. It isn't bad, but the 44th percentile isn't good either, especially for a high school boy whose parents want him to go to college. This boy does have a learning difficulty in the sense that he is a little below the average for his local competition and he is going to have to work hard to be in the golden upper half. Of course, this type of error is more easily recognized when the parents make it! We all know of parents who over-expect for their child, which is a very human fault. We have all tried to break the news gently that their child has limited abilities. But how many times have we made the same mistake ourselves by failing to compare a pupil accurately with his own local competition?

What Is The Pupil's Socioeconomic Status?

The evidence on the positive relationship between socio-economic status (or SES) and academic achievement cannot be ignored, although there is a fatalistic and undemocratic aroma to the subject. Toby (1957) has reported: "Even by grade placement, for every age level, the average grade of middle-class urban children is higher than that of lower-class children." These differences, he says, are as true at seven and eight years as they are at high school. That should make us think of some larger force than individual psychological problems. Davie (1953) found a significantly high correlation between SES and school attendance. Havighurst (1944-1945) participated in a series of group investigations, all with the same result: Children from high SES homes did better on a wide battery of tests and achieved more education than did children from lower SES homes. Tested ability by occupational class shows the same correlation, namely the higher the occupational class, the higher the tested ability.

I am sure you know the mass of evidence in this area, all of it sobering. It seems to indicate that SES and tests of school achievement are positively related; that SES and intelligence test scores are positively related; that SES and the pursuit of education is positively related. Why this is so is not something to argue at this moment. But it does create problems in the school culture. Davis (1950) has been vigorous in calling attention to the conflicts between educational values and the values of lower-class children. Many of our lower-class pupils have a good hand I.Q. but a low head I.Q. and they don't fare well in school. Davis (1950, p. 30) has charged: "The conception that aggression and hostility are neurotic or maladaptive symptoms of a chronically frustrated adolescent is an ethnocentric view of middle-class psychiatrists. In lower-class families, physical aggression is as much a normal, socially approved and socially inculcated type of behavior as it is in frontier communities." How many aggressive problems were referred to us this past year in which we ignored a possible SES factor?

The evidence so far suggests that lower SES pupils enter our school culture with the odds against them. An unfortunate chain of events may start when this pupil has his first learning experience. Perhaps in kindergarten he is a child who does not follow instructions readily, take initiative, or share group responsibility. In the first grade he may not learn to read as quickly as others, is restless in the classroom, distracting, and the beginning of a discipline problem to his teacher. Because of his poor academic achievement, and probably a relatively low intelligence test score, he may be considered a slow learner who needs to be retained in one of the elementary grades. Thus may begin a chain of educational failures which will close, as far as the school is concerned, at or about the age of sixteen when this same pupil will leave school, two grades behind his age, without a high school diploma. He will leave behind him a series of frustrated teachers, guidance counselors, principals, and the school psychologist, who have tried to cope with a pupil who did not like school, did not succeed in it, and who did not respond to discipline, encouragement, counseling, psychological therapy, or, as a matter of fact, to any attempts of school culture either to change his attitudes or to educate him to the level of which he was capable. We need new educational methods for such pupils. The school psychologist at least must grasp the social forces at work and realize that there is more to a pupil's life and future welfare than his ability to succeed by school standards. The courageous school psychologist may even help such a pupil succeed within his own social class mores, rather than within those of school society.

What Is The Pupil's Cultural Background?

Does he come from a cultural group which has strong feelings, pro or con, about education and the authority of the school? In what way will his cultural background affect his reactions to school? How will he stand with his peers? Will he experience prejudice, either for or against himself, because of his cultural background? What will be the effect of his socioeconomic and cultural background?

All of us have seen these children who run head on into difficulty at school, not only with the learning process, but with school authority and with their peer society. All of us have known the boys like Jerry, from a lower SES background, and from the cultural group in town held in least respect. It would be hard to say which factors pushed Jerry into a chronic pattern of rebellion at school, his defiance of those nice middle-class lady teachers, or his show of bravado in fighting all school authority. Jerry had only one role with his peers, that of a strong man, and it was a role he played to the hilt. By fourth grade, he had left no other role for himself. His parents did not believe in school or its culture. Jerry saw no chance for himself to succeed socially at school, so his understandable reaction was to put up a good fight, and a good fight it was, lasting from kindergarten to the ninth grade when he left school.

Yes, he was seen by psychologists, and social workers, and psychiatrists, and so were his parents and older sister. And he was seen by principals and guidance counselors, and teachers who tried to befriend him, and coaches who tried to interest him in sports. But I have no pleasant ending to report to you. Jerry failed in school culture and I think we failed him, but I am not prepared to conclude that his basic problem was psychological, as I have defined it. It seems to me that his basic problem stemmed from social forces characteristic of many more pupils than just Jerry and his personal reactions were secondary to those factors. I may add that the social forces were sufficiently strong to make any type of psychological or therapeutic help unsuccessful, which might be a diagnostic sign in itself that the primary problem is not psychological in nature.

What Is This Pupil's Social Role With His Peers?

This question needs to be asked, and answered, before we can decide that a psychological problem exists. Of all the questions overlooked, this seems to be the most frequent. It isn't that the question isn't asked, or that teachers and counselors don't try to give their picture of the student's social status. It is more that they often don't know, or know enough. The fourteen-year-old boy who is a discipline problem to the adults in school may have a very important reputation with his peers, far more than his neighbor who offers no problems. By important reputation I also mean a good reputation, with both the top and the fringe cliques in student society. He, in short, may be one of the "good guys," even though he is flunking two courses and often in the principal's office. To understand another youngster's poor marks and rebellious attitude, we may have to understand how he is struggling to make it into a clique where such behavior will gain more status than by being a "nothing." There is a certain courage, after all, in defying adult authority, even if it doesn't win friends among the faculty or win favor at home. At the high school age, as we all know, the student wants to win favor with other students and not with us, as Gordon (1957) has so ably described.

The importance of a pupil's sociometric status is becoming more and more evident. One of the most interesting studies has been contributed by Buswell (1953) showing the relationship between sociometric status and scholastic achievement. She found that kindergarten pupils showed no correlation between social acceptability and achievement test scores, but when she repeated the study on the same pupils six months later in the first grade, the social structure had changed. By the fall of the first grade, when the emphasis on achievement begins, the high social acceptability group showed higher achievement score than did the low social acceptability group. She repeated her experiment on fifth grade pupils and then again when they had become sixth-graders. The high social acceptance group received higher achievement scores both times. When I.Q. was controlled, however, there were no differences between groups.

Now, what does this type of evidence suggest? It suggests a disturbing circular relationship among I.Q. school success, sociometric status—and if we look behind the I.Q. we know it is related to SES. It seems to say that "Them that has, gits." Then we come to the evidence contributed by Gronlund and Holmlund (1958) who began with a sociometric study on sixth grade pupils. Seven years later, when these same pupils were in high school, the authors found a positive relationship between sixth grade high sociometric status and (1) continuing in high school until graduation, (2) academic rank, (3) participation in extra-curricular activities, (4) participation in varsity sports, (5) leadership positions in school affairs, and (6) I.Q. In short, high sixth grade sociometric status was a rather good predictor of high school success. Finally, Bedoian (1953) adds a link to mental health in an interesting way. Among sixth grade children he found the more popular children had higher mental health scores than did the unpopular ones.

What Is The Status Of This Pupil's Physical Health?

I hope I don't need to stress the grave importance of ruling out physiological dysfunctioning before leaping to psychological conclusions. As a group, I think psychologists are becoming much more alert and diagnostically precise in picking up organic factors, particularly in the area of brain damage or cerebral dys-functioning. But let us not stop there. A child who is physically ill, as all parents know, is just not himself, and he doesn't have to have brain damage to show it. I think of Tommy, a thin nervous white-faced little third grader whose pediatrician referred him to the school psychologist for psychological problems. Yes, there were problems at home, plenty of them, and it would have been the easiest thing in the world to leap to a psychological conclusion. But a thorough history suggested little relation between his nervous symptoms and strife at home. His pulse and blood pressure were abnormally high, but they did not vary with pressures at school. Further medical studies were undertaken before the physician discovered that Tommy was severely hyper-thyroid. With proper medical treatment. Tommy's symptoms subsided. The problems at home remained.

There is increasing evidence on the relationship between physical disabilities and behavioral symptoms. Eisenberg (1960), after reviewing the studies in this area, feels that abnormalities in pregnancy and delivery have occurred in significantly higher proportions in those children with behavior disorders and reading disabilities than in matched control groups. Recent EEG work suggests children with behavior disorders display a higher than expected frequency of abnormal brain waves. A number of studies indicates a higher incidence of physical disabilities among children of lower I.Q., and lower I.Q. seems associated with lower SES. Strauss and Lehtinen (1955) and the more recent studies by Pollack (1957a, 1957b, 1958, and 1960), Krupp and Schwartzenberg (1960), Taylor (1959) and Haeussermann (1958) suggest improved diagnostic techniques which can be applied in schools.

Is This Pupil Going Through A Normal Developmental Phase?

One of our bibles seems to be that small report by Macfarlane, Allen and Honzik (1954) which gives us some idea of the pattern of behavior problems of children up to fourteen years of age. Why should we leap to psychological conclusions about a ten-year-old girl who is displaying a symptom common to her age that usually disappears by the age of fourteen? Or take the matter of speech difficulties. They seem to be common to boys, starting between the ages of three to five. How do we decide one speech difficulty is just a developmental phase and another is not? How do we decide who needs therapy and who should have treatment judiciously postponed? Which adolescent rebellion is normal, and therefore healthy, and which suggests an internal problem of a potentially pathological nature? The pupil who hangs onto the adults around school, but fails to make it with her peers, may be going through what all mothers call a phase, but is a deeper illness showing itself? This is where our judgment, our diagnostic skills, and our knowledge of the published evidence, are so badly needed.

Is This Pupil Reacting To Some Unrecognized Situation Within The School Environment?

Is he new to the school and struggling to establish himself with his peers? Is he lost in his subjects because of a difference in curriculum, or some academic area he has missed? Does he feel out of place? Is this little first grader upset because she's afraid of a dog on the way to school? This fourth grade boy, who is reported so defiant and troublesome in the classroom, is said by the gym teacher to be a fine sport and a leader. It turns out that this same boy was blamed by his teacher for an incident earlier in the year, one which he did not do, and his sense of fair play was outraged. His defiant attitude turns out to be a localized reaction within the school. In another classroom, we uncover one of those unusual class groupings, one that from the point of view of social psychology is unhealthy. The dominant clique is run by two surreptitious bullies who have turned the class against the different boys. What we have, unknown to adult eyes, is a secret police state. Reorganizing the class produces some amazing changes in children who were thought to have deeper psychological problems.

Is The Student Reacting To Some Unrecognized Situation At Home?

If he is not reacting to some unrecognized situation at school this becomes a necessary question. We all have been struck so many times by the things that trouble children which adults never even imagine. Our perspective is so different. Most of us have outgrown the witchcraft and mythology of childhood which can have a terrible grip on a child. I am thinking now of an entrancing eight-year-old girl, Anna, who was reported listless and irritable at home and in school. Anna had epilepsy and knew she did. She had to take medicine which was bitter. She hated to take it, but was scared not to take it. Behind her fear was a deeper one. Her beloved pet dog had died of a chronic disease, one which had ended in a fatal convulsion. Anna had nursed him tenderly and had been heartbroken. What no adult realized was that Anna thought she had the same disease as her dog and that she, too, was going to die. This was not helped by her older sister's teasing, for her older sister, like so many children, would tease in her most sensitive spot—namely, that her other pets were going to die the way her dog had. What the older sister did not realize was Anna's belief that she, too, was going to die. Cruel? No, not cruel, just children and children's perceptions of life. More of the exact nature of Anna's own illness was explained to her, and a better tasting medicine was used along with generous dashes of orange soda, and Anna was a very relieved little girl. She had a problem, maybe even a psychological one in that it stemmed from her own misperceptions, but one that was not unnatural and thus easily corrected with adequate information.

Is This Student Just A Different Child?

So many interesting adults, and so many creative ones, were not good at school, outstanding members of their social groups, active in extracurricular activities, or good at sports. Some of these same adults were very introspective children, 'odd balls,' poor at school work and teased mercilessly. Out of these differences have come wells of creative ability and unique perceptions which have enriched all of our lives. Sometimes one difference between these children and those with psychological problems is the degree of inner happiness. This is not always true, but sometimes the different child is not so pained by his difference, as he is by all the efforts to make him un-different, and by the disappointments to his parents when their efforts fail.

Walter, now sixteen, is such a boy. He was born to be an architect. His life is the design of buildings and interiors. For reasons which are not clear to me even now, he and his mother have never hit it off, but his father has tried to take his part in an ineffectual way. Life at home has been a vicious triangle for years, and that is a psychological problem. Yet much of it stems from the fact that Walter is different. He is a poor student at everything except art. He is only a fair athlete. He is not the all-American boy his father really wanted and his aesthetic interests arouse his mother's antagonism. Both parents have sent him to schools to reform him into a regular guy. They will not accept an unusual educational pattern for him. They find his dreaminess and lack of practicality a constant irritation. And Walter? Well, Walter lives for the day when he can be what he wants to be and be respected for it. In the meantime his life is very miserable. But the distinction I am trying to make is that I believe Walter would be a changed boy if he had lived in a different environment. Even today, he is a happy and engaging lad when he is in the company of adults who appreciate his qualities. With his peers? Well, you can guess. At boarding school or at public high school, Walter's type of boy usually has a hard time. Because of his lack of practicality, his naivete, he is often the butt of jokes and horseplay. Walter won't come into his own until he is an adult, and we will just have to pray that proper treatment may keep him from being too badly scarred.

Psychological Problems?

I share the concern that I'm sure most of you have, that many children who are different, and wholesomely different, are being diagnosed as psychological problems. Where do we draw the line? When is a difference interesting and refreshing; when is it pathological? When does a lack of social acceptance indicate an absorption with some future interest; when does it mean an unhealthy pattern?

I do not want to leave the impression that I don't think psychological problems exist. Of course they do, from little ones to big ones. Once a major illness is present, it isn't very hard to recognize it or diagnose it. As a matter of fact, I have always been amazed by the very limited number of ways in which people show mental illness. But it is a far different matter to separate the incipient schizophrenic fourteen-year-old from the healthy fourteen-year-old going through a developmental phase. Not all aggression is sick, not all withdrawal is sick, not all introspection is sick, not all underachievement is sick.

But before we use our professional skills to reach a diagnostic decision, I am suggesting we owe it to ourselves, to our pupils, to their families, to our teachers, and to our profession, to be very conscientious about our opinion. It should mean a great deal, if we keep high standards and avoid throwing labels around sloppily. I am suggesting these ten questions, and there are probably more, which we might ask ourselves before we say a pupil has a psychological problem. We can ask ourselves

1. What is the evidence to indicate that any problem exists?
2. What is the pupil's learning ability?
3. What is the pupil's socioeconomic background?
4. What is the pupil's cultural background?
5. What is the pupil's social role with his peers?
6. What is the status of this pupil's physical health?
7. Is this pupil going through a developmental phase?

8. Is this pupil reacting to some unrecognized situation in the school environment?

9. Is this pupil reacting to some unrecognized situation in his home environment?

10. Is this pupil just a different child?

If we can answer these ten questions satisfactorily, then we may be entitled to push our search into the psychological realm. As we search for psychological causes, I hope we can do so in the spirit of the British Committee on Maladjusted Children (1955) whose report begins

> Maladjustment is not the same as unconventionality or oddness of behavior or belief, which may not do a person or his fellows any harm. As Sterne pointed out in *Tristram Shandy*, "have not the wisest men in all ages . . . had their hobby-horses; . . . and so long as a man rides his hobby-horse peaceably and quietly along the King's highway, and neither compels you or me to get up behind him,—pray, Sir, what have either you or I to do with it? A man's idiosyncracies may even be a sign of self-confidence and strength, and lend attractiveness to his character."

References

Bedoian, V. H.: Mental health analysis of socially over-accepted, socially under-accepted, average, and underage pupils in the sixth grade. *J Educ Psychol, 44:* 366-371, 1953.

Buswell, Margaret M.: The relationship between the social structure of the classroom and the academic success of the pupils. *J Exp Educ, 22:* 37-52, 1953.

Davie, J. S.: Social class factors and school attendance. *Harvard Educ Rev, 23:*(3)175-185, 1953.

Davis, A.: *Social Class Influences Upon Learning.* Cambridge, Harvard, 1950.

Eisenberg, L.: Emotionally disturbed children and youth. In *Children And Youth In The 1960's.* Survey of papers prepared for White House Golden Anniversary Conference on Children and Youth, Washington, D.C., 1960.

Gordon, C. W.: *The Social System Of The High School.* Glencoe, Illinois, Free Press, 1957.

Gronlund, N. E., and Holmlund, W. S.: The value of elementary school sociometric scores for predicting pupils adjustment in high school. *Educ Admin and Supervis, 44:* 255-260, 1958.

Haeussermann, Else: Developmental potential of pre-school children. New York, Grune, 1958.

Havighurst, R. J., and Janke, L. L.: Relation between ability and social status in a midwestern community, I. Ten year old children. *J Educ Psychol, 35*: 357-368, 1944. (See also Warner, Havighurst and Loeb, and Janke and Havighurst, below.)

Janke, L. L. and Havighurst, R. J.: Relations between ability and social status in a Midwestern community. II. Sixteen-year-old boys and girls. *J Educ Psychol, 36*: 499-509, 1945.

Krupp, G. R., and Schwartzberg, B.: The brain-injured child: a challenge to social workers. *Soc Casework, 41*: (2)63-68, 1960.

Macfarlane, Jane W.; Allen, Lucille, and Honzik, Marjorie P.: A developmental study of the behavior problems of normal children between twenty-one months and fourteen years. *Univ Calif Publ Child Develop,* Los Angeles, U. of Calif., 1954, p. 2.

Pollack, M.: Brain damage, mental retardation, and childhood schizophrenia. *Amer J Psychiat, 115*:(5)422-428, 1958.

Pollack, M., and Goldfarb, W.: The face-hand test in schizophrenic children, A.N.A. *Arch Neur Psychiat, 77*: 635-642, 1957a.

Pollack, M., and Goldfarb, W.: The patterns of orientation in children in residential treatment for severe behavior problems. *Amer J Orthopsychiat, 27*:(3)538-552, 1957b.

Pollack, M., and Gordon, E.: The face-hand test in retarded and non-retarded emotionally disturbed children. (Manuscript from the author: shorter version in press, *Amer J Ment Def*)

Report of the Committee on Maladjusted Children. Ministry of Education, London, 1955. p. 3.

Strauss, A.A., and Lehtinen, Laura E. (Eds.): *Psychopathology And Education Of The Brain-injured Child.* New York, Grune, 1947, vol. I.

Taylor, Edith Meyer: *Psychological Appraisal Of Children With Cerebral Defects.* The Commonwealth Fund. Cambridge, Harvard, 1959.

Toby, J.: Orientation to education as a factor in the school maladjustment of lower-class children. *Soc Forces, 35*: 259-266, 1957.

Warner, W. L.; Havighurst, R. J., and Loeb, M. B.: *Who shall be educated?* New York, Harper, 1944.

Chapter 6

The Identification Of Emotionally Disturbed
Elementary School Children

WAYNE R. MAES

$\mathbf{M}$ENTAL HEALTH specialists have devoted many hours to identifying emotionally disturbed children in elementary schools. It is clear that individual psychological analysis is both costly and inefficient. There are not sufficient psychologists available nor sufficient funds to employ them in large enough numbers to accomplish the task of identifying the children in elementary schools who are in need of preventive or remedial mental health experiences.

Numerous efforts have been made to develop group survey techniques which could effectively and efficiently identify elementary school children in need of psychotherapeutic assistance. One of the more recent and more comprehensive of these studies was conducted by Bower, Tashnovian, and Larson (1958) in selected elementary schools in California. They collected data on pupil behavior which past research had shown to be related to emotional disturbance and which teachers could readily gather with a minimum of assistance from trained clinicians. Data were collected on 192 emotionally disturbed children and 4,871 children not previously identified as emotionally disturbed, all of whom were in grades four, five, or six. (The criterion of emotional disturbance was that of having been previously identified by a school clinician as emotionally disturbed.) The sources of data collected by Bower and their effectiveness in dif-

Reprinted from *Exceptional Children*, Vol. 32 (1966), pp. 607-609. By permission of the author and publisher.

ferentiating between the emotionally disturbed and normal children appear in Table I.

TABLE I.

SOURCES OF DATA IN BOWER'S STUDY

Reading achievement (California Achievement Test)*
Arithmetic (California Achievement Test)*
Intelligence achievement (California Achievement Test of Mental Maturity—short form)*
Sociometric status (a class play)*
Teacher rating—behavior*
Teacher rating—physical*
Self-concept (thinking about yourself)
Age-grade relationship
Absences from school
Socioeconomic status of the family

*Statistically significant difference between the emotionally disturbed and normal children.

The authors suggested that the significant variables in Table I could profitably be used to identify emotionally disturbed children in grades four through six. A system of weighting the above variables based on the sizes of the respective critical ratios was developed. Total scores for individual pupils were derived by summing the weighted scores for the variables.

The following limitations existed in the procedures which Bower employed in analyzing the data:

1. The weights were not cross validated, and therefore they capitalized on random error, thus causing the predictability of the variables to appear spuriously high.

2. Assigning weights based upon the sizes of the critical ratios (a) does not identify suppressor variables which do not correlate with the criterion variable but which do contribute to prediction, (b) may assign too much weight to variables which are highly intercorrelated, and (c) necessitates the inclusion of each of the significant variables when a fewer number may predict just as effectively.

Using the basic techniques developed by Bower, a two phase study was conducted to determine the effect of the following on identification of emotionally disturbed children in grades four, five, and six: (a) employing a different statistical treatment of the data and (b) making additions and modifications in the data collecting instruments.

The Sample

All pupils in grades four through six in the Lansing, Michigan, public schools who had been previously diagnosed as emotionally disturbed were identified. This group was comprised of pupils who had been identified by the local school district psychological services staff and those identified by the community child guidance clinic. Each of these pupils had been identified through an intensive individual diagnostic study. Only those pupils who were thought to be sufficiently disturbed to require individual psychotherapy were considered emotionally disturbed. In this manner, 91 emotionally disturbed children were identified in grades four through six. Because the limitations of time and money obviated the study of all of the children, a random sample of 44 was selected. Insufficient data were available on four of the emotionally disturbed children so that the final sample consisted of 40 emotionally disturbed children and their 548 normal classmates in 22 different classrooms.

Phase I

Data were collected on each of the pupils in the present sample on the variables which Bower found significantly differentiated between the emotionally disturbed and normal pupils. Using Bower's method of assigning weights, a total score was derived for each child on the combined variables. A point biserial correlation was computed between these weighted scores and the dichotomous variable, emotional disturbance-normality. The correlation was .27, significantly different from zero at the .01 level. This provided a cross validated index of the prediction of Bower's weights.

The emotionally disturbed and normal groups were randomly divided in half, creating two groups of emotionally disturbed children with 20 in each group, and two groups of normal children with 274 in each group. A multiple regression analysis was computed on the significant variables in Bower's study on one of the emotionally disturbed and one of the normal groups. The variables, in decreasing order of prediction, were teacher rating —behavior, arithmetic achievement (California Achievement Test), intelligence (California Test of Mental Maturity—short form), a class play, teacher rating—physical, and reading achievement (California Achievement Test).

The last three variables contributed negligibly to prediction of the criterion variable. Consequently, the beta weights on only the first three variables were used to derive weighted scores for the remaining two groups of 20 emotionally disturbed and 274 normal children. A point biserial correlation was computed between the derived weighted scores and the criterion variable. The correlation was .21, significantly greater than zero at the .01 level.

The point biserial correlation of .27 computed with Bower's weights on six variables was not significantly different from the correlation of .21 derived from use of three variables identified through multiple regression analysis in the study. The use of the three variables (teacher rating, arithmetic achievement, and intelligence) is preferable, because much less time is required in the collection of data, while prediction is not significantly reduced.

Phase II

Two modifications were made in the instruments used for data collection prior to this analysis: (a) Chi squares were computed on each item on the teacher rating of behavior and physical status, and only those items were included in this analysis which significantly differentiated between the emotionally disturbed and normal children. (b) A self-concept inventory, Projective Self-Concept Scale, designed for the purposes of this study, was also included in the analysis.

The emotionally disturbed and normal groups were randomly divided in half, creating two groups of emotionally disturbed children with 20 in each group, and two groups of normal children with 274 in each group. A multiple regression analysis was computed on the first group of 20 emotionally disturbed and 272 normal pupils. The variables, in decreasing order of prediction, were: teacher rating, intelligence (California Test of Mental Maturity—short form), arithmetic (California Achievement Test), and self-concept.

The last two variables made a negligible contribution to predicting the criterion variable. Beta weights on the first two variables were used in deriving weighted scores for the remaining two groups of 20 emotionally disturbed and 274 normal children. A point biserial correlation was computed between the derived weighted scores and the criterion variable. The correlation was .32, significantly greater than zero at the .01 level.

The prediction achieved with two variables (teacher rating and intelligence) is as effective as Bower achieved through use of six variables which required a great deal more time in data collection. This prediction may appear to be inflated by the circularity of the criterion measure (diagnostic study of children referred by teachers and others) and the teacher rating scale. The effort of this circularity is considerably reduced by the following: (a) Some of the emotionally disturbed children were identified by the local child guidance clinic as a result of direct referrals from parents. (b) With few exceptions, the emotionally disturbed children no longer had the teacher who had initially referred them. (c) Many pupils identified by the teachers as having emotional problems were not considered by the psychologists to be sufficiently emotionally disturbed to warrant referral for treatment, so they appear in the normal rather than the emotionally disturbed group. (d) Some of the emotionally disturbed children were referred by teachers for other than emotional reasons (e.g., intellectual or reading diagnosis).

Table II indicates the extent to which these two variables can assist in the identification of children who are sufficiently emotionally disturbed to require treatment. If all children with a weighted score of .1000 or higher were referred for diagnostic study, 15 would be identified as emotionally disturbed, while 56 would not. Approximately one of every five children referred would be identified as sufficiently emotionally disturbed to require psychotherapy.

TABLE II.

WEIGHTED SCORES ON TEACHER RATINGS AND INTELLIGENCE
AS PREDICTORS OF EMOTIONAL DISTURBANCE

Weighted Score	Emotionally Disturbed		Normal	
	Number	Percent	Number	Percent
.1000-.3070	15	75	56	21
.0500-.0999	4	20	54	20
.0014-.0499	1	5	164	59
Total	20	100	274	100

Reference

Bower, E.; Tashnovian, P., and Larson, C.: *A Process For Early Identification Of Emotionally Disturbed Children*. Sacramento, California State Department of Education, 1958.

Chapter 7

A Method Of Identifying Maladjusted Children In The Classroom

TED CHRISTIANSEN

T HE INCIDENCE of maladjustment (defined in this paper as emotional disturbance and social maladjustment collectively) is estimated to be 2 to 12 percent of the total school population, depending upon the research study examined. These figures pertain to serious maladjustment. The incidence of mild maladjustment is reported to be much higher.

The 2 to 12 percent estimate means that the classroom teacher may expect as many as four children in a class of thirty-five to be seriously maladjusted. It is essential for the welfare of the maladjusted child and for the proper education of the other children in the classroom that the seriously maladjusted child be identified early and referred for psychological diagnosis and treatment. Although there is much disagreement as to what constitutes serious maladjustment and how best to measure it, most researchers believe the classroom teacher is best qualified to handle the initial screening process.

It is the purpose of this paper to present a check list that can be used by the classroom teacher as a screening device to identify the seriously maladjusted child. The check list is based on the assumption that maladjusted children differ from normal children in the number and nature of their adjustment problems. An adjustment problem arises when the child interacts with significant people in the home, school, or peer-group setting. The

Reprinted from *Mental Hygiene*, Vol. 5, (1967) pp. 574-75. By permission of the author and publisher.

normal child, in general, makes satisfactory adjustments to conflict situations that develop in his interpersonal relationships. The maladjusted child, however, fails to resolve many of these same conflicts.

The presence of adjustment problems is revealed by deviations in the child's regular pattern of behavior. Even with normal children such deviations occur, though they are not chronic in nature or intensely exhibited, since the conflict is eventually resolved. Some of the behavioral deviations that may appear in children with adjustment problems are shown in the check list that follows:

Check List Of Behavioral Deviations In Children With Adjustment Problems

1. Underachievement in school that is not related to physiologic or other logical causes.
2. Chronic displays of unhappiness or depression.
3. Destroys the property of others.
4. Frequently lies or boasts.
5. Often steals things.
6. Disrupts normal classroom procedures constantly.
7. Frequent absence or tardiness for which no physiologic or other sound reason can be found.
8. Relates poorly to peers in cooperative situations.
9. Shows withdrawal characteristics such as excessive timidity or quietness.
10. Daydreams frequently.
11. Shows unusual anxiety, fearfulness, or tenseness.
12. Shows a preference for working and playing alone.
13. Highly sensitive to the reactions and criticisms of others.
14. Tires easily or appears to be drowsy much of the time.
15. Has an unkempt or slovenly appearance.
16. Tries too hard to please others.
17. Constantly strives to gain the attention and approval of others.
18. Overly concerned with a sense of order and consistency. Tends to resist change.
19. Shows fear of getting dirty.

20. Displays facial or other bodily twitchings or tics.
21. Complains of headaches, stomach-aches, etc.
22. Appears to be incapable of having fun.
23. Speaks incessantly of a dislike for school.
24. Immature and irresponsible in dealing with others.
25. Defiant, impertinent, or disobedient in class.
26. Teases, fights with, or bullies other children.
27. Loud and boisterous.
28. Possesses an irritable temperament, often erupting in temper tantrums.
29. Overly competitive with others.
30. Frequent displays of jealousy.
31. Has trouble with the police.
32. Uses profane language.
33. Has deep feelings of inferiority or inadequacy and reveals these feelings in his behavior.
34. Associates mainly with younger children.
35. Inattentive in class, or has a short attention span.
36. Easily gets discouraged or flustered in some learning task.
37. Displays bizarre or unusual behavior.

This check list is a valid screening device for maladjustment when the teacher uses certain criteria as guides in the identification process. The most important criteria in identifying serious maladjustment are the number, type, and frequency of behavioral deviations. Research has not provided an answer concerning the number of deviations that a child must manifest before he is classified as seriously maladjusted. Typically, however, maladjusted children show a multiplicity of behavioral deviations.

Research studies have shown a positive correlation between maladjustment and the extent to which a child's behavioral deviations diverge from accepted norms. This means that the child who exhibits the more unusual or serious of the deviations listed above is the child more likely to be maladjusted. Since normal children also manifest certain of the behavioral deviations shown in the check list, the frequency with which a deviation is displayed becomes an important factor to consider. When a child consistently shows a pattern of deviating behavior, the presence of serious maladjustment must be suspected.

In summary, it is important that referral for psychological diagnosis be made when the behavioral deviations of a particular child can be related to one of the above three criteria; and diagnosis is mandatory for children whose pattern of behavior relates to three or even two of these criteria.

Chapter 8

Psychiatric Examination Of The Child

MARVIN I. SHAPIRO

THE PSYCHIATRIC EXAMINATION of a child may superficially bear very little resemblance to the psychiatric examination of an adult patient. Nonetheless, the interview with the child—although it may be conducted on the floor during a game of jacks or with the patient sitting on the examiner's lap sobbing over a broken toy—remains essentially a reapplication of basic principles of interviewing techniques in a different setting.

In developing an understanding of the emotional aspects of a child's difficulties, the pediatrician, general practitioner, psychiatrist or other worker may at first feel uncertain in his approach to the child. Many unexpected, disconcerting situations develop, and it is often not clear what to look for during the contact with the child. Frequently all that is obtained from the examination is an impressionistic recollection of some outstanding trait or performance rather than a well-considered appraisal of the child and the problem. The mental status examination is useful in evaluating the personality of the adult patient. There has been no comparable standardized guide, however, for the psychiatric examination of the child.

The purpose of this communication is to present a form for the diagnostic evaluation of a child which organizes the many inferences that may be drawn from interaction with the child. Space limitation prevents a discussion of the many specific contributions which have been made on this subject, but special mention

Reprinted from *Mental Hygiene*, Vol. 43 (1959) pp. 32-39. By permission of the author and publisher.

should be made of the monograph titled *Diagnostic Process In Child Psychiatry* (1957). The writings of Erikson (1950), Sullivan (1954), A. Freud (1946), Lippman (1956), Gill (1954), Witmer (1946) and Nixon have also been drawn upon freely.

Background

Before taking up the examination itself, it will be useful to review some general concepts that help put the diagnostic activity into proper perspective in the process of helping a child by means of psychiatric intervention.

The study of a child's difficulties must include an evaluation of the familial and environmental factors. In this paper, however, the focus is upon the child himself. It is helpful to keep in mind that while the doctor is going about his work the child is also busily appraising the doctor, and that the conclusions formed by the child will enter into the clinical behavior the doctor is observing.

The psychiatric examination differs from the medical or laboratory examination in that psychiatric examination, diagnosis, and treatment go on simultaneously and cannot be separated from one another. Like a juggler, the examiner needs to coordinate the many aspects of his relation to the child. The emphasis in this outline will be upon organizing the information originating from the interview in such a way as to enable the doctor to act most effectively in behalf of the child and his problem. It is planned to consider what takes place during the psychiatric examination of a child, what is to be observed and tested. The problem of *how* to conduct the examination is outside the scope of this paper, as such skills are best gained under supervision and no fixed procedure for this can be easily described.

Prior to the examination, the doctor should have some general plans to help him organize the raw data of the child's behavior. He should have some ideas, obtained from a previous contact with the parents, as to what to expect. The purpose of the examination is to determine the nature of the problem, whether or not treatment is indicated and if so, who is to receive it—the child, the parents or both. An effort is made to categorize the problem in the classification system used in general psychiatry, and the doctor accumulates the evidence that permits him to diagnose the presence of organic brain damage, a psychotic disorder, a psychoneurosis, etc. When psychopathology is found, the doctor evaluates its severity, seeking to clarify whether the disturbance is a situational response and transitory or whether it has become part of the child's personality. The examiner's estimate of the treatability of the disturbance or of the child's capacity to change is just as important as the recognition of psychopathology.

With this as our orientation, we can turn to a consideration of the psychiatric examination. It is to be anticipated that the items suggested in this study are not to be used during the interview in the same order in which they appear in the outline. Rather, the form may be useful as a mental check list of the various elements which enter into the examination.

Identification

This is an orienting statement which forms the background and reason for the clinical evaluation of the child. The subsequent interview will attempt to answer the question implied here. Where the parent has a host of complaints regarding the child, it is important to identify the primary difficulty which is the most disturbing to the parent.

The Outline Of The Psychiatric Examination Of The Child

IDENTIFICATION
Name, age, sex, religion, color, ordinal position, reason for referral, who referred, first or second examination, etc.

APPEARANCE
Build, facial expression, clothing, health, defects in hearing, vision, etc., personality traits, mannerisms.

INTERPERSONAL RELATIONS
Interaction with parent—waiting room, degree and type of anxiety upon separation, response to reassurance, reaction upon rejoining parent.

Interaction with examiner—attitude: arrogant, suspicious, cooperative, etc.; capacity to relate; type of relation: trusting, controlling, erotic, etc.; role taken and role assigned to doctor; feeling aroused in reaction to patient; beginning compared to end of hour; first interview as compared to last.

CAPACITIES

Intelligence—estimated level: knowledge, imagination, grasp of situation; potential capacity.

Affects—mobility, appropriateness, predominant moods, shame, anger, depression, anxiety, etc., shifts in tension, somatic expressions as sweating, blushing.

Motor—coordination, gait, muscularity, use of hands, body, activity pattern, inhibited, immature, hyperactive, etc.

Speech—clarity of diction, of ideas, defects, vocabulary, pressure, spontaneity, voice quality, etc.

CONTENT

(Attitudes, feelings, ideas, etc.)

Towards clinic visit—reaction to visit, grasp of purpose, awareness of difficulties, reaction to symptoms, feelings about return visits, participating in planning.

Towards self—Behavior, appearance, body, sex, intellect, worries, fears, preoccupations, etc.

Towards others—parents, siblings, relatives, peers, teachers.

Towards things—pets, hobbies, possessions, money, food, school.

PLAY AND FANTASY

Play—approach to and interest in toys, toys used, mode of play: incorporative, extrusive, intrusive, etc.; manner of play: constructive, disorganized, nurtural, etc., distractibility, play disruptions, etc.

Fantasy—wishes, dreams, daydreams, fantasies, ambitions.

CLINICAL IMPRESSION

Descriptive—summarize personality structure.

Dynamic—major areas of conflicts, mechanisms of adaptation.

Statistical—use standard nomenclature and code number (Diagnostic, 1952).

PROGNOSIS

Benign, malignant, acute, chronic, with treatment, without treatment.

DISPOSITION

Further diagnostic studies, need for treatment, treatability, psychiatric therapy, environmental control.

TREATMENT

Individual, group, collaborative, consultative; frequency and estimated duration of therapy, goals, family management, countertransference impressions, general approach.

Appearance

A vivid description of the impression that the child creates helps to establish a mental picture of the kind of child being examined. The items listed make no attempt to exhaust the description possibilities. Some further items could include family resemblances in the facial expression, whether the child appears older or younger than his stated age, details of body care such as bitten nails or unkempt hair. Gross neurological signs such as facial assymetry, disturbances of gait or nystagmus will suggest further medical investigation. The first few minutes of the interview may be regarded as having a far greater degree of intensity and therefore more significant influence upon the remainder of the interview than any other similar few minutes during the examination. Aichorn (1935) has empasized the importance of the quick impression in the beginning moments of the interview when recognition of the dominant attitude and feelings of the child enable the doctor to respond most appropriately to the child.

Interpersonal Relations

Observation of the child in the waiting room often furnishes valuable clues as to the nature of the parent-child relationship. of handling the child, the reaction of the child and the parent the attitude of the parent as expressed in voice tone and manner of handling the child, the reaction of the child and the parent to the separation—all these are noted in the first few moments of the study.

As a general procedure, it is preferable to plan for at least two diagnostic interviews. While one may be sufficient (and at another time three or four sessions may be indicated), two interviews permit the examiner to observe the changes in the child's responses to his visits. A child who remains detached and solidly defensive in successive interviews presents a different task in the planning of therapy from the one who shows a progressive ability to relax and to relate. The former indicates that the character formation has already become involved and the child will probably require individual therapy regardless of any subsequent alteration in parental attitudes and behavior. In the latter case, the changing nature of the relationship indicates a greater elasticity of the child's personality. This in turn suggests that the attempt to change the parents' attitudes and relationship to the child will be an important part of the treatment plan.

The feelings aroused in the examiner in reaction to the child are another valid source of data. At the descriptive level, a child may appear to be silent and inhibited. Yet one child may be frozen with fright, another rigid with anger, and still a third provocatively teasing. The most sensitive recorder of these differing moods remains the emotional response of the examiner.

Capacities

Here is described both the endowment that the child possesses and his ability to use it freely. This includes the enduring assets as well as the outstanding liabilities which are observed in the child. The level of functioning and the degree of stability in maintaining this level form a base line against which future progress or regression can be measured. The manner of functioning that the child demonstrates may suggest the therapeutic approach to be used. One child may be overintellectualized and need help in relation to isolation of emotional feelings. Another may act impulsively, indicating difficulty in controlling motor activities. Still another may be unusually sensitive and shrink from close contacts with people.

The examiner is alert for fluctuations in the level of performance such as flashes of intelligence, which help in the differential diagnosis of a brain-injured child or a mentally retarded one.

Content

It is helpful to gain some understanding of the child's ideas and feelings about coming to see the doctor. The preparation of the child for the examination should be reviewed beforehand with the parents. It is usually quite revealing to observe the results of preparation, not only in terms of the child's personality but also in terms of the parent-child relationship. There are many possibilities to explore: The child may not have heard what was said to him, or he may have distorted the information, or the parent may have been unable to be direct with the child in this matter.

During the examination the child should be prepared by the examiner for other procedures such as psychological tests, and for future visits. The child's ability or inability to express his feelings about such important figures as his parents helps the examiner to map out the sensitive areas in the child's living experiences. The overall total response of the child to the new situation throws light upon the character formation and the defenses that the child characteristically uses in meeting life's stresses. The child's appropriate or inappropriate response to the clinic setting furnishes an opportunity for estimating the capacity to adapt.

The doctor needs to be familiar with the series of problems that each child meets in growing up and to evaluate the current difficulties in terms of the successful or unsuccessful integration of these successive stages of psychosexual development. The individual problem may appear in the form of a currently unrealistic belief about the world or about himself. It may show up as an exaggerated feeling or absence of feeling, or an inability to act, or a preoccupation with one particular activity, or indeed any combination of any or all of these. Once identified, the tendencies should be cautiously tested to see whether it is flexible and reversible or whether it has become isolated from the influences of daily living and part of the character of the child.

Throughout all of his efforts to understand the child, the examiner does not simply probe for factual material but creates the atmosphere which is most favorable for a spontaneous interchange of matters of interest to the child.

Play and Fantasy

The child's fantasy life and play activity offers significant indicators of the unconscious determinants which enter into his behavior. Through these media, as through dreams, the needs and wishes that are too anxiety-provoking to be directly expressed find discharge. A child can be encouraged to share his fantasies by such questions as "If you could make three magic wishes, what would you wish for?" or "What do you want to be when you grow up?" or "What is your favorite program on television?" The doctor can express his interest in hearing about dreams which the child enjoyed and dreams which were frightening to him. This tension-releasing function of fantasy and play is not only of service to our diagnostic purpose, but also indicates the therapeutic openings which can be used in helping the child gradually express his desires and fears more freely.

While the emphasis in this paper has been upon a verbal interchange, at times it may be desirable to use play materials such as dolls, clay, or pencil and paper to help the child express himself. The experience and personal preference of the examiner will help decide the choice of such aids. A few dolls in a family scene may help the child relate how he feels about an emotionally charged aspect of his home life. If he shows an interest in drawing pictures he may be asked to tell a story about them. As the child talks, the examiner listens for the particular affect, such as shame or anxiety or anger, which appears as a persistent thread woven into the fabric of the stories and dreams. It is this thread that is so important in understanding the painful feelings against which the child needs to defend himself.

The mode of play item has been adapted from Erikson (1950) and refers to the principal way that the child functions or, to put it differently, to his main style of life. For example, the hyperactive child who is unusually curious and prematurely pugnacious, who literally gets into everything, may be using this intrusive form of behavior to express unresolved phallic strivings. Sudden alteration or disintegration of a play activity is carefully noted as a sign of increasing tension and the examiner relates the disruption in play to what has just preceded it.

Clinical Impression

These separate diagnostic impressions summarize the significant findings which have emerged from the examination. The child is described as to what type of a person he is and how he tends to deal with his difficulties. From the review of his observation and participation, the doctor also infers what the sources of the difficulties are. The value of a statistical diagnosis lies more in the direction of recording information about similar clinical problems in order to gain a broader base for our understanding, rather than of being of immediate clinical use with the child.

The diagnosis of psychopathology in the child is less definitive than the diagnosis of psychopathology found in the adult. The immaturity of the child and the flexibility of his defenses allow for a shifting of patterns of response to stress. An understanding of this prepares the doctor for the discrepancies he will often meet where the child's reported problem is so different from what is actually observed clinically. The interview is part of a total dynamic interplay of forces, and the relatively isolated sample of behavior which is noted will limit the scope of conclusions to be made. Still, a working hypothesis that allows practical, realistic action to be taken can almost always be synthesized from the various data that have been accumulated up to this point.

Prognosis

A projected course of events may be considered in terms of a historical review of the problem as it has developed up to the present time. While the doctor is unable to predict every adaptive stress that the child will face, he may be able to anticipate some. For instance, it may be expected that an eight-year-old patient who shows a potentially psychotic disorder will have considerable difficulty in handling the problems of adolescence, and perhaps may be unable to manage them with success. Social and economic realities, the stability of the family unit, the intelligence and concern of the parents are some of the significant factors to be weighed in the prognosis. To these the doctor adds his judgment of the malignant or benign quality of the child's difficulty as it appeared during the examination.

Disposition

Here the doctor recommends the next step to be taken in the management of the child's problem. The primary decision to be made is in regard to the treatability within the setting where the child is examined. In a clinic where different workers may see the child and his parents, the assignment of the collaborating therapist is considered. Recommendations for further medical studies are also made when necessary.

Treatment

Once the need for and the feasibility of psychotherapy has been established, further details of treatment are to be considered. The decision of who is to receive treatment—the child, the parent or both—is important. The type and frequency of therapy—whether supportive or uncovering, individual or group —should be considered. The goal of therapy and the problems that might be anticipated should be recorded as well. These matters are not regarded as fixed and unalterable but are to be changed when indicated.

Discussion

While the technical problems of interviewing do not lend themselves readily to didactic analysis, it may be fruitful to reflect upon some of the special situations which often arise in work with children.

Recognizing that the child often comes unwillingly, the doctor is prepared to meet and help his patient, who is frequently most uncooperative. If possible, the doctor sees the child alone in order to observe how he handles himself when he is on his own. With some children, however, the separation may stir up such an overwhelming amount of anxiety as to threaten to disrupt self-control. In these situations the parent is asked to accompany the child until a tolerance for the separation is developed. The principle here is the same as is found in all fields of medicine: The doctor himself should do no harm and must not introduce a new traumatic experience into the problem.

Should the child angrily refuse to accompany the doctor to his office, the doctor responds as appropriately as possible to each specific situation. He accepts the child's anger as an expression of anxiety over the examination. At the same time, he helps the child avoid feelings of shame which could arise afterwards if infantile, regressive behavior were allowed to control the situation. This is accomplished by the firm insistence that the examination be carried out. By his own direct participation the child has the opportunity to see that his fears about it were unrealistic. In the case of a preschool child the examiner may simply pick up the child in the waiting room and carry him into the office. This, however, would be humiliating for a child of school age, who is no longer accustomed to such physical control by parent-figures; here the doctor would be acting more appropriately to take the child firmly by the arm and lead him into the office. This illustrates an important point, namely, that the doctor needs to adapt his own behavior and expectations concerning the child's performances to the age and personality of each patient he sees. The needs and problems of the preschool toddler are different from those of the adolescent, and each requires a modification in the clinical approach used by the doctor.

The question of the use of physical force is often a source of personal difficulty in professional work with children. The doctor is ready to act whenever necessary to keep the situation within limits of comfort and safety. If verbal controls do not suffice, then physical control may be required. The confident readiness and unambivalence of the doctor is actually reassuring to the child, who may have anxiety over his own lack of self-control.

The real dependence of the child upon adults requires that the doctor be aware of his dual role. He is both a parent-surrogate as well as a physician and cannot remain completely impersonal in his relation to the child. In an interview with an adult patient who breaks down and starts to cry, the doctor waits until he has regained composure. In the case of a young child, however, the doctor does not remain so detached, but offers the child his own handkerchief or draws him close for physical comforting. In working with the preschool child, the physical nearness of the examiner may be used to help establish the relationship. It is often of value for the examiner to pick up a child who is sitting alone and feeling very alone and hold him on his lap. If a child remains absolutely silent in the face of the examiner's attempts to relate to him, it may be helpful to gently take the child's pulse rate. A racing pulse suggests that the child is struggling to control inner tension, while a relatively normal pulse rate indicates a greater degree of ego participation in the resistance.

In this fashion the diagnostic process demands active participation by the doctor so that bits of behavior can be properly evaluated. A careful consideration of the physiological factors, psychosexual development and cultural background is necessary for the analysis of any one clinical problem.

Since the major portion of this paper has been centered around the facets of examination and diagnosis, a reconsideration of therapy during the interview should be added to restore balance in this matter of helping a child in difficulty. Since the child is most often brought to the clinic because of the parents' concern, his initial position is a passive one. The symptomatology for which the parents are seeking help may in no way correspond to the worries or concerns that the child has about himself. Part of the purpose of the visit, therefore, from a therapeutic point of view, is to interpret the interview in terms of what the child himself wants or is worried about or would like to be helped with. We seek, at all times, to engage the child's own participation in the therapeutic process. If this concern with the child's own preoccupation is lacking, the examination will tend to remain an objective description of the child and his functioning, and the child's own emotional investment will be minimal. Ideally, his contact with the doctor should be a constructive experience in living for the child. It should expand his trust of adults and begin to supply the help he needs.

References

Aichorn, August: *Wayward Youth.* New York, Viking, 1935.

Diagnostic and Statistical Manual: Mental Disorders. Washington, American Psychiatric Association, 1952.

Erikson, Erik H.: *Childhood and Society.* New York, Norton, 1950.

Freud, Anna: *The Psychoanalytic Treatment of Children,* London. Imago, 1946.

Gill, Merton: *The Initial Interview In Psychiatric Practice.* New York, N. Y. U., 1954.

Group for the Advancement of Psychiatry: *The Diagnostic Process in Child Psychiatry.* Report 38, August, 1957.

Lippman, Hyman: *Treatment Of The Child In Emotional Conflict.* New York, McGraw, 1956.

Nixon, Norman: personal communication.

Sullivan, Harry Stack: *The Psychiatric Interview.* New York, Norton, 1954.

Witmer, H. L.: *Psychiatric Interviews With Children.* New York, Commonwealth Fund, 1946.

SECTION C

DYNAMICS

Chapter 9

Three Forces In Psychology And Their Ethical And Educational Implications

PAUL BRUCE

P RACTICALLY all strands of our society are being influenced by theories and research from the field of psychology. Probably the most blatant example of this influence is seen in the women's magazines which month after month headline lead articles by "experts" advising and analyzing the psychological problems of our day: sex, marriage, child rearing, narcotics, alcoholism, etc. Even more significant than this is the more subtle influence psychology is having in such fields as advertising (*à la* Vance Packard's *The Wastemakers*), human engineering in industry, psychotherapy and counseling, and, of course, in our schools. Maybe one measure of this impact is the amount of critical attention psychology (in the name of mental health) is getting from the ultra-conservative elements who, indeed, find the influence from psychology to be threatening the *status quo* of a bygone era.

The point I want to make is that if through psychology humans can be influenced in certain directions, then the ethical problem arises of evaluating these directions in terms of their being desirable or not. And if through psychology the process of education toward certain goals becomes more effective, then it becomes imperative that these goals and the determination of these goals be carefully evaluated.

Reprinted from *Educational Forum*, Vol. 30 (1966), pp. 277-285. By permission of the author, publisher and Kappa Delta Pi, an honor society in education.

Now, the typical psychologist (or I might better say the typical scientific psychologist) does not like to admit the ethical implications of his discipline; he prefers to don the robes of scientific impartiality and limit his consideration to the quest for truth as he finds it. But I don't think we should let him get away with this. We need to face up to the ethical implications ourselves, and we need to ask the psychologist to face up to the ethical implications of their theories and research and even to take a stand regarding them.

To illustrate and further define this issue, I want to discuss three forces or schools of influence in psychology today and indicate the ethical and educational implications of their formulations as I see them. These are associationism—particularly as represented by reinforcement (S-R) theory; Freudianism or classical psychoanalytic theory; and the third force which is relatively new and has no consistent label as yet, but goes under the names of humanistic psychology, perceptual psychology, existential psychology or neo-Freudianism. I will present these three schools of thought briefly as theoretical models and ask the reader to realize, as with everything else, that the adherents and practitioners who represent these models modify the theory to fit their own needs and perceptions.

Associationism

Associationism in psychology developed during the latter part of the nineteenth century out of the thinking of such philosophers as Herbart, who described the mind as a complex of isolated sensations, ideas, thoughts, decisions, and feelings bound together by the process of association. With the aid of a new interest in the use of animals for observation and experimentation, psychologists, first under the leadership of E. L. Thorndike, developed theories of behavior most familiarly represented by the stimulus-response formula. Thus, Thorndike proposed that every new idea, every new feeling or sensation is a response to a preceding idea, feeling, or sensation. Under this system, memory or learning was explained as a series of stimulus-response connections, particular stimuli calling forth the specific responses. Various laws or principles of learning were developed which explained the establishment of a bond or association between stimulus and response. For example, reward or punishment, repetition, need satisfaction, reinforcement, conditioning, etc., were postulated as effecting learning and could be used to elicit certain desired behavior patterns.

This school of thought has persisted though modified and developed, and today it remains the most popular theory (at least among scientific and academic psychologists) and perhaps the most influential force representing psychology in society today. In our schools and colleges, the prevalent use of repetition as in drills (e.g., write each spelling word five times); the use of workbooks and tests which provide the stimulus and require the student to provide the "right" response which is subsequently approved or disapproved; the extensive use of a system of rewards and penalties (as in the way grades are typically given); all of these reflect the influence of this school of thought. More recently a whole new medium has been developed and is currently bing promoted—that of programed learning or more popularly termed teaching machines. Based primarily on B. F. Skinner's reinforcement theory (a refinement of association), programed learning involves the careful presentation and division of the subject matter into extremely small units so that the student is frequently rewarded by correct answers and can move along independently at his own pace.

In advertising, political campaigns, public relations programs, etc., the principle of conditioning is used very effectively. Briefly, the principle of conditioning states that if a stimulus and response are associated enough times together, this association will be learned. Thus, if you hear a brand name associated with a product enough times, you will automatically think of the brand whenever you think of the product; and if the terms "liberal," "socialist," "civil libertarian," "progressive education," "life adjustment," are associated with the concept of the Communist menace enough times, then these labels and those to whom they apply become tainted with the same attitudes ascribed to Communism.

Thus, when addressing themselves to the problems and issues of our times, these psychologists, believing people's behavior to be a result of the forces exerted upon them, find their answers in terms of the manipulation of these forces. The ethical problem implicit in this system, of course, is that somebody, other than the persons affected, must decide the desired direction the behavior is to take. This necessarily calls for a "great man" philosophy of dealing with people—somebody who knows where the people should go. This system calls for leaders who are supermen of a sort, skilled in the manipulation of forces to get people to behave in the ways desired by the knowing few.

And so in schools, for example, we have developed specialists and experts who are determining what the children should learn in the various subject areas, and other experts who are predigesting what will be programed in the teaching machines. In the Midwest they now have airborne educational television by which one *expert* teacher can serve schools in six states (7000 school districts; over five million children); meaning that where used, all the children are getting the *same* presentation of the *same* curriculum at the *same* time!

One of my students wrote the following, which perhaps overstates the kind of teaching which follows from this system wherein learning is thought to result from having students respond to well-ordered stimuli:

> Teaching too often becomes the process of carrying, pulling, showing, and assisting pupils along to the end of the course. *Teachers* do the reading, the explaining, the thinking, the talking, the appreciating, the devising, the planning; the problems are *teacher*-worked, the reasons are *teacher*-thought-out; the beautiful is *teacher*-selected. All the pupils do is to remain passive, to listen, to copy, to memorize, and finally to recite or to write at a stated time what they have managed to cull out of an extended dictation!

B. F. Skinner, a prominent scientist from this force in psychology, wrote a novel some years ago entitled *Walden Two* in which he gives a fictional account of what he regards as a Utopian community in which the learnings of the behavioral sciences are fully utilized in all aspects of life—marriage, child rearing, ethical conduct, work, play, and artistic endeavor. Skinner's conception of paradise is a large rural colony where democracy is replaced by behavioral engineering. The common theme of this novel and of some of his other treatises is that the psychologist possesses the means of social control and must use these means effectively for the welfare of society. Let me quote what Skinner has his hero say in this novel:

> Well, what do you say to the design of personalities? Would that interest you? The control of temperament? Give me the specifications, and I'll give you the man! What do you say to the control of motivation, building the interests which will make men most productive and most successful? Does that seem to you fantastic? Yet some of the techniques are available, and more can be worked out experimentally. Think of the possibilities! . . . Let us control the lives of our children and see what we can make of them . . . (Skinner, 1948).

In another paper Skinner elaborates the implications of his theories; he states,

> We must accept the fact that some kind of control of human affairs is inevitable. We cannot use good sense in human affairs unless *someone* engages in the design and construction of environmental conditions which affect the behavior of men . . . (Skinner, 1955-56).

As you can see, Skinner's projection of his system is garbed in benevolence; however, the ethical question still remains as to who is to determine the *desired* direction behavior should take. And presumably this molding of human behavior would be the function of the schools, and we ask if this is the function we want education to perform.

Classical Psychoanalysis

If associationism is the most popular force among academic and scientific psychologists, Freudianism (classical psychoanalysis) has been the most influential among the clinical psychologists, and psychotherapists and counselors. Although few accept the theories exactly as Freud postulated them (which would be impossible anyway, since Freud modified and even contradicted his own theories throughout his lifetime), yet the main tenor of his system remains and poses some ethical questions.

Psychoanalysis originated in the field of medicine as a result of attempts to find some cure for the neuroses and in revolt against the dominant somatic or physiological explanations which were popular in the nineteenth century. Some psychiatrists were becoming convinced that such causal factors as brain lesions were not to be found in their patients, and they began to substitute such factors as emotional stress, weakness of will, suggestibility, and irrational habits as explanations. Soon hypnotism was introduced and accepted by some elements of the medical profession particularly when dealing with such neurotic conditions as hysteria. It was on this medical scene with an interest in neurology that Freud began his productive but controversial practice in Vienna. Influenced by the French schools in Paris under Charcot and later in Nancy under Janet, Freud built up a practice dealing primarily with hysteric patients, experimenting with hypnosis and eventually giving this up, developing his own techniques and corresponding theoretical formulations.

The point I want to bring out in this very brief historical sketch is that psychoanalytic theory originated and was developed as a result of studying and treating mentally disturbed, upper-class Europeans during a period referred to as the Victorian era. In other words, Freud's sampling from which he drew his conclusions was anything but representative of the human race.

With his medical background, it is not surprising to learn that Freud believed that the nature of man is essentially biological; man is born with certain instinctual drives which can (though they frequently don't) work themselves out as a person grows. Freud classified the instincts under two main headings: the *life* instincts (*Eros*) and the *death* instincts (*Thanatos*). The life instincts include hunger, thirst, and sex, the latter being considered the most driving. The principle operating here is the pleasure principle or self-gratification. The death instincts include hate, aggressiveness, and self-destruction.

According to Freud, the *psyche* is divided horizontally into *conscious* and *unconscious;* and vertically into what he labels the *id, ego,* and *superego.* Gradually the child's unconscious fills with things forgotten or suppressed because they are unpleasant, and more importantly, with emotions and drives which are too painful to be tolerated in the consciousness. The *id,* entirely unconscious, is the most primitive and concerned only with the gratification of drives. The *ego,* almost entirely conscious, develops from experience and reason, interacts with the environment and acts as a check on the *id*. The *superego*, largely unconscious, is the restraining force, the conscience, and consists of the attitudes and moral codes absorbed unwittingly in childhood. Neuroses, then, result from a lack of harmony among the *id, ego*, and *superego*. Neuroses can develop as a result of lack of gratification of the instinctual drives (the *id*), or as a result of a weak *ego* structure and thus poor reality contact, or as a result of a too severe *superego*, which is the product of too strenuous socialization of the child at the hands of harsh, punitive parents.

In spite of the magical, fable-like quality of the theory, its distinctive, widely-accepted contribution to our understanding of human behavior is the significance the theory attributes to the unconscious.

The ethical implications of this theory are of greater or lesser significance depending on how literally we accept its assumptions and principles. Probably the most crucial implication stems from the proposition concerning the instinctual drives. Freud wrote,

> . . . Men are not gentle, friendly creatures wishing for love, who simply defend themselves if they are attacked, but . . . a powerful measure of desire for aggression has to be reckoned as part of their instinctual endowment. The result is that their neighbor is to them not only a possible helper or sexual object, but also a temptation to them to gratify their aggressiveness, . . . to seize his possessions, to humiliate him, to cause him pain, to torture and to kill him; . . . who has the courage to dispute it in the face of all the evidence in his own life and in history? (Freud, 1930).

According to this view, man's *finer* sentiments and strivings are only sublimations of animal instincts which lurk beneath the surface of his civilized veneer.

If this be the nature of man, then we cannot look to nature to provide us answers to our ethical question—the definition of good and evil. Traditional Christian doctrine provides an out with its supernatural definition of good and evil. But Freud rejected religion and referred to it as the "mass obsessional neurosis," and deplored society's religion-based concept of morality. Furthermore, denial, or even worse, restriction of man's nature (as viewed by Freud) leads to mental illness indicating we cannot look to the antithesis of the Freudian assumption for a solution.

Interestingly enough, much of the recent clamor against permissiveness and "life adjustment" in the schools (neither of which ever existed to any great extent in actual school practice) has been misdirected when "progressive education" and John Dewey are blamed. (Dewey argued for an experimental, experience-centered, activity, problem-solving approach to education.) Actually the permissive, life adjustment emphasis stems largely from the Freudian influence whereby parents and teachers are admonished not to thwart or deny the expression of a child's instinctual drives or else his *psyche* will become crippled and pave the way for adult neuroses.

On the other hand, acceptance of the Freudian notion of the inherent primitive, animalistic, aggressive nature of the child leads many teachers and administrators to be preoccupied with the problem of control and discipline sometimes to the exclusion of concern over the learning process.

Another implication derives from the deterministic nature of the theory. The underlying causal factors of behavior are primarily unconscious and irrational. Man's motives are something other than they appear on the surface, and his thinking is easily distorted by inner desires and passions of which he is not aware. How then, with the minimizing of man's rational powers, with the denial of free will, can the individual be held responsible for his actions or behavior? Anna Russell catches the spirit of the problem posed by Freud's psychic determinism when she sings in her "Psychiatric Folksong,"

> At three I had a feeling of
> Ambivalence toward my brothers,
> And so it follows naturally,
> I poisoned all my lovers.
> But now I'm happy; I have learned
> the lesson this has taught;
> That everything I do that's wrong,
> Is someone else's fault (Mowrer, 1960).

This view (shared with associationism), that man is the product of forces beyond his control, undercuts the basic convictions underlying democracy and democratic relations among men. Democracy just doesn't make sense (and wouldn't work) unless man is basically free, and active (and not just reactive), and capable to some degree of making rational choices and decisions and being responsible for his actions.

Third Force: Humanistic Psychology

Throughout the development of psychology as a formal discipline during the past sixty to seventy-five years a number of psychologists have started rebellions of some importance against what they considered the dominant deterministic and analytic trends in psychology represented by associationism and psychoanalysis. Until recently, these psychologists did not represent a unified system or school. In the last few years, however, these various groups have been coalescing into an increasingly comprehensive theory of human nature, into what Abraham Maslow calls a "Third Force." This group includes the so-called neo-Freudians who emphasize man's nature as being primarily social and cultural rather than biological or instinctual; the Gestalt or field theorists who emphasize man's interaction with his environment as a unitary function which cannot be understood in a piece-meal fashion, as they claim the associationists would have us do; the organismic psychologists who, like the Gestaltists, insist on considering the individual as a whole; the perceptual psychologists and existential psychologists who emphasize the uniqueness and integrity of the individual and of his very personal and unique interpretation of his life and environment. As all of these movements place great significance on the individual human being and on distinctively human qualities (as opposed to animalistic or mechanistic qualities of the other two forces discussed above) the label "Humanistic Psychology" seems appropriate.

In contrast to the other two forces, many of the propositions of this third force stem from a study of man (as opposed to animals) and a study of psychologically healthy (rather than neurotic or sick) men. For example, A. H. Maslow, although beginning his career in the study of abnormal psychology, developed his present theories while studying psychologically healthy people and while studying the healthiest experiences and moments (which he called peak experiences) in the lives of average people.

Basic to this humanistic force in psychology is the conviction that man is essentially *good* if permitted to develop his natural humanistic qualities. Only when his nature is distorted by pathological conditions, rejecting parents, constant failure and rebuff, or a repressive culture does man become aggressive and cruel. *Good* in this context is equated with *nature*, thus anything conducive to bringing out man's inner nature is desirable. *Bad* or abnormal is anything that frustrates or blocks or denies the essential nature of man. Putting it another way, Maslow equates what we *ought* to be with we *can* be, and he states further that by substituting the concept of what one *can* become for the term *ought* or *should*, the matter becomes open to empirical, scientific investigation (Maslow, 1954).

Space does not permit me to be more definitive regarding the inner nature (and thus what would be defined as desirable) in man. Writers such as A. Combs, A. Maslow, and C. Rogers do this well in their writings.* Suffice it to say that research being done in anthropology, psychiatry, sociology as well as psychology is coming up with some consistent findings. For example, there is wide-spread agreement that the following are characteristics of psychologically healthy (self-actualized) people: they can be described as loving, self-accepting, well integrated, fully functioning, creative, autonomous, reality-centered, adaptable, among other characteristics.

The other two forces we have discussed have built systems describing man as he *is*. Humanistic psychology has added the dimension of looking at what man can *become*—a look at not only the *actualities* but the *potentialities* as well. Also in contrast to the other two forces which look upon man as *reactive* to the forces in the environment or to the *psyche*, humanistic psychology looks upon man as being active and having the capacity, at

---

*See the 1962 Yearbook of the Association for Supervision and Curriculum Development (N.E.A.), *Perceiving, Behaving, Becoming*, which includes papers on this topic by Combs, Kelley, Maslow, and Rogers.

least to some degree, to evaluate and choose. While agreeing that human behavior is influenced by the environment and culture, humanistic psychology emphasizes that the ultimate effect of the environment and culture is in large part determined by the individual's unique view and attitudes of these external factors. That is, I am influenced by my world as I see it, not as you or anyone else sees it nor as the world may *really* be.

This view of man as having a large potential for freedom is consistent with the democratic conviction that the ordinary man given access to factual information *can* evaluate public issues with some degree of objectivity and rationality rather than as a robot conditioned to think and behave in certain ways. It is assumed that the freedom granted by democracy to the individual to make decisions is not just an illusion.

Similarly, the view of man as free and active is basic to a philosophy of education which emphasizes the development of young adults capable of rational problem solving, creativity, and critical evaluation. Applying the insights of this force in psychology (compared to those of associationism), teaching would involve facilitating learning rather than directing learning; it would involve uncovering new vistas rather than covering what is already known; it would involve asking pertinent questions rather than telling what is already thought out; it would involve helping children learn rather than making children go through the motions of learning (Combs and Snygg, 1959).

Obviously, the ethical implications of this third force are part and parcel of the system it proposes. Unlike the other two forces, it does not beg the question of values. A commitment to a criterion for determining value—that which corresponds to basic human nature—underlies the entire movement. Some will claim that this takes the movement out of the jurisdiction of science. Maslow argues otherwise. He claims that the scientific approach can and should be used to develop greater understanding of man's basic nature, and thus a science of values *is* possible. Erich Fromm writes

> The thesis is that values are rooted in the very conditions of human existence; hence that our knowledge of these conditions, that is of the "human situation," leads us to establishing values which

have objective validity; this validity exists only with regard to the existence of man; outside of him there are no values (Maslow, 1959).

In summary, let me make this observation. The diverse views of human nature as neutral, evil, or good have important ethical and educational implications. Whichever view one accepts, it is apparent that man is a highly educable creature and that his development for good or evil can be greatly influenced by environmental conditions. But here agreement ends. If man is by nature hostile and aggressive, society through the school must shape him by exerting stringent controls; if, on the other hand, man's natural tendencies are for good, society through the school can best achieve its purposes by structuring the environment in such a way as to allow the child considerable freedom for creativity and self-development.

References

Combs, A. W., and Snygg, D.: *Individual Behavior*, Rev. ed. New York, Harper, 1959, pp. 401-402.

Freud, S.: *Civilization And Its Discontents*. London, Hogarth, 1930, pp. 85-86.

Maslow, A. H.: *Motivation And Personality*. New York, Harper, 1954, p. 344.

Maslow, A. H. (Ed.): *New Knowledge In Human Values*. New York, Harper, 1959, p. 151.

Mowrer, O. H.: Sin, the lesser of two evils. *Amer Psychol, 15:* 301, 1960.

Skinner, B. F.: Freedom and the control of men. *Amer Scholar, 25:* 47-65, 1955-56, p. 56.

Skinner, B. F.: *Walden Two*. New York, Macmillan, 1948, p. 243.

Chapter 10

The Teacher And The Withdrawn Child

ORVAL G. JOHNSON

Wickman's early study (1928) indicated that teachers were not aware of the seriousness of withdrawal in young children and that they were much more concerned with the child who was a behavior problem in class. They felt that the problem child was much more of a mental health risk than was the withdrawn child. Hobson's study (1937) about a decade later lent support to the findings of Wickman. A more recent study by Stouffer (1952) repeating Wickman's procedures, indicated that teachers had advanced considerably in their knowledge of good mental hygiene principles. The present study is an attempt to shed light on the extent to which teachers understand the needs of the withdrawn child.

Every experienced elementary school teacher has had to cope, at one time or another, with a child or with children in her classes who would be termed "withdrawn." These children seldom or never volunteer for any assignment or special activities and when placed in such activities they frequently function in a listless and inhibited manner. When left to their own devices they frequently resort to solitary, unconstructive activities which are often irritating to those about them. They may tap with their pencils, finger their hair, gaze out the window, doodle with their pens or pencils, and in countless other ways appear to be discharging the tension and energy which other children are putting into more constructive and socializing activities. The

Reprinted from *Mental Hygiene*, Vol. XL, No. 4 (1956), pp. 529-534. By permission of the author and publisher.

pattern of withdrawal, once initiated, tends to reinforce itself and to become more and more pronounced as time passes. The child has less and less contact with other children of his age and becomes less and less capable of functioning with others to his own satisfaction. It is important, then, that the pattern of withdrawal be broken up as early as possible. This study presents an analysis of the techniques which are reported by one group of teachers at the first and second grade levels to bring the withdrawn child into better social contact with the other children in his classroom.

The data for this study were gathered through the use of a simple questionnaire which was sent out to the first and second grade teachers in the public schools of Jackson, Michigan. After giving some background information on the problem of the withdrawn child, the following instructions were given and questions asked:

> On the attached sheet, will you please describe clearly but briefly any procedures, techniques, maneuvers, etc., which you have found particularly effective in bringing the withdrawn child into the group. Please be specific. These should be things you *do,* rather than principles by which you are guided. Describe what materials, if any, are involved. Techniques which you have developed as a result of your own experience are likely to be of most value. Nevertheless, specific techniques which can be used in the classroom are the objectives of this request. Feel free, therefore, to consult with colleagues or to jot down techniques which have been mentioned in courses you have taken, remembering that your own experience is probably the best criterion of what is a good technique for this purpose. Make as many suggestions, and describe as many techniques, as you wish. It is hoped that there will be at least one suggestion from each person who receives this request.

Thirty-two teachers responded to the questionnaire with 137 suggestions for dealing with the withdrawn child.

The question arises, are the thirty-two teachers who responded to this questionnaire similar in important respects to the forty who did not respond? If we are to make generalizations about teachers from the results of this study, we must have some assurance that the teachers who responded are representative of other first and second grade teachers. According to t-tests, the mean ages of the responders and the non-responders are not significantly different, nor are there significant differences in years of experience. Performance ratings by supervisors were not markedly different for the two groups. A chi-square test of the distributions of the two groups according to amount of formal training was not significant, although it closely approached significance at the .05 level, the responding group having a slightly higher academic attainment. There are, therefore, no statistically significant differences in the above-mentioned respects between the responders and the non-responders.

Although each technique was aimed *ultimately* at bringing the withdrawn child into better social contact with his peers and his teacher, the techniques could be classified according to certain sub-goals which were vital to the attainment of the overall goal of bringing the withdrawn child into closer contact with the people about him. There were seven of these sub-goals or intermediate objectives (including a "miscellaneous" category). They are listed below in the order of frequency with which they were mentioned:

1. *Develop the child's confidence in himself; provide ego support and enhance the child's self-concept.* Seventy-six of the 137 suggestions, or 55 percent of the total, were placed in this category. Because such a large number of the responses were included in this classification, this category was broken down into sub-categories as follows:

    (a) *Directly praise the child for things he has done, taking every opportunity to give legitimate praise.* Several teachers reported that they would even praise a child for such behavior as "being such a good rester."

    (b) *Give the child recognition.* Although this is closely allied with the giving of direct praise as described above, it involves a somewhat different class of activities. For example, one teacher made a special point of talking "to" a withdrawn boy by looking directly at him now and then during group sessions. Other teachers would call on him first to be "It" in a game, and others might call the group he is in by his name, i.e., "Tom's group."

    (e) *Confer some responsibility on the child.* "Confer" is used advisedly, as against "impose." Emphasis was placed on the fact that this responsibility should involve tasks which the child perceives as real and important.

(d) *Find areas or activities in which the child feels secure enough to participate.* Some children were able to talk relatively freely about their families when questioned. Some children first participated in group activities when they described their pets at home or were asked to bring them to school. Other children were drawn out through art activities.

(e) *Ask the child for suggestions and advice in areas where he is able to be helpful.* Teacher-pupil planning was described as one activity which was often helpful in getting a child to participate.

(f) *Inform the child of the progress he is making.* Although this is closely related, again, to the direct praise described in (a) above, it is somewhat different in that it is a more objective description by the teacher of the progress that the child is making. She points out, for example, that he is able to do certain things which he was not able to do before. This may also involve sending evidence of good work home to the parents.

(g) *Help the child when he needs it, and not only when he asks for it.* If the teacher is perceptive enough to know when the child needs help, she may be able to help him avoid many traumatic failure experiences.

2. *Manipulate the environment to encourage the child's contact with his peers.* Some variation of this approach was advocated in 13 percent of the responses. Some teachers make a point of placing the withdrawn child in group activities with friendly children. He may be seated near outgoing, friendly boys and girls. The child is often placed in a very small group to make it easier for him to communicate with the others in the group. Some teachers directly encourage other children to play with the withdrawn child.

3. *Wean the child gently away from withdrawal and toward participation* (10 percent of total suggestions). The child is protected from traumatization, from being pushed faster than he feels capable of moving in the direction of participation with others. Thus, the child is allowed to participate in groups first, where he is able to remain relatively anonymous and yet participate in the group. Later, when the teacher feels he is ready for individual participation, he may be encouraged to perform individually. If individual participation is required by the activity at a particular time in class, one teacher's technique is to "wait until others have made mistakes before asking him." Some teachers protect the child against the ridicule and teasing of his classmates. Another technique for "gentle weaning" is to start the child on

activity which is primarily or solely physical. It is usually some
activity which he can do by himself and which does not at first
require communication with others. It amounts to starting the
child with some form of "parallel play" and bringing him along
from that stage of development. Later on, he is given activities
which require the help of one other child, and through this
gradual process the child is brought into active communication
and participation with the group.

4. *Help the child to understand his need to participate and share
   with others.* The specific technique most frequently used here
   was to talk directly with the child, pointing out how much more
   fun it would be for him if he were to join the others. Nine percent of the suggestions were in this area.

5. *Develop feelings of security in the classroom, helping the child to
   feel "at home" with the teacher and with other children.* This
   may involve conversing with the child about things with which he
   is familiar, directly assuring him that he is needed and loved by
   the teacher and the rest of the class, smiling, and providing
   enough freedom within the room so that the child does not feel
   that he is hemmed in by regulations and restrictions. One teacher
   reported that she had taken a withdrawn child home with her for
   dinner and the evening to help the child develop feelings of security with the teacher in the classroom.

6. *Set a pattern of relaxed calmness in the classroom.* Four of the
   137 suggestions were classified in this group. All four of these
   suggestions were given by one teacher, and included "using soft
   but clear voice tones" and "moving at a moderate speed."

7. *Miscellaneous suggestions.* These are responses which did not
   appear to be classifiable in any of the other categories, and include the following: Provide a good example of acceptance of,
   and communication with, the withdrawn child; set standards of
   achievement within the child's capability and keep the child challenged; work from an understanding of the home situation; suggest to the family that the child have a physical examination.

The material presented above may be said to represent the
thinking of thirty-two first and second grade teachers about how
best to deal with the withdrawn child. We have no adequate
evidence as to whether or not the thinking which is presented in
this study is transformed into effective action. The teachers'
responses to this questionnaire tell us what they know about how
to deal most effectively with the withdrawn child. Evidence that
at least some of the teachers are practicing the techniques which

they describe may be derived from the fact that many of the teachers, in reporting their techniques, described specific cases in which they were used, frequently giving the name of the child.

The results of this study have some interesting implications with regard to the mechanism of withdrawal in children at the first and second grade levels. We must consider, first, that these suggestions for handling the withdrawn child come from people who are practitioners dealing with "normal" children in a "normal" setting. That is, these are not children who have been referred to a hospital or child guidance clinic, and their withdrawal cannot be considered pathological. With most of the children, the withdrawal appears to be an adjustment mechanism which is amenable to change without prolonged and intensive psychotherapy. As indicated above, 55 percent of the suggestions could be classified as "ego-supportive," but many other suggestions which were not classified in this category nevertheless had a strong element of ego-support in them. From this, we may conclude that the teachers in general feel that the withdrawn child needs most to develop confidence, or, in other words, to develop a different and more flattering self-concept. The implicit reasoning behind the techniques used by the majority of the teachers appears to be that the child withdraws because he feels inferior in the kinds of activities taking place in the classroom. There is a need in every child to maintain a favorable self-concept, and the withdrawal is a protective mechanism to prevent failure and a consequent lowering of the self-concept. Thus, by improving the child's self-concept (increasing his confidence in himself), the teacher encourages the child to participate with other children and also makes him more able to tolerate failure. The child who is not severely traumatized by failure in a group situation is able to participate, and in the process is likely to achieve some successes. This is why children who are once brought into participation with the group, under the guidance of a supportive adult, are usually able to continue under their own power as members of the group. The extent to which ego-support is recognized as a necessary element in the socialization of the withdrawn child is indicated by the fact that only three out of thirty-two reporting teachers did *not* report some kind of ego-supportive technique.

Summary

This study has reported the results of a questionnaire sent out to thirty-two first and second grade teachers concerning techniques for helping the withdrawn child. The 137 suggestions gleaned from the responses were classified according to seven categories of techniques. It was found that a majority of the suggestions involved providing ego-support to the child and enhancing his own self-concept. Some implications of this study for the mechanism of withdrawal in young school-age children are suggested.

References

Hobson, C. V.: How much do teachers know about mental hygiene? *Ment Hyg, 21:* 231-242, 1937.

Stouffer, G. A. W.: Behavior problems of children as viewed by teachers and mental hygienists. *Ment Hyg, 36:* 271-285, 1952.

Wickman, E. K.: *Children's Behavior And Teachers' Attitudes.* New York, Commonwealth Fund, 1928.

Chapter 11

The Acting-Out Boy

Ruth G. Newman

In November of 1953, the children's branch of the National Institute of Mental Health, under the direction of Dr. Fritz Redl, took on its first group of patients.* They were six hyperactive boys of nine to thirteen years of age with behavior disorders of a kind both troublesome to society and destructive to people and property; in a loosely descriptive word, "delinquent."

Since that time there have been two other patient groups. The second group included boys from ten to twelve years, while the age range of the boys in treatment currently is eight to eleven years. It was planned that the first two groups be studied for dynamic diagnosis—a term intended to include in addition to the usual battery of psychological, educational, and physiological tests including an electroencephalogram, sample observations of the child in school, on the ward, in therapy, in groups, and individually, by participant observers and non-participant observers, the study of notes and records through conferences, case studies, discussions, and progress reports at regular intervals by all those concerned with the care of the child (therapists, group workers, teachers, caseworkers with parents and foster parents, child care workers, research workers) so that all might share in bringing to light as much significant data as possible concerning

Reprinted from *Exceptional Children*, Vol. 22 (1956), pp. 186-190, 204-205, 215. By permission of the author and publisher.

*These observations were made on the learning difficulties of boys with severe behavior disorders as they are exhibited in a special school at the children's research branch of the National Institute of Mental Health, Bethesda, Md.

the patterns of behavior and fantasy material operating in the child.

The boys in the present group will be maintained here until they have been cured or as long as residential treatment is useful to them and to our research needs.

All of the boys who have been admitted to the children's branch have shared a common pathology to which the phrase "acting-out" has been assigned. By this is meant a type of behavior where an impulse or fantasy, conscious or unconscious, is immediately acted upon whether or not it be an appropriate or realistic response. The inner controls which serve to inhibit most people from such behavior are undeveloped in these boys. They lack the ability to postpone, regulate, or foresee consequences. Such behavior appears as involuntary as the flare up of a firecracker once it is ignited. The child seems no more able to muster up controls, to stop or to alter his act, than the firecracker can stop itself from exploding.

More specifically, the kind of boy included at the children's branch for treatment and study is physically and verbally assaultive. He has frequently run into difficulties with authorities—be they school, police, or juvenile court—and he has frequently been brought to the attention of various social agencies. He may have established a reputation as thief, vandal, fire-setter, bully, bed-wetter, and sometimes a combination of these. His rages seem to come from nowhere and are expressed with the violence and variety of a three-year-old. No matter how old he is or how tough he tries to be, he appears infantile and, like an infant, he demands that his needs (often contradictory) be met instantly and absolutely. He has more likely, though not necessarily, come from a less privileged socioeconomic level. Through his history has run an inescapable line of affectional deprivation, which is more often than not embellished by tragedy and a series of traumatic and rejecting experiences.*

The basic research at the children's branch of NIMH is planned to cover three areas of these children's lives: (a) to

---

*The boys who have been admitted to NIMH have been committed to us through the courts, through welfare agencies, or by the parents' temporary release to the welfare agency, for the purpose of committing the child to us.

study the acting out boy in a total living situation; (b) to study him in individual therapy; and (c) to study his learning difficulties as they exhibit themselves in school. It is only with the third area that this paper is concerned. It should be made clear that this study is at the observation gathering stage and few scientifically measurable statements can yet be made. At the present time, even the tentative observations that have been gathered must be confined to the life on our ward in this particular residential setting, situated in a large clinical-research hospital.

In order to understand the school program and its problems, it is necessary to have a brief picture of the way in which these boys live at the National Institutes of Health. Life for the boys is not only distinct from non-institutional life in a home setting where a child attends a regular school or even a special class, and perhaps goes for therapy hours to a clinic; it is also distinct from a residential treatment home which is built specifically to house children, whose facilities are child centered, and whose prime concern is clinical rather than a combined goal of research and treatment that is attempted at NIMH.

The group is housed on part of the fourth floor of a gigantic new clinical center. In order to have any sports and games, or just outdoor play, the children, with adequate adult escort, must leave their locked ward, go through halls and elevators where they encounter patients from the other divisions of the clinical center, various employees of the Institutes, as well as expensive and enticing research and clinical equipment. A normal child would find such a setting a difficult one in which to adjust comfortably, and these children, not as aware of the needs of external reality, are nontheless affected by the form of life in such a place. Therefore the environmental factor must be considered in any generalizations that are made.

Nevertheless, taking into consideration this special setting, observations have led to certain hypotheses concerning the learning difficulties of the "acting-out" boy, the creation of a school program to fit his learning needs, and the problems a teacher will have in working with him individually, or in a group.

Since the difficulties that surround learning are of major clinical and research importance in working with the acting-out boy, a school program was planned whose goals were to attempt to overcome these difficulties and to study their source, manifestations, and cure. In order to offer these children an opportunity to learn, according to their abilities and interest, teachers needed to be equipped to handle the emotional and educational needs of these particular children in such a way as to help them learn how to relate to other children, as well as to the adult, in a flexibly structured environment, as well as to help the children develop assets and increase their frustration-tolerance level in learning and structured situations. Obviously the selection, training, and supervision of such teachers are a prime concern in launching a school program.

Past School Background And Experience

In order to create a suitable school program, it was necessary to understand what "school" and "teachers" had come to mean to these boys. Their past school experience had to be evaluated in order to determine sensitive areas, special resistances, as well as any positive experiences.

The concept "school" for every child carries with it the values, aspirations, and motivations he has brought from his home, his culture, and his neighborhood. School may be a place to avoid home scrutiny, a place to fail, or a place to strive; a way to make friends, a battlefield for bitter competition, or withdrawal; a way to feel more competent by learning, or to be shamed by ignorance. Adults will be thought of as kind, indulgent, easy to manipulate, unfair, strict, or mean. Other children will be sought out as rivals, buddies, followers, or leaders, or will be avoided. How school comes to mean what it does for each child will be something more than the total of his home and school experiences and will depend on his ability to deal with the reality that confronts him.

The pathologically acting-out boy has little ability to deal with reality without severely distorting it. His concepts of school, teachers, and peers have developed from the damaging experiences he has lived through and from his distortions of additional experiences which have, in turn, led him into more damaging experiences. Therefore, his perception of "school," "teachers," and "learning" has been weighed down by the same anger, resentment, defeat, and refusal that he has taken from, and brought to, his other living experiences.

In every case, the children at the children's research branch had experienced serious difficulties in school. Only two out of the total sixteen had had no severe academic problems (these two were operating at grade level according to standard school achievement tests) but notwithstanding, even these two had been in trouble because of behavior: inability to conform to regulations, or routine, to follow directions, or to relate to other children and adults. The other fourteen, in addition to the above behavior problems, had been unable to learn academic subjects. Reading, that tremendous hurdle for so many emotionally disturbed children, had been impossible for many of them. Arithmetic, with its demand for concentration, logic, and accuracy, was frequently a hopeless task. Some boys could not write, most could not spell. None of the boys had been able to comply with directions, to organize material, to complete a task, or to sustain an effort.

In some cases no standard tests could be administered, in others the tests had to be administered in unusual ways. Where possible Standard Metropolitan Achievement Tests, Stanford Achievement Tests, Gale Oral Reading Tests, Munroe Silent Reading Tests, were given.

16 Boys	Expected Grade Level	Actual Grade Level
(1) 13-year-old	8th grade	8th grade
(1) 11-year-old	6th grade	6th grade
(1) 12-year-old	7th grade	5th grade
(1) 11-year-old	6th grade	4th grade
(1) 10-year-old	5th grade	3rd grade
(1) 10-year-old	5th grade	4th grade
(2) 11-year-old	5th grade	3rd grade
(2) 9-year-old	4th grade	1st grade
(1) 8-year-old	3rd grade	kindergarten
(2) 10-year-old	5th grade	3rd grade
(2) 9-year-old	4th grade	2nd grade
(1) 12-year-old	7th grade	3rd grade

For a classroom teacher, who brings to the classroom his own expectations, cultural values, and emotional investment, to have a child in her school such as the ones described above is a strain, indeed. In all probability, it will be this child who disrupts class activities, destroys property, hurts himself and other children, is unable to remain quiet, refuses to be involved in group work, and who gives up on any set task. To complicate matters the teacher may well be puzzled by the fact that the child's behavior has little to do with his intelligence quotient. This child may be quick or slow, able to grasp a difficult idea, and remain blank at a simple one, or he may assimilate nothing the teacher says. Even when the boy is permitted to initiate his own task he probably will not be able to complete it, and may at any time, for no reason at all, or no apparent reason, play havoc with the lesson-plan for the day. Any failure may bring him to fury and success reassures him, if at all, for no more than a minute. The teacher's reaction to the child has little to do with personal attractiveness. The boy may look like an angel; speak, at times, with courtesy, and be capable of disarming charm; he may be unattractive, gross, sloppy in apparel, or he may have speech defects, tics, or unpleasant physical habits.

Regardless of his mental endowments or personal appearance, he takes more of the teacher's time and energy than any other child in the room. He is the child who is first sent to the principal's office, often with such regularity that the principal sees him as much as his classroom teacher.* He is the child over whom many hours of consultation and testing are spent. His parents, or foster parents, or the agency responsible for his care is frequently called and invited for conferences.

The school may be aware of other types of emotional disturbance, but it is the hyperactive, aggressive, behavior problem for whom drastic measures are taken. The course of action usually taken is suspension and the inauguration of a visiting teacher program, or he may be put in a special class. Few school systems have special classes for the "emotionally disturbed."

---

*One of the NIMH boys reported that he liked third grade because he spent every day in the principal's office and never had to do any work.

More often he is put in classes for the brain-injured, the physically handicapped, or the retarded, where it is hoped that he will cease to be a torment for anyone but the special teacher to whom he is assigned, and that, incidentally, he may be able to learn.

All of the boys at the children's branch have lived through most of the above school experiences. Each experience has solidified their concept that they live in a hostile, rejecting world, peopled by adults who can be defeated by their behavior. In their knowledge of the adult's helplessness and anxiety, they become convinced that they are unable to be helped, that they are unloveable, unreachable, and hopeless. They cannot afford to be aware that they have participated in creating this own rejection—to do so would be to give up the defense they have been able to maintain at such great cost—if I am unloveable, I will hate, and punish you; if you will not give me what I want and need, I will not take what you want to give me. In school, this means a strike against learning, a strike against those who teach and against those children who succeed in complying. By virtue of these children's distortions and experiences, school has become a hostile, rejecting, need-denying place where *not* to learn is a natural response and where to learn evokes defiance, rage, and failure.

The Special Class, The Special Teacher

Sometimes, during this school history, the acting-out boy may be placed in a special class for the emotionally disturbed. Where such classes exist, they contain a large proportion of the type boy included in this study. In such a class, or in a school like the one at NIMH, the acting-out boy will encounter the special teacher.

When a teacher departs from ordinary classroom teaching and undertakes to teach the emotionally disturbed child, his expectations for himself are distinctly different from those he would have in teaching an average class. Aside from a probable determination to succeed where others have failed, to turn his pupils' past failure into success, change attitudes, inoculate the child with learning as painlessly as possible, he may have decided to teach emotionally disturbed children because of his own personal motivations. He may have had painful school experiences of his own, or may be unhappy with large groups, and comfortable only in small ones. His own need to be specially treated, to be nonconformist, to "fix people up," to help, or to change them, may have had a determining role in his vocational choice.

The acting-out boy has as great a skill as the proverbial schizophrenic for feeling out anxious areas in others and in discovering those goals that the teacher desires for himself. Since the child is a past master at the art of defeating others as well as himself, unless the teacher becomes aware of his motivations and expectations, he may well be made so anxious that he ends by being unable to teach, thus confirming the child's conviction that no one can, or will, help him. Thus, the teacher will need to evaluate how realistic his expectations of himself and the children are in the light of their actual performance and his own limitations. In the experiences with the three groups of boys at NIMH many occasions have arisen where it is this kind of interaction between child and teacher that has temporarily brought learning to a standstill.

Notwithstanding what inner drives the special teacher brings to the group, he has usually had extra training in the use of techniques and materials and will be called upon to use all these and many others he has never learned. He requires the ability to plan ahead and then to scrap all plans and develop others on the spot. He needs a variety of approaches and techniques from which to draw.

Limit Setting

If the school is situated in a residential-treatment setting, such as exists at the children's branch, where the exhibition of the acting-out pathology is part of the treatment, in contrast to a day public school setting where an overload of acting-out behavior cannot be tolerated, and on occasion encouraged, the boys will frequently behave in a most disorganized fashion, and the teacher may fear that like the creator of a Frankenstein monster he has let loose more than he can handle, or more than is beneficial to the child. He may be concerned that he has participated in destroying rather than building up controls. He will have to wend his way through a morass of behavior and his consequent feelings in order to establish what limits are essential for the welfare of the boys. For with these boys, even with a permissive atmosphere, that seeks to examine rather than repress pathological behavior, the establishment of appropriate limits is an essential part of setting the stage for learning.

To discover the limits that are appropriate for each child at any given moment presupposes the living through of many anxious periods and many failures. It becomes necessary to distinguish what behavior is acceptable as an expression of present disorder, what must be tolerated as a necessary evil for the time being, and what must be stopped immediately. Such decisions are delicate and open to human error at best. Since timing is a major factor the task requires skill, knowledge, experience, intuition, and self-respect. One second too late is plain too late and one minute too early, while preferable, may be equally ineffective. To help the acting-out boy build his ego controls and increase his ability to avoid the disintegrating experiences of his past, appropriate, and well-timed limits must be established even to the point of physically removing the child from the class.

Closeness

It has been learned that closeness is a serious problem to acting-out boys. In all of his school experience, the acting-out boy has demanded the teacher's complete and absolute attention. He has insisted on being the first, having the most. Because of his demands, derived from affectional deprivation in his past, he both craves a one-to-one relationship and fears it. Thus, an essential part of his learning is to afford him the chance of an unshared one-to-one relationship and to help him feel safe in using it.

Proceeding on the premise that a child must learn how to relate in a one-to-one relationship before he is able to relate and learn in a group, periods each week have been set aside for each child at NIMH for individual tutoring. The need for such a program is the more important when it is recognized that no matter how small the total group, each of these children's levels of attainment, methods of learning, interests, and motivation vary to such a degree that only by some strictly individual help can they assimilate any of the academic skills. (The range of grade level ability in reading alone in the current group runs from ninth grade to first grade.)

The goals of the tutoring sessions are many: to give the child the individual attention he has been demanding; to indicate to him that adults are not necessarily enemies but may be the instruments by which he can feel and become more adequate; to give him, by materials and techniques, specific remedies for his particular educational deficiencies and make it possible for him to learn according to his own perceptual pattern; to give him enough quick successes without the need to compare himself with others so that he will increase his toleration for frustration and build up sufficient controls in learning to be able to complete a task, lengthen his attention span, and broaden his motivating interest.

In carrying out the individual tutoring program it has been repeatedly noticed to what an extent this coveted one-to-one relation becomes threatening at the very moment it becomes meaningful. Closeness is often met by the very child who has demanded it the most vociferously, with panic and resistance.*

---

* One child in the first group after having established a good one-to-one relationship with his tutor, became frightened of the very closeness he sought. He refused to come for his tutoring period unless a male counselor was with him and when, unavoidably, he was left alone with her he flew into a tantrum, threw books and crayons, ran from the room, fled down the hall screaming that the teacher was trying to kiss him. It took three months of cautious, non-pressing proffering of the relationship, before the child could feel safe enough with this teacher to ask for the help that had always been offered. Then, careful to combine distance with closeness, the teacher could proceed with the tutoring and the child was able to begin to learn how to learn.

A boy in the current group began his tutoring sessions by making clay models and then dictating stories about these creatures which he was able to read back. He liked this creative method of making his own reading text and he proceeded with poems and stories. He was momentarily proud to have written them and to be able to read them. As the stories became more personal and meaningful to him, he grew panicky and threw over the whole method that he had been able to use so well. He refused tutoring sessions and lashed out at the teacher. He only felt safe to tutor when he was offered the most routine drills and exercises that he had hitherto rejected with violence.

A teacher may feel bewildered when a child who has clamored for individual attention pushes him away, rejects the offer, screams insults, and runs in panic. Rejection is never easy to take, and to be assimilated, the dynamics behind the child's behavior must be understood.

Closeness implies the establishment of a relationship, an experience which to all these children has been impossible or devastating. To attempt it and fail is far too frightening, and to be made vulnerable by becoming dependent is insupportable, so that at the very moment the relation begins to have significance, the child will push the teacher away or take to flight himself. The child needs to go through long periods of testing out, and of living with nondamaging adults before he will be able to perceive them as friends rather than enemies. To give up his battle before he is ready would be more than his shaky organization could sustain.

If the dynamics are understood by the teacher, it will help him to forestall too close situations and to foresee times when techniques, position, or methods should be altered. The importance of the teacher's awareness of these dynamics cannot be minimized for if the problem of closeness is doubly loaded by carrying the weight of the teacher's problems as well as the child's it may well prove a trap wherein the child relearns the damaging lesson, learned too well already, that is, that he *can* defeat all adults and therefore, no one remains to help him.

Recapitulation Of Educational Evolution

The greater part of the school day at the children's branch involves group activities which center around a series of projects. The goals of these projects are to offer the child an opportunity to relate to a limited number of other children, to form a group wherever this is possible, to relate in a group to a teacher, to provide skills in manipulating a variety of materials, to motivate interest in learning, and to indicate different methods and approaches in handling a given task. The kind of a project that is planned, how it is carried out, and how long it lasts depends on the children's interest and what they are able to do with it at any given time.

In looking over the groups, current as well as past, that have participated in the projects at the children's unit, a pattern of behavior seems to emerge which, if it is indeed a consistent pattern, has many implications.

It has been noticed that when new boys appear at the children's branch there is an inevitable "honeymoon" period. The boy behaves in a rigidly controlled best-school manner. He is reasonably courteous, unenthusiastically compliant, and tries to conceal his academic weaknesses.

When it becomes clear, by means of the other children's behavior, the physical set-up of the school, the attitudes and behavior of the teacher, that this is a different type of school from that which he was used to, the child is, for a while, a bit dazed. He may drop his "Sir" and "Ma'am," he may refuse to work on material he had thought any self-respecting school insisted on, and yet be afraid to participate in the program, language, or attitudes he sees the other children using. He acts lost and restless, and is frequently frightened by his isolation or his blow-ups. He may complain that this is no real school, and that he is getting worse every day; he may express enthusiasm for its difference. Either way he feels unable to share in it.

As he becomes acclimated, he loosens up, or "defrosts." He has an increasing number of blow-ups and shows of violence, frequently on the issue of being "first," or being "best," or being "left out." These blow-ups may be between him and the teachers, or more usually, between him and one or another of the children. His academic level, no matter how high or low it was when he came, falls off. If he reads at fourth grade level, he no longer reads at all, or he tries only encyclopedia material where he is bound to fail. If he reads at second grade level he becomes illiterate so far as use of past knowledge is concerned. If he came to the school as a painter, he stops painting. If he came with skill in arithmetic, he no longer uses it. The period is a disorganized, searching one and he seeks out a level where he can feel comfortable.

Invariably, the teacher offers him a series of projects and materials and, in an effort to reach him at the level where he is, feels frantic as the level changes from day to day, moment to moment. It would be of some comfort for such a teacher to know (if such be the fact in all cases, as it has been with the limited sample of boys at the children's branch) that it is not necessarily the teacher's lack of resourcefulness or insight in reaching these children but that children with this pathology seem to pass through this stage reconstructing for themselves a new perception of school.

Furthermore, it has been observed that these children, in descending the educational scale, break their fall downward at a nursery school level. Though the range of the boys observed has been from thirteen to eight, during this phase they use nursery school and kindergarten materials; their interaction with the other children is of a parallel-play type typical of nursery school children, who can be interested in an activity next to, but not with, another child. They need large doses of complete and unshared adult attention, much as a nursery school child seeks out his teacher to substitute for his missing parents. They use blocks, dramatic play, water, boxes to climb in, or hide in, objects that move, nursery school storybooks, pacifying and passive activities, and simply directed tasks in the manner of a nursery school child.

Since children learn by various forms of play, it is possible, though perhaps fanciful, that if a child has been deprived (because of his life history) of the ability to learn through play, he cannot begin to learn academically until he has lived through the experience of playing with, and manipulating materials that three and four-year-old children find fascinating and involving, and from which they learn so much.

The teacher may feel confused and inadequate when these boys fall from what appeared to be a higher academic level to such an immature use of materials and projects. If he is aware that this descent to nursey school learning through play is an expected development, he can plan for it, and can be less anxious when it occurs. If he is not prepared, he is likely (because of his own panic) to try to stop or alter it too soon, and by so doing may prevent the child from getting what may be an essential background for later learning. Thus, the acceptance of the acting-out child's infantile needs by creatively using them may become a basic part of establishing a relationship with him which in turn may lead to further learning.

This period does end. Its duration varies with the child. He moves up to a first grade level where he still needs to manipulate some of the same materials that he has been using, but he does so in a different way. He sometimes can work in conjunction with another child, or children. Occasionally, at this stage, he is able to follow directions and to complete a short task without destroying the product. Although he is wary of academic learning and group participation, if a proper diagnosis of his particular method of learning has been made, he can make a beginning at reacquiring academic skills on a more secure basis. His attention span will be short, but what he takes in he will be able to assimilate, retain, and use. A series of quick successes may help him to partially erase the failures of the past.

At this point, some recognizable structure and materials reappear; however it is a structure that grows out of the acting-out boy's demands and needs and it is often quite different in method, and materials, from those that are useful in ordinary school classes. Within the boundaries of this simplified and flexible school structure, he begins to be able to function more comfortably. Although he still has blow-ups and times of withdrawal as well as periods when he has to be removed from the classroom, they are less frequent. Many times, in this period, his disintegration can be related to real frustrations in the classroom, to some interpersonal friction between the boy and his peers, or between himself and an adult, to a home visit, or a visit from home, or to an anxious period in his therapy, instead of seeming to come from nowhere as it did hitherto.

Summary

The past two years in planning and executing a school program at the children's research branch of NIMH have yielded the generalizations described above. The observations are not yet precise nor are the implications or applications clear. However, certain tentative hypotheses have emerged that may prove useful in expanding and deepening our knowledge concerning the learning problems of the acting-out boy, the problems of creating a school program appropriate for him; and the problems of the teacher in successfully dealing with him:

1. In order to understand the acting-out boy's perception of "school," "teacher," and "learning," it is necessary to become well acquainted with his life history before entering a residential setting. Only in this way can an appropriate school program be established.

2. The particular means an individual boy can learn, the way he perceives, his motivations, interests, and use of materials, need to be examined closely in order to create a program in which the acting-out boy can eventually succeed in learning.

3. It is necessary to have specially trained teachers who can understand and accept the pathology of the acting-out boy and utilize his assets. It is of primary importance that this teacher be aware of his own motivations, expectations, and areas of anxiety so that he will be able to avoid the pitfall of allowing the acting-out boy to defeat him and thus defeat himself.

4. The acting-out boy needs limits set for his behavior in order that he may avoid disorganizing experiences and may eventually build inner controls. The timing of the limit-setting process is a delicate and important factor in its effectiveness. The distinguishing between the times when it is necessary to set a limit and those where it is necessary to permit the acting-out behavior is equally difficult and important.

5. The acting-out boy demands a close one-to-one relation with the teacher in order to learn, yet, when it is offered he frequently finds it threatening and rejects it. The psychodynamics of this paradoxical behavior needs to be understood and planned for so that the essential relationship of teacher and child does not disintegrate.

6. The acting-out boy needs opportunity to use a variety of materials in a group. When he is given a permissive atmosphere he demonstrates his need to play and to manipulate materials at a three to four-year-old development level before he can proceed up to the educational scale to group activity and academic learning.

7. Once having been accepted at his operating level, and having established the beginnings of a relationship with the adult, the acting-out boy can begin to learn skills and subject matter. He can sustain some frustrations, can complete some short and simple tasks individually and with a group.

8. Set backs are frequent, but the quality of blow-ups and tantrums begin to change in the school settings. Instead of arising for no perceivable cause, they are more often related to traceable factors in the child's current life.

Further study and research of a more detailed and measurable nature need to be carried on in order to determine the validity and implications of the points made above. Nonetheless, the study of the acting-out boy in a special school program within a residential-research-clinical setting provides an excellent opportunity to better understand the problems of the teacher in working with acting-out boys and the problems these boys have in learning and relating.

Chapter 12

A New Look At Overprotection And Dependency

BEATRICE A. WRIGHT

T HE OBSERVATIONS that led me to reexamine the meaning and significance of such concepts as *overprotection, dependency,* and *independence,* are simple and common ones. We know that in work with persons who have severe disabilities there is much emphasis placed on independence training, and understandably so, for to be able to feed oneself and dress oneself can spell the difference between eventual custodial care and living at home. Certainly to be able to earn one's living, that is, to be economically independent, is of vital concern to the individual and society.

Yet it seemed to me, after observing parents in relationship with their children who had severe disabilities as well as the work of several rehabilitation specialists, that the emphasis placed on getting the child to help himself often was all out of proportion to what the child could be expected to do. More than that, the emphasis frequently seemed to provoke a situation that was filled at best with a seriousness of purpose and at worst with a hostile and anxious atmosphere between adult and child that destroyed good-will between them.

As part of the emphasis on independence, it seemed to me that investigators and interpreters of psychological behavior saw overprotection in the natural solicitude of a parent for a child and condemned on all counts whatever they considered to be "overprotection"—its cause typically being ascribed to guilt, and

Reprinted from *Exceptional Children,* Vol. 26 (1959), pp. 115-122. By permission of the author and publisher.

its effects seen in a gamut of undesirable child behavior such as aggression, submission, nervousness, and withdrawal.

These observations led me to wonder whether, in our stress on independence, we were forgetting the importance of dependency needs, and whether the effects of overprotection were as deleterious as they were reputed to be. They led me to wonder to what extent overdependency stemmed from overprotection and to wonder about the best way to help a child overcome excessive dependency and develop desirable progress toward independence.

Wondering thus, I spent hours seeking out the relevant research, and the more I studied the more I became convinced that a reappraisal of the significance of overprotection, dependency, and independence is very much in order, that the commonly assumed relationships do not in fact hold up, at least not in the simple way in which they are presumed.

The first problem facing us is to get at the facts, just as in the case of the four travelers—a sergeant, a colonel, a pretty young girl, and a spinster—who were riding in a train. As the train went through the tunnel, the darkness was punctuated by a kiss and a loud slap. . . . When the train emerged, each one looked about and wondered what had happened. The old maid thought that the sergeant had kissed the young girl, and that she had slapped him for his trouble. The young girl thought that the colonel had kissed the old maid and that she had slapped him in return. The colonel had part of the facts, he knew he had been slapped. He thought that the sergeant had kissed the young girl, and that she, thinking it was the colonel, had slapped him. But the sergeant is the only one who had all the facts. When the train went through the tunnel, the sergeant kissed the back of his hand and slapped the colonel.

I am sure that we shall have only part of the facts, and a very small part at that. But let us see the kind of direction in thinking to which they lead.

The Cultural Position

We can begin by looking at some data pertaining to the position of independence and dependence in our culture. A revealing first step is to pause for a moment and guess at the answer to the question, Does American middle-class society place more or less emphasis on self-help in young children as compared with primitive societies distributed over our globe? The answer can be checked against the facts provided by the cross-cultural study of Whiting and Child (1953):

1. Of 38 primitive societies, 30 allowed their babies to be more dependent than ours.

2. The median age at which serious efforts at independence training was begun for the 38 societies is a little above 3½ years, with American middle class society being placed at 2½ years, that is, fully a year or one-third of the life of the child earlier.

3. With respect to severity of independence training American middle class society was given a high rating for that aspect of independence concerned with the responsibility of the child for taking an adult role in the household economy (e.g., self-help in dressing, performance of chores) and a low rating for fending for oneself without adult surveillance.

4. On such behavior as nursing, weaning, toileting, sex behavior, dependency, and aggression, American middle class society was rated as being extremely low in average indulgence, and rather extreme in the severity of its socialization practices.

A second interesting cross-cultural study presents data on the dependence-independence question from a different perspective (Lambert, Triandis, and Wolf, 1959). Fifty-two societies, on the basis of ethnographic reports, were grouped in terms of the benevolence and malevolence of their deities. Parent and child behavior were analyzed accordingly. It was discovered that

1. Parents in societies with beliefs in aggressive supernaturals were more likely to reward their children for self-reliance and independence and to punish them for the absence of these behaviors than were parents in those societies with beliefs in benevolent gods.

2. There was a general tendency for less indulgent treatment in infancy to be related to predominantly aggressive deities in the cultural belief system, and for more indulgent treatment to be related to benevolent deities.

3. Children in societies with aggressive deities were more self-reliant and independent, but were less nurturant, than were children in those societies with benevolent deities.

4. On three other child behaviors rated, namely, obedience, responsibility, and achievement, no significant differences were found between the two types of societies.

Another way of looking at the cultural evaluation of "independence" and "dependence" is to consider the fact that when people in our society are asked to respond spontaneously to the thought of "independence" and to the thought of "dependence," the former tends to be judged as something positive and the latter as something negative—at least in a global and general sense. Independence goes along with strength, masculinity, leadership, rugged individualism. Dependency, on the other hand, is freely associated with weakness, femininity, indecision, selfishness, and helplessness. No one would be startled to find a book or chapter entitled. "Growing Toward Independence," but one would be rather surprised to find the heading, "Growing Toward Dependence." The shock might be tempered by the assumption of a typographical error, or perhaps by assuming that the chapter dealt with all the bad things which lead children to grow in the wrong direction. If the author argued that children and adults need to grow toward *de*pendence, would the reader take him seriously?

The emotional bias of our culture toward independence, as well as the studies involving cross-cultural comparisons, though not proving that our bias is unwise, does give us pause to wonder whether there is too much stress on independence training in early childhood in our society.

My original concern with the problem of independence had to do with the effects of its stress on the feelings of warmth and friendliness between parent and child. There is some material on this matter, as in the research by Sears, Maccoby, and Levin on child rearing practices (1957). Almost four hundred mothers of kindergarten children were asked individually how much attention their children seemed to want. Whether the child followed the mother around, whether he objected when she left him for a while, and whether he asked for unnecessary help. It was found that those mothers who had an accepting, tolerant attitude toward the child's dependent behavior tended also to be affectionately warm toward the child ($r=.37$). The findings of such studies alone suggest caution in decrying dependency (or for that matter overprotection) without considering the broader relationship between parent and child, the emotional needs of the child, and the ways of achieving a satisfactory dependence-independence balance.

The Value Of Dependency

A great step forward was made when psychoanalytic and other theories stressed the importance of the early period of dependence of the child on his parents and that the need for nurturance in its broadest sense must be satisfied. Nevertheless, dependency as such is usually not posited as a desirable end in itself. Instead, it is seen as a means to emotional security or to ultimately greater independence.

We should like to extend the emphasis on dependency by submitting that dependence in itself is a value, that it is essential in many important kinds of interpersonal relations. People, for instance, should be able to rely on others, to ask for and accept help, to delegate responsibility, but these relations occur naturally only when the person has learned how to become dependent or, what may be more euphemistic, has learned that there are many occasions when dependence is indeed laudable. Dependence becomes then not only a second best alternative, but a valuable end in itself. The physical realities of life as well as the needs of psychological man require that he be dependent on others as well as independent from them.

There is evidence that dependence and independence are not polar opposites as organized within the personality, that to rate high on independence does not mean that one must necessarily rate low on dependence. In a study of forty nursery school children by Heathers (1955), for example, the results show that emotional dependence and independence may be either negatively or positively correlated, depending on what specific measures are related.

The notion of a drive toward independence of the right kind and a drive toward dependence of the right kind are not antithetical. The "do it yourself craze" may just as aptly apply to interpersonal relations as it does to material constructions.

Evaluating Overprotection

Let us now examine the problem of dependency and other personality characteristics from the point of view of *overprotec-*

tion. In any study of the attitudes and behavior of parents toward their children, overprotection is likely to appear as one of the main categories. Moreover, the generalization can probably be made that parents tend more frequently to be overprotective towards their children who have a disability than towards those who don't. A study by Shere (1954), of thirty pairs of twins, one twin of each pair having cerebral palsy, may be mentioned. Among the twins, thirteen children with cerebral palsy were judged to be overprotected, whereas none of the nondisabled twins was so judged.

But our problem first begins. Overprotection is obviously bad, for it is so by definition. Too much of anything is too much. But it is also clear that the judgment as to whether the child is being overprotected depends upon who is doing the evaluating, as well as the culture and times in which he lives. The independence given children today would have been considered excessive by the Victorian master. Socioeconomic class lines influence standards of protectiveness. The adolescent tends to regard any parental guidance as overprotective. A neighbor may regard a parent as underprotecting his deaf or blind child when the parent allows the child to cross city streets.

Even if we take specific criteria of "overprotection," such as those listed by Shere (1954), it becomes clear that a point of view enters the judgment. For instance, consider the first two of her ten criteria of overprotective parents:

> 1. They are highly child-centered; they are eager to sacrifice themselves (and the rest of the family) for the "good" of one particular child.
>
> 2. They are continually helping the child, even when he is fully capable and willing to help himself; they bathe, dress and undress him; they feed him.

The observer may feel that the parent is sacrificing himself too much or helping the child too much, but the parent may not see the situation that way at all. He may feel that it is not a sacrifice; and he may feel that the child is not fully capable of self-help in the instances cited. As the parent sees it, it is the realities of the situation that require his help and protection.

In any case, what is the evidence that overprotection leads to undesirable behavior in children? Let us first look at Shere's work with thirty pairs of twins. In this sample, only the cerebral palsied twin was overprotected. If we take those who were loved *and* overprotected, but not those whose overprotection was accompanied by rejection, it is noted that these children appeared to be friendly, cheerful, with a good sense of humor, and free from aggressive behavior. The overprotected children who were rejected had none of the positive qualities of the children who were accepted, though overprotected. The first possibility to keep in mind, therefore, is that so-called overprotection, when coupled with warmth and acceptance, may not be so bad after all.

In many respects the behavior of both types of overprotective parents (rejectant vs. acceptant) in Shere's study was the same. Both kinds of overprotective parents tended to keep the cerebral palsied twin a baby. They discouraged curiosity and protected him not only from dangers—real or imaginary—but also from new experiences. They did not often explain family policies to him or give him any voice in formulating them. The criteria for distinguishing between these two kinds of parents lay in the rapport which existed between parents and child, in the demonstrations of affections, and in the direction of parental criticism. The overprotective parents who really rejected their child did not enjoy him, and he did not enjoy them. They saw, primarily, the child's shortcomings.

The fact that overprotection occurs in homes differing widely in degree of worth and acceptance has been clearly demonstrated in the appraisal of parent behavior by means of the Fels rating scales (Baldwin, Kalhorn, and Beese, 1949). This fact is necessary to stress because overprotection not infrequently is assumed to stem from such negative attitudes as guilt and rejection without considering the possibility that love, care, and concern may be equally likely if not more likely to be the underlying feelings. The negative connection is made by laymen and scientific workers alike. There is, for example, an investigation (Fitz-Simons, 1935) of parent-child relationships in which overprotection was specifically "used to refer to the type of attitude which might be described as disguised rejection, or is thought to be negative" (p. 17). Thus, if the parent's behavior indicated that he spends much time with the child, protects him from unhappiness, and is concerned about the child in the child's absence, etc., this was rated as a positive relationship when there was evidence of genuine affection, but as overprotection when there was evidence of rejection.

The automatic connection between overprotection, and guilt and rejection, is due to at least two significant factors: First, it has been demonstrated in many experiments, that a priori relations tend psychologically to have the same sign, i.e. cause and effect are perceived as both negative or both positive (Heider, 1958). It is a much more complex cognitive act to perceive that something undesirable can proceed from something desirable. In regard to the case at hand, overprotection, being a negative state of affairs, must result from negative antecedents.

The second factor has to do with the climate of the times, particularly in professional circles, which tends to place an onus upon parents in general. "The trouble with children is their parents" represents a commonly accepted dictum. The appraisal of rejection, guilt, and hate fits in much more easily with this negative orientation to the parent.

Returning to the Fels research, we find corroboration of the possibility that overprotection and rejection are not typically found in the same home (Baldwin, Kalhorn, and Beese, 1949). It was found that those homes that were rated high on babying, protectiveness, and solicitousness (the three indulgence variables) were usually warm, though these parents lacked objectivity in their relations with the child. Furthermore, the typically rejectant parent was typically low on indulgence. There were homes, to be sure, in which overprotection was accompanied by coldness and anxiety in the parent. The pattern was particularly clear when solicitousness was rated higher than babying and protectiveness.

To emphasize the point that the significance of overprotection changes with the character of other factors, still another pattern may be distinguished. There were homes in the Fels study that were rated high on indulgence and warmth, and also high on democracy—these homes being described as showing a soft, spontaneous democracy. In contrast, there were homes that were rated high on indulgence and warmth, and high on restrictiveness—these homes being indicative of a domineering, overcontrolling indulgence.

It now becomes clearer why overprotection cannot be indicted or dealt with without differentiating its types. So-called overprotection does not necessarily, or at least does not only, produce undesirable effects in children. In some cases, notably where warmth and acceptance predominate, many aspects of the child's behavior appear highly desirable.

Several observations in connection with David Levy's study (1943) on maternal overprotection are most pertinent. Overprotection in his study was defined by three criteria: (a) excessive contact—"The mother is always there;" (b) prolongation of infantile care—"She still treats him like a baby"; and (c) prevention of independent behavior—"She won't let him grow up, she won't take any risks." His subjects, twenty of them, were selected from the files of an Institute for Child Guidance and therefore, by this very fact, had more than their share of behavior problems. These were cases of "pure" overprotection, those whose parents evidenced guilt or rejection being excluded. These overprotected but not rejected children improved, despite the mother's attitude, as they grew older. Moreover, though the outcome of treatment of these cases at time of case closure was rated as being less successful than the larger group of cases from the Institute for Child Guidance, several years later, during follow-up, the outcome was rated as being more successful. Maturation by itself, evidently, can be a powerful ally in support of the effort toward independence at least in basically acceptant homes.

Parenthetically, it is not without significance that reports on David Levy's study generally ignore these facts and instead report the findings that of his twenty cases of maternal overprotection, eight children were excessively submissive and eleven undisciplined; that overdependency resulted when maternal domination was combined with overprotection, and undisciplined behavior resulted when maternal control was lacking in an overprotective mother. Such findings must be interpreted in the light of the fact that the subjects were cases from a child guidance clinic, and therefore already selected for behavior difficulties, a fact never referred to, to my knowledge.

Another study of parental behavior as an index to the probable outcome of treatment in a child guidance clinic (Witmer, 1933) also supports a new look at overprotection. The analysis showed that when the mother was markedly overindulgent or overprotective the outcome depended on the genuineness of the affection in the home. Failure occurred when the mother showered on the patient the affection and concern she denied her husband. These cases were marked by marital discord or separation. But success is reported to have occurred when the parents were fond of each other and united in spoiling the child. In all of these cases the patient is said to be "a very friendly, outgoing adolescent with many friends, who had good insight into his mother's attitude and wished to break away from her domination (p. 438)."

Certain comments following the presentation of the preceding findings at a convention are worthy of note. One of the discussants felt that he misunderstood the paper because "Dr. Levy, for instance, has stressed the dangers of overprotection for some years past." Witmer replied, "Dr. Levy said yesterday that overprotection is not necessarily dangerous, and that there is a great deal to be said for overprotection if it is not too severe" (p. 444). And yet, more than fifteen years later, overprotection is still anathema.

I do not want to leave the impression that all serious studies of the problem of overprotection favor the overprotective parent. In one study of parental overattentiveness, for example, it was found that the work habits and social adjustment of school-age children who were babied were predominantly poor (Hattwick and Stowell, 1936). Judgments as to babying were based on such comments in the home-school reports as "An only child whom the mother admits has been spoiled," "Mother tried to shield him from life too much." In a second study dealing with nursery school-age children, the results indicated that children whose homes reflected overattentiveness were likely to display infantile, withdrawing types of reaction (Hattwick, 1936). It should be noted that in these studies, the basic feeling of accept-ance or rejection of the child on the part of the parent was not distinguished. Clearly, considerably more systematic investiga-tion is needed on the question of overprotection, investigation that is based upon and results in greater conceptual clarity.

Developing The Independence—Dependence Balance

At this point I should like to be so bold as to suggest that some children during special phases of their development need more of at least certain kinds of behavior typical of an overprotective parent, such as giving the child a good deal of physical contact, being near the child much of the time, and freely helping the child even when he is objectively capable of helping himself. Of course, the behavior of the parent would not then be called over-protective, for, having desirable effects, it would not be excessive.

Support for and some clarification of the proposition may be achieved by examining a study by Stendler (1954) on possible causes of overdependency in young children. Twenty children, six years of age, who were extremely overdependent as judged by teacher ratings and parent interviews were selected for study. Of these children six, or 30 per cent, had mothers who were overprotective. That is, the mothers wanted the child to be de-pendent, consistently encouraged it, and discouraged independ-ent behavior. But the remaining fourteen children, or 70 per cent, were not overprotected. The mothers of these children, on the contrary, wished very much to prevent dependent behavior!

Moreover, these nonoverprotected children, in contrast to the dependent overprotected children, were not dependent on their mothers for physical habits. Rather, they were *emotionally* de-pendent as seen, for example, in their wish for the mother when they went to bed at night.

The life histories of these fourteen children also tended to differ from children in general. The number of major adjust-ments these children had to make during the critical period between nine months and three years averaged four in contrast to a control group that averaged a little more than one. Major adjustment situations were considered to be situations that required unusual adjustment, such as a major physical disability, the permanent or temporary loss of an important socializing agent such as the mother or father, or adjustment to a new socializing agent as when the mother has to go to work.

The mothers of these fourteen children tried to overcome child dependency by forcing independent behavior and by trying not to give in to the child's demands for physical closeness, care, and attention. But of course they could not be consistent in punishing dependent behavior. When the child became too insistent, when he cried too desperately, the parent finally gave in.

The parent is then caught in a bind, in a vicious circle, for as we know such partial reinforcement produces a learning situation most resistant to extinction. Perhaps if these parents tried less, and like the parents of the cerebral palsy children in Shere's study, happily tended their children, they would have had better results.

There is other evidence to suggest that the way to overcome excessive dependency is not by a frontal attack against it. In the Sears, Maccoby, and Levin (1957) study of child rearing practices mentioned earlier, it was found that punishment for dependency seemed only to make children more dependent than ever. It was also found that withdrawal of love as a disciplinary technique was significantly related to the amount of child dependency. One can posit that these two facts are not unrelated, that ignoring or punishing a child's expressions of dependency needs becomes a threat to the child's certainty that his parents love him.

If a direct attack against the child's excessive demands for physical contact, proximity, help, attention, and praise is not the answer, what is? One principle for correction may be formulated as follows: The small, timorous, and partial indications by a child that he is seeking independence should be encouraged in a warm, but not effusive, manner. The small strivings toward independence are manifested in different ways. Of the following list, the fifth manifestation is generally but erroneously considered to be the main evidence of independence. The first four, however, are equally important signs that the child is making use of his own resources:

1. When the child takes initiative in anything.
2. When he tries to overcome obstacles.
3. When he persists in what he is doing.
4. When he wants to do something, to be active.
5. When he wants to do things for himself.

The parent will act far more wisely in being alerted to these manifestations of independence than in being worried and punitive in regard to the manifestations of overdependency. The latter emphasis spells hostility, conflict, resentment; whereas the former means starting with the child from where he is and taking small steps ahead while preserving the warmth of the human relationship. In the case of severe emotional or physical incapacitation, the problem may be complicated by the fact that even abortive attempts toward independence are hard to detect. It may require special environmental manipulations in order that the environment may be brought into the life space of the child and so lure him to reach out.

Where the mother appears to be holding the reins too tightly, either because she is overly anxious, or because she misjudges the capabilities of her child, there are several aids which can be of real value in broadening the horizons of the parent. The opportunity for parents to observe other children like their own child can be a real help in giving them perspective on what they can encourage and allow their child to do with impunity. Extended awareness of what can be realistically expected of the child also emerges through parent discussion groups. After all, how do any of us get a notion about what children are ready for? By observing, pondering, and discussing.

The parent also needs to be informed of special techniques that can aid in the development of his child. For example, the parent of a blind child can well be told that his child can learn to walk more easily if his feet are placed on the parent's shoes, both facing the same direction. Though the child hasn't been able to observe walking, he will be able to feel the pattern when the parent walks. The principle of becoming acquainted with special techniques could be illustrated by many other examples that apply to the child who is deaf, crippled, mentally retarded, and so on. Many of them, like the example of walking, become obvious to the parent only after the technique is described. Many of them are simple to execute.

The idea of creating opportunities for specific kinds of experience can also be discussed with parents. We do not have to think very much about opportunities for moving and exploring when it comes to the ordinary child. But to the blind child, or to the child with marked physical incapacity, indifference on this score will markedly impede his development. These children will often need to be taken to things and to have different aspects of the environment brought into contact with them.

The creation of opportunities is not always easy to effect, even though the plan may appear to be a simple one. For instance, the parent may realize how important it is for his cerebral palsied child to have experience with a variety of adults and may look for a baby-sitter to provide this opportunity, only to have considerable trouble in finding a person who is willing to undertake this duty. Or, the parent may be aware that his child needs the companionship of other children, but, in spite of his efforts to provide interesting play situations for invited children, he may sense a reluctance on the part of neighbors to encourage this. The children themselves may prefer other outlets for their playtime. The rehabilitation worker must be aware that even with the best of intentions solutions sometimes are "easier said than done." Follow-up is necessary to correct the false leads and seek solutions in other directions.

Finally, the judicious use of reading material can be invaluable in imparting to the parent constructive attitudes and factual information—the background necessary towards realizing a healthy balance between striving for independence and striving for dependence.*

Where love is the prevailing underlying feeling, the aids to growth in independence have the best chance of being effectively utilized, for then the predominant effort of the parent, consciously and subconsciously, is geared toward the child's

---

*Berthold Lowenfeld's book, *Our Blind Children* (1956), is an example of the kind of material that can be most helpful to parents in this regard.

needs, not the parent's. Guilt, rejection, and a need to keep a child dependent, on the other hand, instigate behavior which is basically parent-centered, not child-centered. Where the parent is driven by these feelings, the kind of emotional re-evaluation necessary before a comfortable relation between the child and the parent can be reached may require the services of a specialist in psychotherapy.

In conclusion, the principle stressed here that independence must be viewed in terms of the balancing framework of constructive dependency needs suggests a new look at parent-child relations. It suggests that parents, through the pressure of their own principles and those of the specialist, may be pushing the young child too fast and too soon toward the vague and abstract goal of independence. It raises the concern that the priceless quality of warmth in interpersonal relations may be usurped by the calculated zeal to teach the child independence. It suggests that ratings of overprotectiveness, which appear as central findings in research reports, may be unduly weighted by the high cultural premium placed on independence. It presses us to investigate the kinds of dependency that should be fostered during the different phases of the entire life span of a person's development. It points up the possibility that we may have overrated the negative consequences of so-called overprotection in warm and accepting homes, and that overprotection cannot be considered in isolation from other parental attitudes. It suggests that the way to overcome excessive dependency needs in children is not by a direct denial and campaign against them, but by the strengthening of the child's natural urges to explore, to overcome obstacles and to achieve the satisfaction of accomplishment. These are manifestations of the drive of independence that are as important as the all too often sole emphasis on self-help. It reminds us that our so-called coddling of children lies less in babying in early childhood and more in the possibility that we do not allow sufficient opportunity and challenge for the strengthening of the constructive urges toward the many manifestations of independence well paced to the child's development. Above all, the problems and paradoxes raised fairly beg for greater clarification on the research front of such concepts as dependency, independence, and overprotection.

In this discussion we have done a good deal more than search for the facts. We have also tried to interpret and evaluate them. But this is not unlike the situation of the sergeant and the other passengers on the train. We may be sure that not only did each of them search for the facts, but also that each of them carried away his own evaluation of their implications.

References

Baldwin, A. L.; Kalhorn, J., and Breese, F. H.: The appraisal of parent behavior. *Psychol Monogr, 63:* No. 4 (Whole No. 299), 1949.

Fitz-Simons, M. J.: Some parent-child relationships. *Teach. Coll. Columb. Univ. Contr. Educ.* No. 643, 1935, p. 17.

Hattwick, B. W.: Interrelations between the pre-school child's behavior and certain factors in the home. *Child Develop, 7:* 200-26, 1936.

Hattwick, B. W., and Stowell, M.: The relation of parental over-attentiveness to children's work habits and social adjustments in kindergarten and the first six grades of school. *J Educ Res, 30:* 169-76, 1936.

Heathers, G.: Emotional dependence and independence in nursery school play. *J Genet Psychol, 87:* 37-57, 1955.

Heider, F.: *Interpersonal relations.* New York, Wiley, 1958.

Lambert, W. W.; Triandis, L. M., and Wolf, M.: Some correlates of beliefs in the malevolence and benevolence of supernatural beings: a cross-societal study. *J Abnorm Soc Psychol, 58:* 162-69, 1959.

Levy, D. M.: *Maternal overprotection.* New York, Columbia, 1943.

Lowenfeld, B.: *Our Blind Children.* Springfield, Thomas, 1956.

Sears, R. R.; Maccoby, E. E., and Levin, H.: In collaboration with E. L. Lowell, P. S. Sears, and J. W. M. Whiting. *Patterns Of Child Rearing.* White Plains, New York, Row, Peterson, 1957.

Shere, M. O.: An evaluation of the social and emotional development of the cerebral palsied twin. Doctoral dissertation. Univ. of Illinois. Univ. Microfilms, Ann Arbor, Michigan. Publication No. 9140, 1954.

Stendler, C. B.: Possible causes of overdependency in young children. *Child Develop, 25:*(2)125-46, 1954.

Whiting, J. W. M., and Child, I. L.: *Child Training And Personality.* New Haven, Yale, 1953.

Witmer, H. L.: Parental behavior as an index to the probable outcome of treatment in a child-guidance clinic. *Amer J Orthopsychiat,* 3: 431-44, 1933.

Chapter 13

Understanding The Child With School Phobia

BEATRICE LEVISON

IN RECENT YEARS increasing attention has been directed towards a clinical condition in children called "school phobia." The term itself refers to a state of acute anxiety about going to school. The word "phobia" suggests that the anxiety is localized, its focal point being an irrational fear of attending school. As is characteristic of phobias, the acute panic about being in school is an assumed cloak which hides the real source of anxiety. The school situation is invested with symbolic meaning and the response is not to school but to the private, though consciously unknown, meaning with which it has been endowed by the child.

The anxiety is expressed in a variety of ways. A child in a state of acute panic might turn pale, start to tremble, be unable to move or feel impelled to flight. Psychosomatic symptoms usually are associated with school phobia, even in the less acute states. The most frequent complaint is abdominal pain which may be accompanied by dizziness and vomiting. Enuresis, diarrhea, dysmenorrhea and sleep disturbances are frequent manifestations of the child's disturbance. These symptoms may disappear on days when the child is not required to go to school.

Phobia was one of the first syndromes recognized and treated by Freud in his study of hysteria. Sullivan (1953) has said that "when there is anxiety, it tends to exclude the situation that provoked it from awareness." In all types of phobias there seems

---

Reprinted from *Exceptional Children*, Vol. 28 (1962), 393-397. By permission of the author and publisher.

to be substitution of a real and therefore avoidable danger, for an unconscious internal and consequently unavoidable one. The individual can therefore free himself from anxiety by channeling it toward an external object or situation. In phobia, the fear is allowed to penetrate the consciousness on condition that its true nature is not revealed. The person displaces or projects the fear of his impulse or its consequences onto an external situation which becomes the symbol of his more general fears.

Johnson, Szurek, Falstein, and Svendsen (1941) demonstrated that, as a phobia of childhood, school phobia was primarily a problem of separation anxiety related to an ambivalent attitude toward one or both parents. Thus, attempts to understand this condition are doomed to failure if efforts to discover the origins of the phobia are confined to investigation of the school situation itself. As in most phobic conditions, the fear has internal origins and is not explained by various features of the avoided locale. School phobia appears suddenly and dramatically in youngsters who seem to have been making a good school and life adjustment.

Truancy And School Phobia

A school phobia is very serious in our culture since the school is so large and important an area of life. A necessary distinction should be made between truancy—the reluctance to attend school—and school phobia. A study done by Talbot (1957) suggests that "school phobia is basically not a fear of school but a fear of leaving home—primarily a problem of separation from the mother. It differs from truancy in that the child has terror about being in school. He may flee school in a panic but unlike the truant, he dashes straight home to mother." Persistent truancy is generally not of a phobic nature though it frequently is an indication of serious environmental difficulties, emotional disturbance, a deviant subculture or severe deprivation.

Even in cases of obvious phobia, a child must feel external as well as internal dangers. The onset of the phobia is generally coincident with a reality situation—an attack by bullies, a harsh teacher, school failure, or illness in the home. These environmental factors serve merely to canalize and fixate an intense and preexisting anxiety state.

Not attending school reduces anxiety and provides secondary gains. Here, too, environmental factors may be the hook in reality on which the child hangs his fears. When conflict exists between parents, the child may imagine or fear physical assault on the mother by the father, which the child by his presence feels he could prevent. Lightly made threats of abandonment by the mother for misbehavior may intensify his fear of losing her during his absence from home. A preschool age sibling in the home frequently arouses fear of displacement in the mother's affections. The greater the child's secondary gain from his illness, the more he will delay returning to school and resist therapy.

While these environmental factors may exist at home and be the child's expressed concern, they serve only as reinforcement for the underlying conflict. Strong ambivalent feelings toward parents are always present. Fear of separation from the mother, repressed hostility toward her, resulting in fear for her welfare in his absence, and the wish to separate the mother from the father, or to dominate and control her at all times, may be some of the unconscious reasons for staying home.

The school itself, in some cases, may have only accidentally become the object of the phobia. The child may have experienced a violent attack of fear in school and, remembering this attack in its sensory context and wishing to avoid its recurrence, will avoid the site where the crucial attack occurred.

Characteristic Family Patterns

There is wide agreement by investigators about the dynamic intrafamilial and intrapyschic patterns found in studies of the family of the child with a school phobia. The patterns uncovered by Talbot (1957) in her study of twenty-four middle-class children from small families, all treated at the Queens Center of the Bureau of Child Guidance, are characteristic.

In most instances, the family constellation was deeply inbred and a high degree of interdependence characterized the relationships between the parents, child, and grandparents. There was a marked lack of interest in things outside the immediate family. Parents, children, and grandparents lived an insular existence in close physical proximity to each other. Mothers and fathers were neurotically involved with their own parents, frequently giving second place to the needs of their own families. Marital adjustments tended to be on an immature level, each partner feeling neglected and resentful of the attention paid to the child by the other. There was a high incidence of preoccupation and concern with death on the part of both parents and children, with a seeming inability to differentiate between fact and fantasy. "Death" and "going away" were equated in their minds and fears expressed that their evil thoughts and wishes might be carried out during their absence. Finally, there was an intensely neurotic involvement of mother and child, each clinging to the other both physically and psychologically.

Most mothers were ambivalent in their feelings towards their offspring, with separation as difficult for the mother as for the child. Lack of consistency in dealing with their children was a prevailing pattern and contradictory handling of their children was extreme. The mothers could run the gamut from kissing to slapping within a few seconds and the children were the victims of correspondingly inconsistent standards and expectations. Confused by the unpredictable and infantile behavior of his parents and deprived of much-needed parental strength and support, practically every child in the study felt rejected.

It is small wonder, then, that in the struggle to emancipate himself from his mother, the resentment and hostility growing out of, or causing, the struggle are projected by the child to the teacher and the school where its consequences are emotionally less painful.

Role Of Therapy

In past years the syndrome of school phobia often proved very refractory, frequently persisting for months and even years after the onset of treatment. This resulted in serious disruption of the child's education, hampered his social adjustment, perpetuated the distorted family relationships and provided the groundwork for severe character disturbance in later life. As a result, interest was aroused in learning more about the treatment and management of school phobia in the hope that such knowledge could facilitate preventing intervention.

Investigations begun by Waldfogel, Tessman, and Hahn (1959) produced results which added new dimensions to the thinking on school phobia. Not long after they began their investigations, Waldfogel and associates discovered a striking and unexpected relation between the remission of the acute symptom and the promptness with which the treatment was begun.

Twenty-six cases of school phobia were seen in the first two years of the study. In those cases where treatment was initiated shortly after the symptom appeared, school attendance was resumed after a few weeks in most cases. If, however, treatment had been postponed for a semester or more after the onset of the phobia, the symptom continued long after treatment had begun. Also noteworthy in this study was the fact that the most seriously disturbed children and families were found in the group that was already beyond fourth and fifth grade. Although signs of trouble often had appeared earlier in the school careers of these children, they had been ignored, only to erupt in a more virulent form later on.

On the basis of these observations, an exploratory program was undertaken to identify cases of incipient school phobia in order to provide preventive help *within the school* when this was feasible. Only children demonstrating signs of widespread personality disturbance would receive more extensive therapy in a clinic setting.

Attendance At School

Earlier investigations, such as the studies done by Talbot (1957) and Klein (1945) had demonstrated that the timing of the child's return to school was of prime importance in the treatment of a school phobia. The sooner the child is gotten back to school—even if only to step inside the building—the more favorable is the prognosis.

Once a good treatment relationship is established with the child, the goal should be to return him to school at the earliest moment possible—at any level of school participation the child can tolerate. This implies a lack of rigidity on the part of both the school and the parents. Real progress for such a child might mean just sitting in the principal's office for a short period each day, or having his mother in the classroom, or participating only in art or in music.

Waldfogel and his associates enlisted the cooperation of the Newton, Massachusetts Public Schools for their study and a field unit of the Judge Baker Guidance Center was installed in their Division of Counseling Service. A total of thirty-six children with symptoms of school phobia were referred to the Judge Baker field unit during its two years of operation. Of these, sixteen received therapy in school, four received therapy in the clinic, five had made a spontaneous recovery when contacted and eleven received no therapy.

Every effort was made with all these children to keep them in school during the course of their treatment despite the fact that this often caused considerable distress to both children and parents. The therapist operated directly within the school, offering support to the child in the feared situation. He also worked closely with the principal and teacher with a view toward altering whatever reality factors existed which tended to aggravate the child's fears.

A follow-up study conducted one year later revealed that fourteen of the sixteen children who had received therapy in school were symptom-free, as were all four of those who had received therapy in the clinic. Four out of five who had appeared to make a spontaneous recovery were still symptom-free. Only where there had been no therapeutic intervention was there a difference. Of these, only three out of the 11 remained symptom-free at the time of follow-up.

The success of this effort, though admittedly based on a small sample of the population, has implications which give the school tremendous potential for early detection and prevention of emotional disorders.

Seriousness In Adolescence

Despite the impressive amount of agreement expressed by independent observers on the etiology, dynamics and clinical course of the school phobia syndrome, the *severity* of the disturbance may differ sharply in individual cases. As noted earlier, the most severely disturbed children were found in the group that was already beyond the fourth or fifth grade. These are preadolescent or adolescent children for whom there is a poor prognosis.

Eisenberg (1958) states that when a school phobia occurs in adolescence it represents "a much more serious intrinsic disturbance of general adjustment." Coolidge, Miller, Tessman, and Waldfogel (1960) characterize the adolescent's school phobia as "the symptomatic manifestation of a severe character disorder." In their experience it is preceded by a long history of unmet dependency needs which has seriously interfered with the development of the ego. The outbreak of the acute symptom is in reality an expression of panic in the face of adolescent pressures, usually accompanied by massive regression. Treatment must involve the parents as well as the child and, in addition to individual psychotherapy, must usually include management of all aspects of the child's environment. As in all cases of school phobia, it is desirable for the child to return to school as quickly as possible, but with these children one must be prepared to accept a longer absence. Time is needed to help them mobilize their resources and establish a clearer sense of their separate identities. Since some degree of chronic incapacitation is already involved, there is not the same urgency for getting the child back in school. If outpatient psychotherapy is unsuccessful, then separation and treatment in a residential setting may become necessary.

Role Of The School

Although school phobia appears in conjunction with widely varying degrees of emotional disturbances—ranging from transient anxiety to severe character disorders—and generally requires skilled psychiatric help, what must not be lost sight of in these situations is the positive and constructive role the school can play. Lippman (1956, p. 100), discussing cases treated at the Wilder Child Guidance Clinic, states that "without cooperation from the school, treamtent of school phobia is extremely difficult." A sensitive and flexible teacher can contribute immeasurably to the readjustment the school-phobic child has to make. An understanding of the underlying dynamics in such a situation coupled with a sympathetic and intelligent approach to both parent and child can hasten recovery. Rarely does the child with a school phobia voluntarily return to school and the parents are often ill-equipped to manage his return without help from both the therapist and the school.

School phobia reflects a neurotic relationship between mother and child in which *both* suffer from separation anxiety. It is in large part the mother's clinging to the child which makes severing the dependency tie so difficult for the child. Consequently, she too will grasp at straws designed to keep the child at home. The fear of retardation as a result of lost time, fear of being the object of ridicule by his peers or of return to a strict teacher can all be rationalized by the mother, as well as the child, into valid reasons for refusal to return to school. In such situations, cooperation from the school is essential. If assurance can be given that the school will take special measures to help the child overcome his fears, some of the mother's resistance may be dissolved in the process.

By regarding these parents and children as troubled human beings in need of understanding and help, administrators and teachers within the school can render a vital and constructive service in the efforts to treat cases of school phobia.

References

Coolidge, J. C.; Miller, M.; Tessman, E., and Waldfogel, S.: School phobia in adolescence: a manifestation of severe character disturbance. *Amer J Orthopsychiat, 30:* 599-607, 1960.

Eisenberg, L.: School phobia: diagnosis, genesis and clinical management. *Pediat Clin N Amer, 5:* 645-666, 1958.

Johnson, A. M.; Falstein, E. I.; Szurek, S. A., and Svendsen, M.: School phobia. *Amer J Orthopsychiat, 11:* 702-711, 1941.

Klein, E.: The reluctance to go to school. In *Psychoanalytic study of the child.* New York, Int. Univ. Vol. I, p. 263, 1945.

Lippman, H. S.: *Treatment Of The Child In Emotional Conflict.* New York, McGraw-Hill, 1956.

Sullivan, H. S.: *Conceptions Of Modern Psychiatry.* New York, Norton, 1953.

Talbot, Mira: Panic in school phobia. *Amer J Orthopsychiat,* 286-295, 1957.

Waldfogel, S.; Tessman, E., and Hahn, Pauline B.: A program for early intervention in school phobia. *Amer J Orthopsychiat, 29:* 324-333, 1959.

SECTION D

CURRICULAR AND FACILITY ADAPTATIONS

Chapter 14

Conveying Essential Messages To The Emotionally Disturbed Child At School

RUTH G. NEWMAN

T HE PHRASE "the emotionally disturbed child," is used to cover a multitude of miseries: the child who sits and stares off in space; the bully who makes other children miserable and who cannot stand the least bit of criticism or attack himself; the child with the 140 I.Q. who never gets his work done and who can't learn to read; the child who crouches by the wall on the playground, so shy, he does not even dare look longingly at the group playing kickball for fear the teacher will urge him to play; the child who gets the weeps every time an adult speaks to her; the child who flies into a tantrum when someone else is first in line; the child who, having done something wrong, flees down the school hall and out the door in panic; the child who does well academically, but gets so nauseated every morning at eight-thirty that she cannot get to school; and, of course, the child who so discumbobulates the class and the teacher by clowning or breaking, fighting or tearing apart, that both he and the school feel that hours spent in the classroom are an utter horror and complete failure.

A Portmanteau Term

Granted that "emotionally disturbed" is a portmanteau term, ranging from severe crippling to the minor "slings and arrows of outrageous fortune," it nonetheless is a term that eliminates

---

Reprinted from *Exceptional Children*, Vol. 28 (1961), pp. 199-204. By permission of the author and publisher.

many other kinds of disabilities. For instance, although an emotionally disturbed child may, and often does, test at a minuscule level, he possesses a basic intelligence, potentially capable of learning at his own age level. Thus, though his behavior may sometimes parallel that of the mentally defective, especially since the mentally defective have as great a range of behavior patterns as anyone else, his problems are not the same as those of the retarded. The term does not, in itself, include the physically handicapped or organically damaged, though these children, too, may and frequently do, suffer severe emotional disturbances.

Both the defective and the physically handicapped may benefit from the therapeutic teaching methods devised from the understanding of the emotionally disturbed. Likewise, the emotionally disturbed may profit from the application of methods found useful with the retarded or the brain damaged. It is not necessary to exclude areas of overlap, for those are areas where the findings in one aspect of a disabled child are helpful in working with a child whose disability is different. Yet because of the history of the work done with the disturbed child, the mingling and mixing of techniques and groupings, theories, and approaches have often befogged the primary issues and thus failed to get at the source of the problem and to treat it. Although an antihistamine may relieve symptoms of the flu, it doesn't cure it.

It has been our custom for practical reasons, and until recently for reasons of ignorance, to lump all disabilities in the same "special class" in a school. And sometimes the emotionally disturbed child does seem better. He has been removed from the pressures of a large, normal group. Some of the new methods and approaches may attract or fit him. The specialness of the situation, itself, may fill a basic need. The structure of the special class setting may quiet much of his symptomatic misbehavior. Moreover, (and let's face it, this fact is as operative as any other) he has been taken out of the hair of some teacher who has been trying to teach a class and has been prevented from doing so because of his presence. In the special class where odd behavior is a premise, the teacher feels called upon to try to handle him, if only custodially.

But all this is not actually dealing with the emotionally disturbed child's basic difficulties in the classroom. Symptoms, not causes, are being handled, and the apparent improvement may be illusory or temporary, in which case the illness may break out later in a form more difficult to reach. Sedation is fine, but if the headache comes back to hamper and haunt when the aspirin is gone, we had best look to the cause.

Many School Settings Available

Once he has been properly diagnosed, there are many school settings in which the emotionally disturbed child can be therapeutically handled, if his ills and his total life climate are adequately appraised. A certain kind of emotionally disturbed child can work best in a regular school class under a skilled teacher who has adequate supervision and support from the principal and from trained consultants. This is especially true where the child, while attending school, is being given individual treatment by a professional, connected with the school or outside, but one who is able to work closely with the teacher and the child's parents. Another child cannot do well in an ordinary public school but needs the protection of a small and especially programmed private school, be it a day school or a boarding school. And then there is the child who cannot function at any kind of regular school, no matter how well programmed, even with the additional help of psychiatrist, psychologist, or social worker. Such a child may require a special class or, when the case is extreme, a residential treatment center—of which there are all too few.*

---

*Because an intensive scrutiny of the extreme case of human behavior and dynamics often leads to a clearer understanding of the entire range of difficulties, the six-year study of the severely disturbed hyperactive boys between the ages of nine and fourteen in total residential treatment at the National Institute of Mental Health provided many insights into the learning and school adjustment difficulties of emotional disturbance. The Child Research Branch, which operated from 1954 to 1960, was under the direction of Dr. Fritz Redl. It devoted itself to the study of the total life of the hyperactive child; i.e. his daily program, his internal and external difficulties, and forms of treatment, as well as his learning and school problems. The children selected for a long-term treatment program, which was one of three programs developed, had been, along with their other ills, completely and utterly unable to make a go of any school program whatso-

In appraising the entire range of school settings which includes emotionally disturbed children, from a regular class to an intensive, total-treatment residential center with a school program, certain basic principles become clear. Without an awareness of these principles and without grappling with their implications, though children may be maintained in a school setting and may even make some progress, their basic disturbance and potential for health and growth is only being met accidentally, and its success cannot be duplicated for the use of other children.

Then, let us assume that the aim of a school program for the emotionally disturbed is to do its appropriate part in treating the child along with other forms of treatment, such as individual therapy, group work, program planning, and work with the child's parents (very intensive work if the child lives at home). Let us assume—and it would be the golden age of work with the emotionally disturbed if this assumption were in fact realized in the majority of cases—that communication is good among all aspects of the child's treatment life, all the varied disciplines and people involved. Let us assume that there are united goals, no matter how different the approaches and the language used to express these goals by the various disciplines represented.

Moreover, let us assume that these overall goals maintain the hope that the child will change in the direction of increasing success in living, increasing awareness of his worth, increasing ability to realize his assets and accept his limitations, increasing ability to independently function and at the same time ask for, and use, help from adults and peers. We can further hope that he will ultimately become aware of the fact that he has something to give and something to receive and that though frustrations come, gratifications come also, and future rewards can be more satisfying than immediate gratification.

---

ever. For three years they attended a specially planned school on the hospital ward. For two years thereafter, they were introduced to carefully selected schools, in the community. The clinical staff worked closely with the teachers and principals of these schools and gave the children and the teachers sufficient support so that these boys could both learn and, for the most part, maintain themselves in school without damage to themselves, their classmates or teachers.

Basic Principles

If these are the goals, there are some basic principles of which all people concerned in the treatment of the emotionally disturbed child will be aware. The school people particularly, administrator, teacher, tutor, and supervisor, will have to work daily with these principles and focus upon them in the long, hard, discouraging, one-step-backward, two-steps-forward course from illness to health.

The Emotionally Disturbed Child Can Learn

The emotionally disturbed child has already learned. He has already learned many unfortunate and unhappy things that have interfered with what we, society, would like him to learn. What we would like him to learn cannot be learned without the presence of a complex of factors; factors involving such things as the mental health of his parents, or at least one parent, of his and his parent's physiological health, their economic and physical situations, their conflicts and concerns, their needs and deprivations, their manner of handling life and the manner in which life has handled them, their constitutional make-up, and their economic and cultural opportunities. In any event, these children have not had the climate to teach them what we would like them to learn. Look deeply into any case history of a severely emotionally disturbed child, and you will be surprised that the child survived at all. In accordance with the human organism's adaptive ability, these children have learned what life has taught them about people, objects, danger, helplessness, terror, and survival.

Extinction Of Old Patterns

Extinction of old patterns, even in the simpler instances of lower animals is never as simple as that comfortable *tabula rasa* on which one prints precisely what one wants to print. The old learnings of these children have come out of bitter experiences with the world and the people in it—experiences not so readily ignored. For indeed the behavior patterns that these children have developed for themselves, be it intense withdrawal into a world of their own making or hostile attack, or diffuse, ill-coordinated stabs at the environment, have been the only way they have had to deal with the problems that beset them. To relinquish these tools for survival, regardless of how uneconomical, how unhappy, how inappropriate and self-defeating they may be, simply because we ask them to do so, is an absurd simplification of human processes. To any self-respecting emotionally disturbed child relinquishing these tools seems stupid, blind, and consequently enraging or ridiculous just as if we were to ask a man to jump from a plane using a parachute with a broken shroud.

Demonstration Of New Patterns

We in the school program need to demonstrate to the emotionally disturbed child over and over again that his old learnings are no longer valid, his situation is different, the adults in it are different and the old patterns are not workable, useful or necessary. We need to demonstrate that the world is not totally hostile, that adults are not necessarily ungratifying and untrustworthy, that he, the child, is not hopeless, or unacceptable no matter what he does and that hope exists in the world without ultimate disappointment. We need to convince him that a realistic evaluation of who he is and what he can and cannot do, while pretty terrifying to contemplate, has its gains and its rewards and that adults can help him with skills he wants so that with these skills he can feel less helpless and can elicit respect and love.

Reinforcement Of New Learning

Until such a constant demonstration of a benign world gets through to him, saturates him, and is reinforced day after day, there is no reason to expect that unlearning will take place and that we can extinguish the perception of the world as malevolent. Until we succeed in this task he will revert to his natural mode of reacting as surely as a Pavlov dog salivates at the ring of a bell until the effect of the bell ring has been extinguished by removing its reward and transferring it to some other stimulus. Until that time, there is not much hope that the new methods of handling anything that life offers will be available to him. He will not even give them an honest try. This does not mean we don't keep indicating by demonstration, not talk, alternate modes of

behavior. It merely means they will not click until the kaleido-
scope of his life has been shaken up and he sees the world with
new colors and pieces.

How do we convey the message that school is a benign place
to a child who thinks the whole world is a dreadful place and
school the ultimate in dreadfulness? School is the place where
all your faults shine through, where you are challenged and exposed, where you have to wait when you can't wait, sit still when
you must move, keep quiet when you must scream, or let someone go ahead of you when you must be first. Further, you must
share the teacher when you can't share so much as a chocolate
bar, do something over and over when you can't even do it the
first time, follow a direction when you don't hear a direction, do
things the way people say when you are too angry to do what
anybody says, love your neighbor when you can't even love yourself, think when your mind wanders, listen to an adult droning
on about something you're not interested in when your thoughts
are creating fantasies of power, violence, or escape.

School Is A Place Where Gratifications Exist

Somehow, day after day, regardless of the subject matter being used—blocks, paints, books, wood, arithmetic, writing, clay,
or songs—each small part of the whole daily school design, must
convey the information that gratifications exist. At first the gratifications must come immediately in the wake of the task. Later
the interval between the problem and its fulfillment can lengthen
out. At first the task must bring with it success, no matter how
easy the job. Later the success can be postponed. Some errors
can be encompassed on the way to success, some snags met and
handled. Part of the reward of tolerating frustration need not be
verbalized; it just happens that the subject matter becomes more
interesting and involving as more frustration can be tolerated.
The timing on this problem is tricky, for if one waits too long
the child properly feels belittled and contemptuous of the
teacher as well as of himself.

School Is A Place With A Predictable Environment

The school must convey the message that it is a place the child
can handle, because it is a place that can handle the child. This

means that a structure exists, no matter at what level or what the personal design of the teacher, in relation to the child's needs. This structure is maintained and the teacher indicates clearly, and without guilt, that certain things can go in school, certain things cannot, and that school is a place of safety and learning. In other words, the structure relays the message that, what is appropriate at school at a given period, despite the effort for the child, is less boring in school than out of school.

School As A Place Where Help Is Available

School becomes a place where personal interests can be explored and developed. It is a place where help is available to get something going that a child wants to get going, and to get it completed once started. There is help not to mess up, tear up, destroy relationships, work, or sense of adequacy. The amount of help needed may be enormous—to make a boat out of two pieces of wood may take 90 percent of the teacher's effort and 10 percent of the child's. If the task is important to the child, and if it is important that the child see a completed task in one school period at this time, then it is of no concern that the boat is more the teacher's creation than the child's. Later, more and more of the job will be left to the child. Later, more tasks can be begun one day and completed in two, three, or even more days. The importance of the task lies in the message that the teacher conveys to the child about adults, school, work, effort, and about his own abilities to come through.

Timing In Reference To Props

There is a time for extra supports and a time for no supports. This whole complicated message cannot be conveyed at once. There are times for definitions to be marked according to the child's ability to receive the definitions. A child badly frightened of the very thought of a school room or teacher may well have to spend the first few weeks carrying with him the comic books that later will not be permitted in school as inappropriate. The child whose identity is tied up with an object at a given period of time may well have to bring the water pistol to school just to hold even if he misuses it and, as a result, is bounced from school. He may need the matchsticks or the marbles for whatever magical, protective, or enhancing meanings they have to him. In a while, when the reality has come through that school is not necessarily a terrifying place but instead a place to learn with a teacher who will help, all these props will be excluded along with other inappropriate and no longer necessary behavior.

Timing In Reference To Self-image

There is a time to tell a child about the self-image he conveys. For a while it may be necessary to allow the child to come to school ill-clothed, shirt unbuttoned, belt unfastened, shoes off, socks not matching, and not too clean in order to put across the message that the child himself, no matter how unattractive he thinks himself to be and no matter how unattractive he makes himself is acceptable. To let this go on too long, however, is to convey a poor message, one that says, I don't care how you look, or, anything's good enough for me, or, This doesn't matter. Therefore, when the initial message has been imprinted, the teacher will not allow unfastened belts, unbuttoned shirts, unmatching socks, or unshod feet.

For a while, when the child may be struggling to give up some of his violent physical aggression, he may replace it with language that even the teacher has never before heard. He has to be told this won't do, when the words are said so loudly or so hostilely they can't be ignored. But unless the dirty language itself upsets or excites the child and the class, he may be allowed to stay in class. Later, he will most certainly be removed, because language has its appropriate places, and this language doesn't go in school any more than hitting or kicking go in school. Group reaction, group contagion, specific offensiveness to a particular teacher will determine the timing, when things are no longer tolerated, just as much as the child's own personal needs. It is not useful to the child any more than it is to the rest of the group for him to feel he can powerfully destroy the purposes and meaning of school. At that point, the message that the child can handle school, because the school can handle him, breaks down. Letting too much go by is as poor a communication in his unlearning of old perceptions as is deprivation.

Expected Backsliding

Finally it grows clear that the message, that school is not what the child thought it was when he came, gets through. He is upset by this new perception and doesn't know what to do with it. He tries all his old tricks, out of habit, yes, but also to defend himself against the need to create new ways of responding. Behavior may appear much the same, but the tone of the behavior has changed sufficiently so that the teacher and clinical staff are aware that a difference exists.

Enter—Reality About Self

At this time new learning messages take place. The school, with its defined structure, now is used to define the child for himself, to point out his assets, and also his limitations. He is not superman, not all-powerful; his grandiose ideas for undertaking a project can't work but if he can shave them down to reality-size they can be put into action. A fantasy is fine, but to translate a fantasy into reality requires making the fantasy life-size. One cannot take a tour of the United States looking for turtles simply because one identifies with turtles but one can read about turtles, make maps of the places they live, and find out about these places from books and films. To do even this, skills are needed—one must learn how to read at a certain level, how to look at and use maps, and learn new words. This takes work. It doesn't just come; it comes with help and work. With this work and help, one can grow more able, stronger, less helpless, and more realistically knowledgeable. It may be that a child is terrible at spelling but possesses a genuine skill at manipulating figures and such work goes fast and seems easy and satisfying. Children are in school to explore their own abilities and to increase themselves.

Enter—Reality About The Teacher

The teacher is there not to shame or expose but to help where it is needed because he wishes the child to be adequate and he feels he can be, no matter how many mess-ups and mistakes are made en route. He seems not to take the mistakes as seriously as the child. Mistakes are necessary in learning something new and not simply an indication that a child is stupid, worthless and hopeless. Therefore, when a child has messed up beyond belief on Monday by using bad language, destroying the lesson plan, or getting into a fight with a classmate, he can still start fresh on Tuesday without dirty looks, warning fingers, or resentful reminders. After repetitive demonstrations of all the above amazing phenomena about school and the teacher, it is hardly worthwhile to keep "messing up." He may try (frightening though it may be at first) to respond to encouragement with faith instead of despair, to stick five minutes longer with the work that always seems too hard, to listen to the directions that are given.

The hand on the shoulder that so scared the child for months, may not mean the teacher is going to trap him, pull him close only to turn against him, or demand a closeness which the child can't tolerate. The hand may just be there to give reassurance, encouragement, or a silent warning that the child's behavior is going off bounds. It may be a support, not a trap. The hand may, in time, feel good, and the child will be able to answer with a smile instead of a scowl, curse, or punch.

The Convalescent Emotionally Disturbed Child.

When these messages are conveyed to the emotionally disturbed child and when, given time, patience and opportunities for backsliding, he has developed his own new patterns of feeling and responding, he will learn at school as other children learn. That is to say, he will have his good days and his bad, his easy subjects and his hard ones, his personal dislikes of teachers and peers, and his personal loves.

Often when a child is over the major hump of disease, we tend not to allow him the margin for error and regression that we give any ordinary youngster. We grow wary of any lapse. To be watchful and supportive is a good thing. To be wary and distrustful is another. Our very wariness and anxiety may become an unuseful message to convey. The convalescent emotionally disturbed child has a right to the same mistakes the rest of us make, to the same time lag between a new fact and its assimilation. With a reasonable amount of faith, watchfulness, support and continued interest, once he has stabilized his new perceptions, he not only can, but should, be handled in the same way as other children, without an overdose of specialness.

Summary

It is true that the treated emotionally disturbed child lives with scar tissue. It is true that damages leave their mark. But who does not grow up with damages of some sort? It is true that life may again present him with conditions which may throw him back into his old perceptions temporarily or permanently. But we cannot guarantee that life will not throw the healthiest of us, nor can we know for certain our saturation point.

On the one hand, it may be that he will break again under too much pressure. On the other, it may be that emotional scar tissue is stronger than new tissue and that, just because of his past experiences and his new insights and ability to suffer through storms, he may have greater strength than most. It is the initial communication center that sends the clearest messages, and if, by our demonstration, we have made extinct the original messages, have made them untrue for the child, unuseful and inappropriate, and if we have given reinforcement to more useful patterns and perceptions, the child will choose the patterns most useful to him in living his life.

Chapter 15

Use Of Standard Materials With
Young Disturbed Children

Louise S. Emery

In the past decade, impetus has been given to the development of day school programs for seriously disturbed children. This discussion centers around the program of one such school, the Forum School in Ridgewood, New Jersey, which was established in 1954. It is now state supported and offers services to children excluded from public schools.

The children in this study range in age from five to ten years and have a diagnosis of childhood schizophrenia. Symptoms include autistic, symbiotic, aggressive, or hyperactive behavior. The illness is differentiated from conditions of organic brain damage or mental deficiency, although present diagnostic measurements are not infallible. Implicit in the diagnosis is the possibility that the child is potentially accessible.

The basic aim of the school program is to further the ego development of the child. The essential element in this development is the teacher-child relationship. The tools are many of the standard materials and activities used in preschool programs. These materials can be adapted to the functioning level and the individual needs of the child.

Music And Rhythm

Using the song circle as the first activity tends to give structure to the whole school day. Through music, initial contacts

---

Reprinted from *Exceptional Children*, Vol. 33 (1966), pp. 265-268. By permission of the author and publisher.

can be made with the withdrawn child. Materials are chosen for this period to fulfill goals of self-identification (action songs), development of readiness skills (learning songs), and encouragement of speech (sound songs).

To develop or strengthen self-identification, the first song is one of individual greeting. To the tune of "Happy Birthday," each child is greeted with "Good morning to you, good morning to you, good morning, dear (child's name), we're glad to see you." Along with self-awareness, the names of other children are learned. An action song is used to develop awareness of the parts of the body. To the words "Oh, look, see what I can do," children touch their heads, shake their hands, swing their arms, stamp their feet, or touch their noses, ears, or chins. Each child takes his turn in performing some action, and the group imitates his gestures. The part of the body brought into action is named.

"Looby-Loo" and "Hokey-Pokey" are additional songs used to teach body parts. For some children the teacher must use his own body as an extension of the child's in performance of the motions. Many are resistant to involvement, but progress in self-awareness can be noted in actions initiated by the child and his independent participation in the activity. An identification song which intrigues the children is the nursery song "I see you, I see you." As the song is sung by the teacher, he points to the child on "you" and to himself on "me." The correct use of pronouns has followed many repetitions of this song.

The ABC song, "Today Is (day of the week)," seasonal songs which call attention to weather, nature changes, or holidays provide pleasure in a learning situation. Self-care and articles of clothing are introduced to the tune of "Mulberry Bush," with "This is the way we wash our hands" or "This is the way we put on our coats." "John Brown Had a Little Indian," "Five Little Chick-a-dees," and "One-Two-Buckle My Shoe" serve as introductions to numbers. A clock song, a train song, and "Old Mac-Donald's Farm" have been avenues of experimentation for nonverbal children. Group singing does not demand individual verbalization. One nonverbal child with a strong response to music was frustrated into speech by unfinished lines of his favorite songs. His teacher sang these songs but stopped before the last word of each line. The child had to hear the line completed and supplied the omitted word himself.

Music seems to have unique value as teaching material. Through song the child is helped to recognize himself as a person, taught acceptable play contacts with other children, introduced to academic readiness which he rejects in the classroom setting, provided with speech training under pleasing conditions, and given the opportunity to contribute to a group activity at the level of his capability.

The rhythm period which follows the circle is a welcome change of pace. In the physical activities of marching, tiptoeing, skipping, and skating, excessive energy finds release, muscle coordination is strengthened, and interpersonal relationships are encouraged. Few beginners perform independently. Guidance and support from the teacher are necessary through the period. Some children need a close physical contact as they participate. Others need to be encouraged to join the activity. Some, because of their distractibility or inability to relate, need the reassuring handclasp of the teacher to keep them in the group. Progress may be estimated by the child's increased ability to perform independently.

Clay

Some autistic children are repelled by the feel of clay. If it is to serve as a satisfying manipulative tool, clay must be introduced slowly and carefully. A soft consistency is preferred, for if it is too stiff the child becomes frustrated and refuses to work with it. One successful introduction was a watered-down mixture with the consistency a little thicker than fingerpaint. This very thin substance was presented, because the teacher was aware of the child's need to mess; his only self-initiated activity was water play. Gradually, less water was added until the child accepted clay in its natural form and began to use it to pound and cut. Another teacher rolled out the clay and gave a child a cookie cutter. The child was then able to cut the forms and place them on a tin.

Other children have responded to rhythmically intoned directions from the teacher: "Roll, roll, roll the clay and pound,

pound, pound." As proficiency increases, the children are encouraged to form objects such as balls, baskets, small animals, etc. The teacher verbalizes what is being done. Baskets are filled with clay eggs, and balls are rolled from teacher to child or from child to child. An activity to develop small muscle control is rolling the clay into snake form and twisting it into a mat form (as a braided rug). One child learned to use scissors by cutting the snake-like form into small pieces. Clay is a medium easily handled and, for most children, enjoyable and gratifying. For variety, a flour dough mixture presents a different tactual experience. Adding food coloring to the mixture extends the variation and strengthens color identification.

Pegs

For the ingenious teacher, the pegboard becomes a versatile tool in teaching disturbed children. Through pegs, color recognition can be taught; small muscle control, developed; attention span, increased; form perception, improved; number concept, strengthened; and lateral dominance, practiced. Pegs may be used by a child for quiet play on a one to one basis with the teacher or in a small group where taking turns in placement of the pegs is an aid in the socialization process.

To introduce pegs the teacher places the empty pegboard in front of the child and a small pile of pegs beside the board. Picking up a peg he verbalizes the action: "I'm going to put a blue peg in this hole. Now, it is your turn, Tom. Put a blue peg next to the one I put in." The teacher may have to assist the child on the first few tries. As color recognition increases, the child is able to select the color called and place it on the board.

Simple forms of squares, triangles, and circles may be taught through pegs. A paper pattern placed on the board and outlined with pegs serves as an introduction. After the pegs have been placed around the pattern, the paper form is lifted and the child sees the form shaped by the pegs. He is then encouraged to make the forms without the patterns, starting with a straight line at the bottom of the board and building the verticle lines from this base. When the teacher desires an intimate rapport, he works individually with the child. When socialization is the goal, a pegboard may be shared by three or four children.

Finger Paint

Finger paint is to smear! The seriously disturbed child in this age range seldom uses this medium as a means of communicating feelings or for creative art. The children who need to mess (the ones who find the mud puddles on the playground) revel in finger paint to their elbows and happily cover the large sheets of paper, which are used to encourage breadth of movement. For reasons of economy, the base of the finger paint is liquid starch. This colorless liquid is an easy introduction for the child who becomes upset by dirty hands. After the child becomes accustomed to the feel of the starch and familiar with the sweeping motions, color in the form of powered paint is added gradually; and the child is able to accept the medium. A pail of water nearby to clean hands often was the reassurance needed for one child's beginning. For some children, the teacher spread the paint before they experimented by making designs with a rigid index finger. For other children the teacher's grasp on the wrist to propel the child's hands was enough incentive to learn to enjoy the activity.

Finger paint can be used as a transition from compulsive waterplay to a more constructive activity. It is one avenue by which to bring the child into group activity. It may be used to teach color. As the paint is distributed, the teacher asks the child to identify the color given him. Experimentation in blending colors is a delight to the more aware children. Finger painting gives the child another experience in developing muscle control, whereby the child learns to use both hands simultaneously, attention span is lengthened, and relief from tensions is provided. There is never a demand for design or a finished product. The child's enjoyment and self-satisfaction are the ultimate goals.

Blocks

Of the forty-nine children who have been enrolled in the program over the past eleven years, only two showed any interest in or were able to build with the wooden blocks usually found in every kindergarten. In each instance the structure of the blocks appeared to be related to obsessive phases of their problems. The majority of the children lack the dexterity, the attention, or the awareness necessary for intricate building. Some place one block atop another and delight in knocking them over, but seldom attempt constructive building.

The types of blocks used most satisfactorily in the program are the large, reenforced cardboard blocks (block busters) and the small varicolored, varishaped blocks (parquetry). Highly recommended for durability and easy handling, the block busters have been many things, from protective walls to stepping stones. As stepping stones they are used as a substitute for the walking board to teach balance and control. On initial attempts, few of the children can make this journey without the steadying hand of the teacher. Some put one foot on a block and bring the other foot up to meet it, using the same footwork pattern with which they negotiate the stairway.

Most of the children respond to the challenge of the bright colors and geometric shapes of the parquetry blocks, but some are confused by too much color and too many blocks. Using simplified patterns painted on squares of white show card paper, with two colors instead of the six included in the set, is an easy introduction. These simple designs assure a quick success without too much frustration. As the child becomes adept in matching simplified designs, he moves to the more intricate ones where the six colors are used. These blocks have been used for identification of color; to initiate experimentation in design; to lengthen attention span; and, when two or more children work together, to provide the setting for peer rapport.

Paper

Newsprint, construction paper, wallpaper sample books, and magazines are paper products constantly used in the learning situations. On large sheets of newsprint, children learn to make horizontal and verticle lines and circles with crayons. Often the teacher must begin this activity by placing the crayon in the child's hand and moving his hand to make the lines and circles. The lessening of tension in the child's arm indicates a decreasing resistance to the new activity. Eventually, the child's arm moves freely with the teacher's motions. The child is then encouraged to perform independently. From this beginning of lines and circles, numbers and letters are taught. Lines and circles also form stick figures from which body parts are identified.

Construction paper cut in triangles, squares, circles, and long narrow strips to be pasted on newsprint in a variety of designs appeals to most of the children. As ability to handle paste and the precut forms increases, random designs can form pictures. Circles become wheels, flowers, balloons, or faces; the squares may be houses, boxes, or bodies of cars or wagons.

Wallpaper sample books (discarded patterns from paint stores) provide an excellent practice area to learn how to use scissors, and the weight of the paper is good for beginners. Straight lines in patterns serve as guidelines as children learn to "open and close." Diversity of color and pattern challenges interest. For the more advanced child, the decorative uses of wallpaper are unlimited.

Advertisements in the housekeeping magazines related to items of everyday living are an excellent means for increasing awareness and identification. Through pictures of food, clothing, furniture, people, and family living, children learn to identify objects; increase vocabulary; and recognize color, letters, and words. From magazine clippings, individual children or groups can make posters or wall murals depicting self-care, family pets, foods, clothing, or homes. An advantage of using magazines, as opposed to workbooks, lies in their availability in the home, so that what has been learned in the classroom can become a satisfying activity for after school hours.

Chapter 16

Perspectives For A Classroom For Disturbed Children

LOUIS HAY AND SHIRLEY COHEN

T HERAPEUTIC EDUCATION is a process of nurturing the growth of seriously maladjusted children through a school-based program involving a team of educators and mental health clinicians. The primary objectives are the identification and rehabilitation of emotionally, socially and academically malfunctioning school children. Since disturbed children are rarely limited to one particular area of inadequacy, a suitable program requires a sustained team concerned not only with school experiences but also with the physical well-being, after-school activities and family relationships of these children.

Rehabilitative programs vary with the training, focus, and media available to different professions. In a school setting, the curriculum becomes the primary rehabilitative medium. Through the curriculum, we seek to elicit growing self-insight and healthier relationships to peers, adults, and the social world at large, in addition to academic achievements.

There are, unquestionably, theories and practices designed for application to the general child population which hold for exceptional children. However, we believe that every aspect of classroom functioning should be reexamined in the light of the special needs of disturbed children. If traditional patterns had been effective, there would be no need for special school programs for malfunctioning children.

An abbreviated form of this original manuscript was published in *Exceptional Children,* Vol. 33 (1967), pp. 577-580.

Why Focus On The Classroom?

The classroom is a way of communicating with your children. It is a way of telling them what you think of them, what the purpose of this place is, what needs of theirs are going to be met here. The room is a reflection of the relationship between teacher and children. The classroom is not only an expression of the philosophy of a program but also an important tool in carrying out this philosophy.

When one walks into a room in which the walls are bare, no materials are in sight and screens surround each child's place of work, the guiding philosophy of this program is immediately apparent. It is one of limiting the amount of stimuli with which these children have to deal. This room communicates to children a message involving concern about their self-control and ability to concentrate and achieve. If one enters a room where the walls are covered with children's work, carefully displayed, where stories about the children and pictures abound, then a different emphasis is apparent. Here the room says, I value each one of you; each one of you has an important place in this classroom; I will try to help you value yourself more.

Characteristics Of Disturbed Children Which Have Implications For Room Planning

In planning classrooms for disturbed children, one should take into account the common needs of all children; the needs of the special class, and the particular needs of each disturbed child. We list below several characteristics common to large numbers of disturbed school children which have implications for planning an effective room.

Poor Motor Coordination

"In general the stumbling, tumbling, bumping, spilling, dropping, that goes on reminds one of a group of much younger children—sometimes kindergartners, sometimes those in nursery school" (Montgomery County Board of Education, 1959, p. 21).

To take into account a child's poor motor control would mean to provide wide aisles and pathways for access to all areas which the children use. It would mean eliminating small objects from places where they can easily be knocked down. It would mean storing materials in such a way that they are easy to get at and easy to return. It would mean readying the class to accept and deal with spilled liquids, broken objects, and other accidents.

Hyperactivity

Since many of these children are characterized by diffused mobility, it is valuable to seek movement activities that may be directed and channeled as an area of sublimation. Music, dance, and other forms of rhythmic activities can be combined towards acceptable outlets. Physical activities appropriate to the gymnasium should not be encouraged in the classroom. Such activities complicate the definition of the classroom as a place of learning.

The importance of gross movement activities suggests the need for a large open space within the classroom. Such space can best be provided at special times during the day by the rearrangement of movable furniture or equipment. Large open spaces when not in use can excite and incite children to uncontrolled and inappropriate movement.

Space allowances should include ample movement opportunities for the children while they are seated. Arms and legs need room to stretch and twist. Too often accidental contact resulting from insufficient space allotments is interpreted as aggressive in intent, and therefore results in needless conflict. A hyperactive child and a withdrawn child may need different space allowances. Space can control social distance among those with sharply divergent contact and movement needs.

Disorientation In Space

This characteristic implies the need for a place of anchor for each child from which he can orient himself—a desk and chair which will be in the same place each day. The child's name, clearly printed on the chair with a marking pen, helps avoid confusion and conflict. Disorientation in space also implies the need for consistency in physical arrangement of the room. Labels on closed closets, e.g., "Miss R's Closet," "Everyone's Closet for Games," help clarify expectations and avoid confusion.

The Need To Withdraw From The Group

Disturbed children often find group membership and participation difficult to sustain. The presence of other children or the pressure to interact with them may become too stimulating or threatening. At such times there should be a haven for a child to withdraw to. There are several approaches to achieving this end: a room with one or two partitioned-off cubicles; a room with nooks into which furniture for one or two children can be placed; an L-shaped room so that mutually destructive children need not be constantly within sight of one another; a room in which furniture is arranged so as to provide semisheltered areas. A child who cannot tolerate the presence of a large group of children for an extensive period may be able to work comfortably for alternating periods with two or three other children of congenial tempos in an area somewhat set off from the rest of the classroom.

Withdrawal areas for individual children should be temporary havens. With growth, the need for them will diminish. This area may be furnished with a rocking chair or soft chair, table, phonograph with earphones, hand viewer with assortment of slides, and some stuffed animals. With older children simple games might replace the stuffed animals, and a primary typewriter could be included.

Distractability And Poor Impulse Control

It has been widely noted that many maladjusted children find it difficult to become engaged and to sustain involvement in a particular activity. They are restless and easily distracted. These characteristics may arise from a variety of causes and deserve careful consideration by a team of clinicians and educators working together. However, room arrangements can be helpful to both teachers and children in extending attention span. Materials should not be stored enticingly close to children's desks. Actively centers should be cut off from direct sight when they are not to be used by the arrangement of furniture and room dividers. Care should be taken to prevent mutually stimulating or destructive children from being seated near one another.

Blanket attempts to produce bland and nonstimulating rooms

derive from an oversimplified, stereotyped view of disturbed, hyperactive children. These attempts are often self-defeating. In some cases, they lead to further withdrawal from the real environment and compound a sense of isolation. Nor should this one need for muted stimuli be stressed at the expense of other equally important needs. Responsiveness and tolerance of stimulation varies greatly from child to child, and within any particular child at different times of the day, week, and year. A uniform formula applied to all children is therefore inappropriate.

Lack Of Initiative, Dependence And Inability To Make Choices

Disturbed children often have ego disturbances which manifest themselves as limited self-differentiation and self-knowledge. These children may have poorly developed interests and tastes, find it difficult to make choices and decisions, and demonstrate little initiative. They often depend upon adults who step in to fill this vacuum. The placement and storage of materials has direct relevance to the problem of developing initiative. When materials are kept in closed closets and are selected and distributed by the teacher or a monitor, these children are being deprived of the experience necessary to the development of self-reliance and autonomy.

On the other hand, open shelves with attractive materials may prove too great a distraction for some of these children. In practice, some materials may be left on open shelves in any classroom. These include library and reference books, magazines, drawing and writing paper. Children can be encouraged to help themselves to these materials independently. Other materials such as workshop tools and large jars of paints may require storage in closets to which the children do not have access. There is however a whole range of materials which the children may be encouraged to select from at appropriate times of the day. Among these are arts and crafts supplies, games, and trays of science materials. These materials may be kept in shelves which are covered when they are not to be used, and left open when they may be used. With growth over a period of time during the school year, the children will be able to tolerate more materials in open shelves.

Distorted Or Poorly Developed Social Relations

One of the crucial factors in aiding the development of healthy relationships is the provision of opportunities for mutually supportive children to work together. Traditionally, teachers have based their seating arrangements on size, visual acuity, and alphabetical ordering of last names. More recently, children's own preferences were influential. But the preferences of disturbed children sometimes reflect their pathology. Children's preferences must therefore be used in combination with the insights of the teacher and the mental health team into individual and group dynamics. Proximity to the teacher is also a factor to be considered. Some children need to be close to the adult, while others will do better if they are not in close physical contact with the teacher initially.

Components Of The Room That Require Reconsideration

We have previously suggested that a room becomes the framework for communication between teacher and child, and between child and child. Structure saliently influences function. Adequate structure facilitates the primary goal of rehabilitation while inadequate structure produces an endless return of crosscurrents that interfere with the aims of the program. In thinking of classrooms for disturbed children, one should reexamine every aspect of the physical environment in the light of the special needs of these children. Among the aspects of the rooms that deserve reconsideration are size and shape, sound control, lighting, color, storage facilities, use of wall space, furniture and its arrangement. The relation of the room to strategic school centers such as the gymnasium, toilet, and lunchroom is also a controlling factor.

Location

Children are placed in a special class for the disturbed because they are unable to meet the expectations of the regular class and school. Therefore, every effort should be made to limit the interaction of the special class with the rest of the school until there is evidence of genuine readiness to participate in common school activities. One would then want a room which is in a quiet, lightly used section of the building, apart from the comings and goings of large numbers of children such as is found near the cafeteria, auditorium, or main recreation area.

Many maladjusted children manifest symptomatic problem behavior around toileting. For this reason it is desirable to have toilet facilities adjoining or near the classroom which are reserved for the use of the special class only.

One would also want to look for a room which is close to an exit and not above the second floor, since disturbed children find transitions and transitional movement stressful. A room located on a high floor or far from an exit provides more extensive opportunities for disorder during this transitional travel.

Size

The figure 30 to 40 square feet of floor space per child, which had been accepted as a guide for classroom size in the past, is no longer considered adequate.

> "A major influence in the design of school buildings has been the increase in floor area of classrooms in response to the requirements of the changing elementary education program in recent years. . . . In many cases, where communities have reduced the size of all classes to 20 or 25 pupils, the educational program includes an unusually wide variety of activities. Such schools tend to individualize the program so that more activities with fewer children involved in each are the general rule. The need for space, in such a situation, does not decrease in proportion to the reduction in class size" (Engelhardt, 1953, p. 56).

Registers in classes for disturbed children generally range from five to twelve. A class with ten disturbed children cannot function effectively in one-third of the space allotted a class of thirty children. Programs for disturbed children cannot afford to cut down on the variety of activities made available in the classroom. Moreover, individualized teaching, such as is found in most good programs for maladjusted children, requires more materials and space than does a traditional approach. Additional allowances must also be made for the restlessness and hyperactivity common in this population. They need to move about easily. When aisles are narrow and the classroom is cramped, poking, tripping, and collisions ensue. A more appropriate space allotment for special classes is 55 to 65 square feet per child, with a minimum total of about 450 square feet for even the smallest group.

Shape

In designing or selecting classrooms, serious consideration should be given to nonrectangular rooms. These include L-shaped rooms, rooms with nooks, or two adjoining rooms with an open doorway between them. The advantage of these shapes is that they can allow for more variety in activities while protecting against overstimulation or constant rearrangement of furniture. While a special cubicle for each child is not indicated, two or three cubicles are valuable resources.

Sound Control

In thinking of sound control, one must consider the arrangement of work centers. How many work centers which produce a high level of sound, such as woodworking and block-building, can a room house? What kind of work centers should be located near one another? Which children can be allowed to work together? The answers to these questions should be based on a knowledge that some disturbed children are hyperactive and loud; that some disturbed children may require a greater opportunity for being noisy as part of a coming-out-of-withdrawal phase; that there are striking differences in children's tolerances for loud and discordant sounds; that some disturbed children show an exaggerated, painful reaction to auditory stimuli; that a high intensity of sound will cause withdrawal in some children, loss of control in others. The program must be balanced to meet these needs and tolerances within a particular class.

A "loud" room may be partly the result of hard, sound-reflecting surfaces. This situation can be remedied by the use of porous, sound-absorbing plaster tiles on the ceiling or by an abundance of corkboards about the walls of the room. Sound can also be used to control high sound levels. Quiet music will often set a mood which children will not violate. The whole tone of a classroom can be quieted at times by a reduction in the volume or intensity of the teacher's voice. Screens and room dividers placed between different activity groups can reduce interfering sounds. Children who are particularly sensitive to auditory stimulation can be seated away from noise producing areas and close to quiet ones.

Noise can, at times, be necessary and beneficial. A classroom which is never noisy is a classroom in which important experiences are missing.

Furniture

Fixed furniture does not lend itself to the flexibility called for in the special class. It limits the possibilities for meeting temporary needs and stages of growth. Movable furniture is preferable, but furniture which shifts about easily is a poor choice for some hyperactive children or children with spatial disorientation. Heavy movable furniture, with desks and seats attached, may be a better choice for these children.

Individual physical differences must be taken into account in selecting furniture. Desks and chairs should be ordered in three sizes rather than in one standard size, unless the furniture is adjustable. Desks whose tops open up so that their contents can be readily inspected have a decided advantage over desks with fixed side openings. The former allows the child a better feeling of control over his own belongings. Individual desks are in general preferable to double desks. Double desks make no allowances for physiological differences and require the ability to live in close proximity to another child for long periods. In classes for disturbed children, this may invite endless friction, competition, mutual stimulation towards undesirable ends or a relationship of domination and submission.

Several small tables should be available for group activities. Round tables seem to be particularly inviting of group cohesiveness.

Use Of Wall Space

Bulletin board displays are important tools of communication; tools by which the teacher makes concrete her recognition and respect of the children, their efforts, and their achievements. The care with which children's work is displayed, the effort which the teacher is ready to make to preserve and exhibit it, proves to the children that their work is valued by the teacher. The teacher's attitude forms the basis for the child's own attitudes towards his work and towards the efforts of his peers (Kramer, 1958). When bulletin boards revolve about the children, they begin to get a sense of their own worth. Current events are not only the major occurrences in our city, country, or world, but also events current and important in the lives of these children.

Chalkboards are excellent devices, not only for helping teachers teach, but also for helping children learn. To a restless child who needs a feeling of freedom-of-movement, working at a desk for even relatively short periods of time can be taxing. Chalkboard activities can provide a respite from the cramped and hedged-in feeling that these children get at their desks.

Color And Light

A room for disturbed children should be light, bright, and clean. For many children, a colorful classroom is a happy change from a dreary or disordered home. While little fuss need be made in response to the daily classroom cumulative disarray and untidiness, each morning should be witness anew to a fresh, clean and well-ordered room. These children are particularly susceptible in terms of mood and tone to a depressingly dark and dreary environment. To house maladjusted children in such a place is to reinforce the rejection which they often perceive around them.

Conclusion

It is commonly believed that disturbed children should be exposed to the same activities in the same framework as healthy children. Expose them to accepted standards with vigorous insistence, penalties and rewards, and they will respond and grow into appropriate behavior patterns. Very likely some will. We see the problem differently. To seek immediate adherence to accepted norms is to confuse goals with current readiness. It shows a lack of adequate consideration of the controls of deviant behavior—the gaps in development, constricted experiences, self-defeating defense mechanisms, conflicts, anxieties, physical and family trauma—which results in failure to help large numbers of such children. The room which we have projected is the living space congenial to our goals and approaches towards nurturing children into healthy functioning.

A room is going to be used either well or badly. It is going to contribute either to the difficulties which a class of disturbed children have in living and learning together, or it is going to facilitate their growth in living and learning together. Sensitivity to the implications and effects of the manifold aspects of the physical setting is the best assurance that the physical setting will be used constructively.

References

Cruickshank, W. *et al.*: *A Teaching Method for Brain-Injured And Hyperactive Children.* Syracuse, Syracuse, 1961.

Engelhardt, N. *et al.*: *Planning America's School Buildings.* New York, Dodge Corp., 1953.

Hay, Louis: A New School Channel For Helping The Troubled Child. *Amer J Orthopsychiat, 23:* 676-683, 1953.

Kornberg, L.: *A Class For Disturbed Children.* New York, Bureau of Publications, Teacher's College, Columbia University, 1955.

Kramer, Edith: *Art Therapy In A Children's Community.* Springfield, Thomas, 1958.

Long, N.; Morse, W., and Newman, Ruth (Eds.): *Conflict in the Classroom.* Belmont, California, Wadsworth, 1965.

Montgomery County Board of Education: *Children With Learning Disabilities.* Syracuse, Syracuse, 1959.

New York City Board of Education: *Early Childhood Education.* New York, Board of Education, 1958-59.

Chapter 17

Psychoeducational Processes In Classes For Emotionally Handicapped Children

WILLIAM G. HOLLISTER AND STEPHEN E. GOLDSTON

Is THERE a unique educational methodology for emotionally handicapped children? Are there some specific procedures for working with emotionally handicapped children which differ significantly from those usually employed in the regular classroom? Is there merit to the use of the term "Special Education" in our approach to this group?

In search for answers to these questions, we reviewed and analyzed a sample of program descriptions from schools, located in various sections of the country, that are currently providing classes for emotionally handicapped children. Twelve of the problems reviewed are in public school systems while six are in private day or residential settings (see List 1). In addition, we studied more abbreviated reports from 50 other classroom programs for emotionally handicapped children. A number of the listed programs were visited to supplement our information. We also personally discussed these three questions with a number of the mental health and educational leaders in this field: Birch, Bower, Cruickshank, Deno, Dunn, Jones, Lambert, Mackie, Morse, Newman, Phillips, Rabinovitch, Rashkis, Redl, Reynolds, Rhodes, Trippe, and others.

By gently pursuing the deceptively simple questions, "What are you trying to do with these children? How are you going about the doing? What do you think is happening?," we became

Reprinted from *Exceptional Children*, Vol. 28 (1962), pp. 351-356. By permission of the authors and publisher.

aware that (a) a considerable range of different procedures is being tried and that (b) communication between various investigators and practitioners is extremely limited. It is also evident that a considerable number of schools throughout the nation have initiated classes for emotionally handicapped children but most have not described their activities in sufficient detail to permit a thorough analysis of these programs. Nonetheless, the brief descriptions available provided some clues to the wide variety of approaches and practices now being used.

By focusing our attention on trends or on areas of common concern and practice, we were able to identify certain commonalities and gaps in these various classroom programs. We became aware that some system of description of the various psycho-educational processes being used was sorely needed in order to implement planning, communication, preparation of teachers for such classes, and for evaluative research. Therefore, we undertook the task of organizing the data from existing reports into a "beginning taxonomy" of the procedures and considerations involved in conducting classes for emotionally handicapped children.

The result of our efforts is a lengthy outline of the processes, factors, and procedures being employed or advocated for use in various classes for emotionally handicapped children. Through the insight and courtesy of The Council for Exceptional Children this material has been gathered into a pamphlet entitled "Some Basic Considerations in Planning and Studying Classes for Emotionally Handicapped Children" which is available from their headquarters office. We should like to emphasize that this document is only a preliminary taxonomy which has been collected, organized, and published principally to stimulate the various professions involved to do more definitive work.

It is our hope that this classification of procedures will enable school administrators and teachers to effect more comprehensive planning of their programs and that this outline will help teacher-educators to broaden their programs of preparing teachers to work with emotionally handicapped children. Beyond this, we hope such a taxonomy will set in motion more efforts at program description, some comparative studies, and stimulate research to evaluate these various proposals and procedures.

The Psychoeducational Processes

In our attempt to order the data we had collected, it was necessary to erect a classification of the essential psychoeducational processes we found to be operating in these various programs. Eventually, we settled on the 12 principal processes described below which we grouped into Administration, Pupil Selection and Study, Classroom Operations, and Supportive Operations. We were not able to order our information into mutually exclusive categories nor was it possible to integrate procedures based on such widely diverse premises into a unified approach. The sections that follow represent an attempt to summarize and combine the best features and procedures of the programs studied into a meaningful continuum.

LIST 1

DESCRIPTIVE PROGRAM REPORTS REVIEWED

Public School Classes

California—Fontana Unified School District
New York—New York City "600" Schools—East Meadow Public Schools
Michigan—Lansing Public Schools—Detroit Public Schools
Minnesota—Minneapolis Public Schools
Missouri—Kansas City Public Schools
Illinois—Chicago Public Schools—Quincy Public Schools
Virginia—Arlington County Public Schools
Wisconsin—Milwaukee Public Schools
New Jersey—Wayne Township Public Schools
Massachusetts—Newton Public Schools

Private School Classes

New Jersey—The Forum School, Paterson
Tennessee—Nashville Mental Health Center
Rhode Island—Bradley Home, Providence (residential)
Massachusetts—Gaebler School, Metropolitan Hospital, Waltham
Florida—Montanari Clinical School, Hialeah (residential)
New York—The League School, New York City

Administration

1. *Administrative Processes:* The initiation, organization, planning, coordination, and operation of classes for emotionally handicapped children requires intensive and extensive administrative implementation. Since the development of policy and program in this area involves not only the school administrators and the

school board but also considerable interdisciplinary involvement and community backing, the mechanisms of decision-making and plan implementation need to be clearly formulated. Consideration needs to be given to the following important administrative areas: legal responsibility, need assessment, definition of program goals and objectives, staff and consultant involvement in program development, policy development, designation of administrative and technical authority and responsibilities, administrative placement of the program, responsibilities for liaison and coordination, relationships with pupil-personnel, school health and instructional staffs, staffing patterns, teacher selection, staff role relationships, staff development programs, personnel practices to fit a more difficult teacher role, communication mechanisms, budget, administrative review, program evaluation by staff, as well as provision of such auxiliary services as transportation and food service.

Pupil Selection And Study

2. *Screening and diagnosis*: Need assessment and program development involve provisions for screening the school or community population to detect already emotionally handicapped children and to identify children who are "susceptible or vulnerable" to emotionally disorder so that early or preventive help can be given. A screening program entails defining the group to be screened, choosing the screening methods, training the personnel to be used, interpreting to parents and children, and establishing criteria of what children shall be given individual study. Full development of the diagnostic aspect of the program encompasses not only separate educational, medical, psychological, and psychiatric appraisals but a concerted attempt to define educational and psychological assets and deficiencies. Emphasis is on usable descriptions instead of classification and scores. Such a diagnostic program involves use of referral resources, interpretations and clearances with parents, as well as the difficult task of mobilizing and coordinating the efforts of an interdisciplinary group to evolve a comprehensive diagnosis.

3. *Planning, placement, and continuous assessment processes*: The formulation of recommendations and plans for care and

education, based on the individual needs of each child, is contingent upon integrating diverse diagnostic findings into a meaningful picture of the pupil, and the selection of feasible goals for extending help that are appropriately matched to the resources available. Procedures are required to integrate a multi-disciplinary working diagnosis and plan, to define the range of resources and the indications for their use, to determine placements, and to involve the staff who receive the pupil in the rationale for placement, to translate recommendations into action plans, to interpret to parents, and to evaluate periodically both the diagnosis and the placement.

Classroom Operations

This broad category encompasses a variety of closely related processes, often not mutually exclusive, which foster the education and adjustment of the emotionally handicapped child.

4. *Relationship-building process*: Much of the success of the educational program rests upon the skill and ability of the teacher to establish with the pupil a mutually perceived climate of trust, understanding, and empathy. The various procedures involved in this relationship-building include steps to prepare the child for relationships before entering the class, patterns of introducing new children into the class, methods to increase psychological safety, ways of setting up expected behaviors, factors associated with the grouping process, provision of direct emotional support by the teacher, diagnosing and reinforcing areas of personality strength, utilization of rewards and reinforcement, and group cohesion building patterns.

5. *Motivation-development process*: Emotionally handicapped children frequently require special efforts to free and nurture their motivation to learn and to achieve meaningful relationships with others. Such special efforts include procedures to utilize interest assessment techniques and to employ clinical knowledge of the child's psychodynamics as cues to defenses needing strengthening or impulses requiring reinforcement that can be used as motivations for learning. A group of procedures, varying from those designed to utilize stimulus deprivation to ways of

focusing or heightening responses, have been developed under the category of "motivational lure methods."

6. *Perceptual retraining process*: Distortions in perceptual abilities may be either the cause or the result of a child's emotional handicap. Procedures for diagnosing perceptual deficits are available, and educational methods have been evolved to train or retrain the pupil to overcome some of the perceptual distortions that interfere with his learning.

7. *Classroom behavior management process*: Most emotionally handicapped children show impaired behavior control and capacity for relationships with others. In order to release energy and time for learning, the teacher must frequently provide structure and firm guidance for the pupil's behavior. She needs to use her understanding of individual and group functioning to lessen and prevent maladaptive behavior that interferes with relationships, group productivity, and individual learning. The procedures include structuring expected behaviors, use of peer controls, group-wide guidance methods, control of group misbehavior, and methods for coping with poor individual behavior. Many of the procedures under the following sections also contribute to behavior management in a preventive way.

8. *Behavior reeducation process*: Some antisocial or asocial behavior can be regarded as a defect due to incomplete or improper learning. The amelioration of these disturbances often requires corrective learning experiences provided through a gradual, planned process of behavior reeducation. Emotionally handicapped children frequently must unlearn inappropriate behaviors and learn new behavior patterns which maximize their potential to effect those attitudes and behaviors which will enhance their personal well-being, usefulness, and acceptance. Procedures placed within this process have been grouped as anticipatory guidance education, planned corrective learning experiences, and general education on personal and social behavior.

9. *Academic education process*: The special class shares with the regular educational activities the objective of transmitting our cultural heritage and knowledges. Often, an emotionally handicapped child will have significant capacities and energies still available for intellectual growth. To meet the needs of an

emotionally handicapped child a detailed educational diagnosis is needed in order to develop an individualized curriculum for him. The procedures in this process are tutoring methods, remedial education methods, and the use of special methods and materials. Efforts which increase the child's cognitive, memory, evaluative, and other thinking abilities become ego strengths which can be used by him in coping with and solving some of his life adjustment problems.

10. *Process of rehabilitation to the regular classroom*: The task of social, emotional, and educational rehabilitation to the regular classroom and school life is a gradual process which demands careful planning involving both the special and regular education staffs, the clinical personnel, and the family. The procedures of rehabilitation include the establishment of criteria for transfer, planning for and methods of returning to the regular class, procedures for returning the pupil to the special class as needed, preparation of the regular teacher, and provisions for follow-up guidance and evaluation.

Supportive Operations

Although Administration and Pupil Selection and Study are supportive in nature, the following two procedures are important operations which are supportive to the teacher working in the classroom.

11. *Clinical-educator liaison process*: A special class program for emotionally handicapped children requires a close working relationship between a clinical team and the education staff. Planning for each child is a continuous process, a joint multidisciplinary responsibility, that must progressively deal with the changes in personality and other psychosocial factors affecting the course of the child as he progresses through various stages of his problem and into the rehabilitation process. The following operations implement this process: use of conferences and consultations, use of group and individual supervision methods, therapeutic opportunities and supports for teachers, periodic case reviews, in-service training methods, and joint data collecting and research efforts.

12. *School-home liaison process*: The development of com-

munication with the home and the supplementary extension of special service to the parents complement and extend the impact of the school program and help to mitigate factors in the home which may work against the psychoeducational processes being used at school. Various procedures such as periodic interview programs, use of parents group activities, provision of parent counseling, therapy, casework, or nursing services, as well as the use of parent-aides, and home-school reporting systems are used to effect this liaison.

Summary

Our attempts to explore the current status of educational programs for emotionally handicapped children revealed to us the need for some orderly classification of the various psychoeducational processes we found being used in such programs. We have developed this beginning effort at a taxonomy of the methods used in these classes in the hope that this preliminary outline will be of value to those currently planning and operating programs, and to those attempting to describe and evaluate the procedures being used in these classes. In addition, this categorization may be helpful to those exploring the issues related to the training and qualifications needed for teachers of the emotionally handicapped.

Returning to the three questions posed at the beginning of this paper, we believe there are emerging out of the rich variety of current practices some unique or special procedures for use in these classes, and that the term "Special Education" is justifiably applied to this work. Since a look at educational history reveals that yesterday's special education procedure frequently became today's standard class method, it would be wise to reserve judgment about the eventual use of these procedures in general classes. It is quite possible that some of the motivational lure and perceptual retraining methods along with the process of diagnosing and reinforcing ego strengths and using group development methods might well be the precursors to methods that will some day be used in classes for all children.

We are certain this outline deserves further refinement and elaboration. Improving its semantics and resolving its theoretical heterogeneity will require considerable future effort. In essence, we believe we have outlined an important book needed in special education, a book whose chapter and verse will be written by creative educators and behavioral scientists within the next decade.

Selected Bibliography

Bower, E. M.: The emotionally handicapped child and the school: an analysis of programs and trends. *Exceptional Child, 26:* 182-188, 1959.

Cruickshank, W. M.; Bentzen, F.; Ratzeberg, F., and Tannhauser, M.: *A Method Of Teaching Brain-injured And Hyperactive Children.* Syracuse, Syracuse, 1961.

Hirschberg, J. D.: The roles of education in treatment of emotionally disturbed children through planned ego development. *Amer J Orthopsychiat, 23:* 684-690, 1953.

Morse, W. C.: The education of socially maladjusted and emotionally disturbed children. In W. M. Cruickshank and G. O. Johnson: *Education of Exceptional Children and Youth.* Englewood Cliffs, N.J.: Prentice-Hall, 1958, pp. 557-608.

Phillips, E. L., and Haring, N. G.: Results from special techniques for teaching emotionally disturbed children. *Exceptional Child, 26:* 64-67, 1959.

SECTION E

EXPERIMENTAL PROJECTS AND APPROACHES

Chapter 18

Educational Engineering With Emotionally Disturbed Children

FRANK M. HEWETT

As EDUCATIONAL PROGRAMS for emotionally disturbed children receive increased federal, state, and local public school support and become more widespread, several models for establishing these programs are available to teachers. There is the psychotherapeutic model with a psychodynamic, interpersonal emphasis; the pathological or medical model, which focuses on brain pathology and treatment of measured or inferred organic causal factors; and the pedagogical model, concerned with intellectual development, remedial techniques, and academic goals. Each model has influenced school programs for emotionally disturbed children, and, depending on the intuitive, diagnostic, and curriculum skill of the teacher, has been useful to some degree. The need still exists, however, for a more generally applicable model to handle the ever increasing number of inattentive, failure prone, and resistant children who are being separated from their more readily educable peers for special education. Such a model must be understandable to the teacher, translatable to the classroom, and hold promise for more effectively educating the emotionally disturbed child.

Recently, a model called behavior modification has demonstrated usefulness with exceptional children. Rather than view the emotionally disturbed child as a victim of psychic conflicts, cerebral dysfunction, or merely academic deficits, this approach

Reprinted from *Exceptional Children*, Vol. 33 (1967), pp. 459-467. By permission of the author and publisher.

183

concentrates on bringing the overt behavior of the child into line with standards required for learning. Such standards may include development of an adequate attention span; orderly response in the classroom; the ability to follow directions; tolerance for limits of time, space, and activity; accurate exploration of the environment; and appreciation for social approval and avoidance of disapproval. Promoting successful development of these standards as well as self-care and intellectual skills through assignment of carefully graded tasks in a learning environment which provides both rewards and structure for the child in accord with principles of empirical learning theory (Skinner, (1963) are the basic goals of the behavior modification model.

According to Ullman and Krasner (1965), the behavior modifier has three main concerns: (a) defining maladaptive behavior, (b) determining the environmental events which support this behavior, and (c) manipulating the environment in order to alter maladaptive behavior. In the case of the emotionally disturbed child, his maladaptive behavior is readily distinguished in the classroom by poor concentration, hyperactivity, acting out, defiance, avoidance, withdrawal, and other manifestations that make him a poor candidate for learning. Environmental events which maintain these behaviors might include positive reinforcement and recognition for misbehavior; association of school, teacher, and learning with failure and negative reinforcement; and assignment of learning tasks inappropriate to the child. The third concern, what can be done to change school to remedy both the emotionally disturbed child's maladaptive behavior and its environmental supports, is the subject of this paper.

The Engineered Classroom

In the engineered classroom, the teacher is assigned the role of behavioral engineer; she attempts to define appropriate task assignments for students, provide meaningful rewards for learning, and maintain well defined limits in order to reduce and hopefully eliminate the occurrence of maladaptive behavior. The teacher, then, engineers an environment in which the probability of student success is maximized and maladaptive behavior is replaced by adaptive behavior. The role of behavior engineer has been previously described by Ayllon and Michael (1959), with reference to application of behavior modification theory by nursing personnel working wtih psychotic patients. The engineered classroom concept has been explored by Haring and Phillips (1962), Whelan and Haring (1966), and Quay (1966) with emotionally disturbed children, and by Birnbrauer, Bijou, Wolf, and Kidder (1965) at the Rainier School in Washington. The latter research project was visited by the author and aspects of the engineered design described here stem from these observations. Other authors, such as Staats, Minke, Finley, Wolf, and Brooks (1964), Zimmerman and Zimmerman (1962), and Valett (1966), have applied behavior modification principles to academic teaching.

One of the problems inherent in introducing theoretical concepts and research findings into the classroom is the inevitable involvement of a specialized and often alien vocabulary, as well as a frame of reference for implementation not usual to the educational background of the teacher. This dilemma arises in the psychotherapeutic and pathological models mentioned earlier, where libido, ego strength, and psychosexual development, or dyslexia, perceptual motor dysfunction, and strephosymbolia may be impressive but not always useful terms in the classroom. Successful application of behavior modification principles also requires understanding of such concepts as reinforcement, contingencies, and scheduling; while simple and clear-cut in intent, they are not always easily grasped or accepted by teachers.

The engineered classroom design currently under investigation was introduced in the public school (Hewett, 1966), by a teacher who had no previous exposure to behavior modification theory. It attempts a translation of this theory—not rigidly, but pragmatically—to the school setting. Behavior modification principles are organized in terms of a learning triangle, the sides of which represent the three essential ingredients for all effective teaching: selection of a suitable educational task for the child, provision of a meaningful reward following accomplishment of that task, and maintenance of a degree of structure under the control of the teacher. Figure 1 illustrates the relationship of certain behavior modification principles to these three factors.

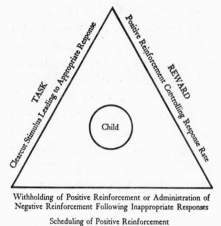

Withholding of Positive Reinforcement or Administration of
Negative Reinforcement Following Inappropriate Responses

Scheduling of Positive Reinforcement

Setting of Contingency for Receipt of Reinforcement

STRUCTURE

FIGURE 1. The Learning Triangle

The engineered classroom design creates an environment for implementation of the learning triangle. Suitable educational tasks are selected from a hierarchy, presented in Figure 2, which describes seven task levels. The first five are readiness levels, largely mastered by normal children before they enter school. The final two are concerned with intellectual skill development which constitutes a primary educational goal with all children.

Emotionally disturbed children are usually not ready to be in school because they are unable to pay attention, follow directions, explore the environment, or get along with others. For this reason, suitable educational tasks for these children must often

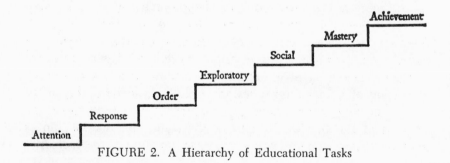

FIGURE 2. A Hierarchy of Educational Tasks

be selected from the five readiness levels. The hierarchy encompasses many fundamental concepts of the psychotherapeutic, pathological, and pedagogical models discussed earlier. However, it attempts to define these concepts in terms of educational operations rather than by psychoanalytic, neurological, or narrow academic nomenclature. In this regard the present hierarchy is a revision of one earlier described (Hewett, 1964). Table I summarizes the seven task levels of the hierarchy, children's problems relating to each, the type of learner rewards available, and the degree of structure inherent at each level.

An assessment procedure enables the teacher to rate the child in terms of specific deficits on the hierarchy shortly after he enters the engineered classroom. This assessment becomes the basis for establishing an educational program for him and provides the teacher with an understanding of his basic learning deficits. This procedure is ongoing and is repeated three times each semester.

In helping an emotionally disturbed child get ready for intellectual training the teacher can profitably use the behavior modification principle of shaping; rather than holding out for the ultimate goal (e.g., student functioning appropriately on the mastery and achievement levels), successive approximations of that goal (e.g., functioning at attention, response, order, exploratory, and social levels) are recognized achievements. The engineered classroom design attempts to provide an environment and program for shaping appropriate learning behavior.

Classroom Description

The engineered classroom should be a large, well lighted room (ideally 1200 to 1500 square feet) with a double desk (2' by 4') for each of nine pupils. The class is under the supervision of a regular teacher and a teacher aide. The aide need not be certified or specifically trained. High school graduates and PTA volunteers have been effective.

The physical environment can be described as having three major centers paralleling levels on the hierarchy of educational tasks. The mastery-achievement center consists of the student desk area where academic assignments are undertaken. Adjacent

TABLE I

DESCRIPTION OF THE HEIRARCHY OF EDUCATIONAL TASKS

Hierarchy Level	Attention	Response	Order	Exploratory	Social	Mastery	Achievement
Child's Problem	Inattention due to withdrawal or resistance	Lack of involvement and unwillingness to respond in learning	Inability to follow directions	Incomplete or inaccurate knowledge of environment	Failure to value social approval or disapproval	Deficits in basic adaptive and school skills not in keeping with IQ	Lack of self motivation for learning
Educational Task	Get child to pay attention to teacher and task	Get child to respond to tasks he likes and which offer promise of success	Get child to complete tasks with specific starting points and steps leading to a conclusion	Increase child's efficiency as an explorer and get him involved in multisensory exploration of his environment	Get child to work for teacher and peer group approval and to avoid their disapproval	Remediation of basic skill deficiencies	Development of interest in acquiring knowledge
Learner Reward	Provided by tangible rewards (e.g., food, money, tokens)	Provided by gaining social attention	Provided through task completion	Provided by sensory stimulation	Provided by social approval	Provided through task accuracy	Provided through intellectual task success
Teacher Structure	Minimal	Still limited	Emphasized	Emphasized	Based on standards of social appropriateness	Based on curriculum assignments	Minimal

to and part of this center are two study booths or offices where academic work may be done without visual distraction. These are carpeted and outfitted with desks and upholstered chairs. An exploratory-social center with three distinct areas is set up near the windows and sink facilities. Equipment for simple science experiments is available in one area, arts and crafts activities in another. Social skills are fostered in the communication area of the exploratory center where group listening activities and games are provided. The attention-response-order center is in an opposite corner of the classroom and consists of two double desks and a storage cabinet where puzzles, exercises, and materials for use in emphasizing paying attention, responding, and routine are kept. Thus each level on the hierarchy has a designated area in the room where specific types of tasks may be undertaken by the child.

Mounted by the door is a work record card holder displaying individual work cards for each student. The room has limited bulletin board displays and looks much like any elementary classroom. The hypothesis that all emotionally disturbed children need a drab, sterile, nonstimulating school environment is rejected in this design.

The class operates five main periods in the minimum 240-minute day required by California for programs for the educationally handicapped. Period I is a ten minute order period (attention, response, and order levels); Period II consists of reading and written language (mastery level), and lasts sixty minutes; Period III is devoted to arithmetic (mastery level) and is sixty minutes in length; Period IV is a twenty minute physical education session; and Period V is for science, art, and communication (exploratory and social levels) and lasts sixty minutes. In addition, a recess, nutrition break, and evaluation period round out the class day.

A floorplan of the engineered classroom is illustrated in Figure 3.

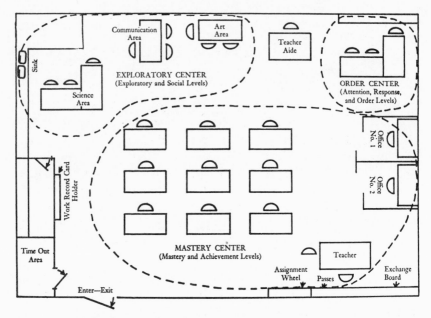

FIGURE 3. Floorplan of an Engineered Classroom

Students

Two types of students have been enrolled in experimental engineered classrooms to date: public school children with essentially normal intelligence from Santa Monica and Tulare in California and the Palolo School district in Oahu, Hawaii, identified as educationally handicapped (underachieving due to emotional, neurological, or learning disability factors) and emotionally disturbed children hospitalized on the Children's Service of the UCLA Neuropsychiatric Institute and enrolled in the Neuropsychiatric Institute School. The public school population consisted mostly of boys with conduct disturbances, neurotic traits including long-standing school phobias, psychosomatic and borderline psychotic problems, as well as minimal neurological impairment. The hospitalized group represented more serious emotional problems and included grossly psychotic and more markedly neurologically impaired individuals. All students were in the age group from eight to twelve.

Engineered Classroom Operations

As can be seen from Table I, the range of rewards possible to offer the child in school includes tangible rewards, social attention, task completion, sensory stimulation, social approval, and task accuracy and success. Normal children arrive in the classroom ready to learn in anticipation of such rewards as approval and accuracy, but emotionally disturbed children often are not motivated in the same manner. Levin and Simmons (1962) found that emotionally disturbed boys were more effectively motivated by tangible rewards of food than by social praise.

Since a meaningful reward for learning is essential in a successful teaching situation and emotionally disturbed children differ so greatly with respect to what is rewarding for them, the engineered classroom operates on the most basic reward level in an effort to insure gratification in school for even the most resistant learner.

As each student enters in the morning he picks up his individual work record card which is ruled into two hundred squares. As he moves through the day the teacher and aide recognize his work accomplishments and efficiency to function as a student by checking off squares on the work record card. The student carries his card with him wherever he goes in the room. Checkmarks are given on a fixed interval, fixed ratio basis every fifteen minutes. A time rather than a task contingency is used because it standardizes the total number of possible checkmarks in a single day, reduces competition, and is useful in alerting the student to the work efficiency orientation of the classroom. Intermittent schedules for rewarding children may be more powerful but, in the author's experience, they have not proven as manageable and practical for the teacher.

Checkmarks are given in very specific ways. Normally, a maximum of 10 is given for any fifteen minute period. Two checkmarks are given for starting the assignment (attention level), three for following through (response level), and a possible five bonus given for being a student (order, exploratory, social, or mastery levels, depending on child's learning deficits). In addition, extra checkmarks might be given a particular child when necessary for motivation. In the main, however, the checkmarks are awarded conservatively by the teacher and attention is called to the specific reasons for the checkmarks being given or withheld. Since social reinforcement may actually be aversive for some emotionally disturbed children, the checkmark system functions as a neutral, nonconflictual meeting ground for teacher and student. The teacher attempts to convey the notion that checkmarks are objective measures of accomplishment and literally part of a reality system in the classroom over which she has little control. In this regard the teacher functions as a shop foreman who pays workers what they actually earn according to standards set by the plant system. The teacher's message to the child is in essence: "That's just the way it is. I work here too." Students save completed work record cards and exchange them on a weekly basis for candy, small toys, and trinkets. An exchange board in the room displays the tangible rewards available for 1, 2, or 3 cards filled with checkmarks.

While the checkmark system remains constant as the primary source of reward in the classroom, every effort is made to provide rewards at the higher levels of the hierarchy. The attention-response-order center offers activities such as tachistoscopic training, decoding exercises with symbol and flag code messages, puzzle making, simple construction kits, design copying with beads, blocks, and many other tasks useful in getting the child to pay attention, respond, and follow directions.

The concept of order is also emphasized through the use of a system of passes to facilitate assignments to the offices and other centers in the room. When the child is assigned to a center he picks up at the teacher's desk a pass which designates the area to which he will move. This pass is hung on the wall by the center during the period of time the child is away from his desk.

The exploratory-social center provides opportunities for multisensory exploration of the environment and communication. Materials for science experiments and demonstrations in electricity, magnetism, animal care, and basic chemistry are available in one section. A listening post, Morse code activities, simple games for two or three children, and a tape recorder are in another section for communication and social tasks. Arts and crafts materials are available in another section. One of the main periods of the class day takes place at this center. Usually the teacher demonstrates several different science experiments each week. These experiments are pictorially illustrated on large cards with simple directions and filed at the center where they may be replicated by students assigned to the center at other times during the class day. Each day, students participate in art and communication tasks as part of the exploratory period.

The mastery and achievement center seeks to engage each child in a certain amount of academic work each day because in a majority of cases emotionally disturbed children have failed to keep pace in acquiring reading, written language, and arithmetic skills. A reading period is held three times weekly and consists of three different activities: individual oral reading with the teacher, independent activity reading for comprehension and development, and word study for review of reading and spelling words. Story writing takes the place of the reading period twice a week. Arithmetic assignments are individually prepared and based on diagnostic achievement test results. Assignment of mastery tasks coincides with the time contingency used as a basis for the checkmark system. Different tasks are assigned individual students every fifteen minutes.

Intervention

In accordance with principles of behavior modification the teacher in the engineered classroom attempts to alter the environment to change maladaptive behavior patterns of students and to foster the development of more adaptive patterns through manipulation of assigned tasks and provision of success and rewards. The basic goal is to keep every child functioning as a student. So long as the child respects the working rights of others and displays a reasonable tolerance for limits of time, space, and activity, he earns a full quota of checkmarks regardless what type of task he is assigned in the room. In order to help individual children earn as many checkmarks as possible, a series of interventions must often be used to alter the learning environment including the nature of the assigned task, type of reward, and degree of structure. These interventions are divided into two categories, student and nonstudent, and involve descending the hierarchy of educational tasks until a level is found that enables the child to function successfully or provides for his exclusion from class.

If at any time during the class day the student begins to display signs of maladaptive learning behavior (e.g., inattention, daydreaming, boredom, disruption) his assignments are quickly changed. Table II summarizes the interventions which may be used in an attempt to foster adaptive student functioning. The teacher may select any intervention seen as appropriate or may try the student at each intervention level until his behavior improves. As long as the child is able to stabilize himself during any of the student interventions, he continues to earn checkmarks on a par with those students successfully pursuing mastery level assignments. He is in no way penalized for the shift in assignment. There appears little need to worry about other children reacting to what might be seen as inequality. They have seemed content to accept the teacher's explanation that "Johnny needs a different kind of assignment to help him learn right now."

When one to one tutoring on the attention level cannot be provided or is ineffective, the child loses his opportunity to earn checkmarks, is considered a nonstudent, and sent out of the room for a short period of isolation. Use of such isolation as an intervention has been described by Whelan and Haring (1966). If the child can successfully tolerate this period (usually 5, 10, or 15 minutes) his card is immediately returned and he may be reassigned at any level depending on the teacher's assessment of his capacities for adaptive behavior at the moment. No lecturing or demand he "promise to be a good boy" is given.

With respect to interventions, a question may arise regarding whether or not removing a child from a more demanding task and assigning him a less demanding task in the classroom actually constitutes rewarding inappropriate behavior. Will not some children misbehave in order to be reassigned to a more inviting exploratory or order activity? In the author's experience with the engineered classroom this has occurred only rarely. When it does, the child is not permitted the choice of an alternate activity but is directly placed in an isolation intervention. In most cases, teachers anticipate such problems by limiting the

TABLE II

HIERARCHY OF INTERVENTIONS TO MAINTAIN STUDENT ROLE

Level	Student Interventions
1. Achievement	Assign student to study booth to pursue mastery work.
2. Mastery	Modify mastery assignment and have student continue at desk or in study booth.
3. Social	Verbally restructure expectation of student role (e.g., respect working rights of others, accept limits of time, space, activity).
4. Exploratory	Remove mastery assignment and reassign to exploratory center for specific science, art, or communication activity.
5. Order	Reassign to order center for specific direction following tasks (e.g., puzzle, exercise, game, work sheet).
6. Response	Remove child from classroom and assign him to a task he likes to do and can do successfully outside (e.g., running around playground, punching punching bag, turning specific number of somersaults on lawn).
7. Attention	Remove child from classroom, put on a one to one tutoring relationship with teacher aide, and increase number of checkmarks given to obtain cooperation, attention, and student behavior.
	Nonstudent Interventions
8. Time Out	Take away work record card and explain to child he cannot earn check marks for a specific number of minutes which he must spend in isolation (never use more than three times in one day).
9. Exclusion	If child requires more than three time-outs in one day or fails to control himself during time out, or if he is verbally or physically abusive to teacher, immediately suspend him from class for rest of day and, if possible, send home.

amount of mastery work given the child, assigning him to an alternate center before his behavior becomes maladaptive.

With most children who become restless and resistant the teacher approaches the child and says, "You seem to be having trouble with this assignment. I want you to earn all of your checkmarks this period so go get a pass for the exploratory (or order) center and I'll give you a different assignment there."

This is an expression of the basic philosophy of the engineered classroom which in essence tells the child: "We want you to succeed at all costs. If you will meet us half way and function reasonably well as a student we will give you tasks you can do, need to do, and will enjoy doing, and we will reward you generously for your efforts."

Discussion And Implications

The engineered classroom design has been developed and observed in four public school systems and a hospital setting for the past two years. It has constantly been reassessed and changed and still is undergoing alteration in an effort to arrive at a practical and useful model for educating emotionally disturbed children. Preliminary observations suggest that changes in work efficiency and adaptive behavior occur quickly. One of the aspects that most impresses observers is the purposeful, controlled, and productive atmosphere in the classrooms. Despite the requirements for a teacher aide, a well organized classroom, and use of tangible rewards, it appears to be a feasible design for use in a public school.

Some educators are reluctant to use the behavior modification model because it has emerged from the experimental animal laboratory and some feel that tangible rewards for learning represent an unwholesome compromise with basic educational values. However, if one objectively and realistically views the emotionally disturbed child as a unique learner, not initially responsive to a conventional learning environment, and often not rewarded by traditional social and intellectual rewards, then reducing one's goals so that he may be included, not excluded, from school, is just good common sense. To fail to teach a child because he lacks capacity to learn is one thing, but to fail because of a lack of flexibility and a realistic assessment of a child's needs, is quite another.

The engineered class design is not viewed as an end in itself. Observations suggest that the value of checkmarks and tangible exchange items soon gives way to the satisfaction of succeeding in school and receiving recognition as a student from peers, teachers, and parents. Transition programs have been worked out where children started in the engineered classroom have gradually been reintroduced into regular classes. While this stage is not wholly developed, it appears to be a natural evolutionary development in the program.

Some criticism of this approach has discounted improvements seen in the adaptive functioning of the children as merely the result of the Hawthorne effect (Roethlisberger and Dixon, 1939); that is, anything novel or different in the environment produces an initial change in behavior. Even though some children have continued to improve for a full year in the engineered classroom, this possibility still exists. The answer to such a criticism is simply, "So what?" If one can create a unique learning environment that produces more adaptive learning behavior in emotionally disturbed children, perhaps we should capitalize on the Hawthorne phenomenon in special education and continuously introduce more stimulating and novel approaches with all exceptional children.

One major problem which has arisen from presenting the engineered classroom design to teachers in the field bears mention. Some of them are so desperate for ideas and dirction to increase their effectiveness with emotionally disturbed children that they react to superficial aspects of the design and somewhat randomly apply them in the classroom. It is not uncommon to hear of a teacher rushing out, buying a large stock of M and M candies which are often used as exchange items, beginning to pass them out rather haphazardly in the classroom, and then waiting for a miracle to occur. Needless to say, such a teacher will have a long wait. Checkmarks and candy are only a small part of the entire design. There is nothing new in the use of gold stars and extrinsic rewards in education, but there is a great deal that is unique in the systematic use of these to foster development of more adaptive learning behavior on the part of resistant and often inaccessible learners.

Behavior modification theory is a systematic theory, not a faddist theory based on gimmicks. To be useful, it must be understood and adhered to systematically, not sporadically. We are still trying to increase our understanding of its effectiveness in the engineered classroom, anticipating considerably more evaluation, exploration, and experimentation before we can be certain of its applicability.

References

Ayllon, T., and Michael, J.: The psychiatric nurse as a behavioral engineer. *J Exp Anal Behav, 2:* 323-334, 1959.

Birnbrauer, J.; Bijou, S.; Wolf, M., and Kidder J.: Programmed instruction in the classroom. In L. Ullman and L. Krasner (Eds.): *Case Studies In Behavior Modification.* New York, Holt, 1965.

Haring, N., and Phillips, E.: *Educating Emotionally Disturbed Children.* New York, McGraw, 1962.

Hewett, F.: A hierarchy of educational tasks for children with learning disorders. *Exceptional Child, 31:* 207-214, 1964.

Hewett, F.: The Tulare experimental class for educationally handicapped children. *Calif Education, 3:* 6-8, 1966.

Levin, G., and Simmons, J.: Response to food and praise by emotionally disturbed boys. *Psychol Rep, 11:* 539-546, 1962.

Quay, H.: Remediation of the conduct problem in the special class setting. *Exceptional Child, 32:* 509-515, 1966.

Roethlisberger, F., and Dixon, W.: *Management Of The Worker.* Cambridge, Harvard, 1939.

Skinner, B.: Operant behavior. *Amer Psychol, 18:* 503-515, 1963.

Staats, A.; Minke, K.; Finley, J.; Wolf, M., and Brooks, L.: A reinforcer system and experimental procedures for the laboratory study of reading acquisition. *Child Develop, 35:* 209-231, 1964.

Ullman, L., and Krasner, L.: *Case Studies In Behavior Modification.* New York, Holt, 1965.

Valett, R.: A social reinforcement technique for the classroom management of behavior disorders. *Exceptional Child, 33:* 185-189, 1966.

Whelan, R., and Haring, N.: Modification and maintenance of behavior through systematic application of consequences. *Exceptional Child, 32:* 281-289, 1966.

Zimmerman, E., and Zimmerman, J.: The alteration of behavior in a special classroom situation. *J Exp Anal Behav, 5:* 59-60, 1962.

Chapter 19

The Elgin Approach To Special Education For Emotionally Disturbed Children

Levi Lathen

The Elgin special class for emotionally disturbed children was one of the first in the state of Illinois. It was opened in the autumn of 1964 with three objectives: (a) reconditioning of deviate, nonintegrative, classroom behavior; (b) attainment of academic achievement commensurate with abilities; and (c) eventual return to the regular classroom with adequate behavioral and academic functioning.

To achieve the goals of the class, the children were admitted at an age amenable to reconditioning (ages 6 to 10), parents became involved in therapy, an effective plan for educational diagnosis was devised, and individual programs of remediation were developed on the basis of diagnostic findings.

The following diagnostic outline was devised and has proven profitable to this program during the past two years:

1. Determination of capacity for learning, using intelligence testing and personality evaluation.

2. Evaluation of achievement.

3. Determination of discrepancy between achievement and capacity.

4. Analysis of diagnosis, which includes an evaluation of perceptual abilities believed to be directly related to classroom achievement and areas of difficulty exposed by psychological and educational testing.

Reprinted from *Exceptional Children*, Vol. 33 (1966), pp. 179-180. By permission of the author and publisher.

5. Plan for remediation, which is directly related to analysis of diagnosis and considers one problem at a time.

A quantitative evaluation of the program nine months after its inception revealed that the class was achieving its goals. New and more flexible patterns of behavior have been learned, enabling more integrative adjustment to precipitating situations. Academic progress is three times as great as it was prior to special class assignment. At this time five of the seven students originally admitted to this class have returned to regular classes.

Chapter 20

Working With Emotionally Disturbed Children In The Public Schools Setting

JUNE B. PIMM AND GORDON McCLURE

Because all children are required by law to attend school, inevitably the problem must be faced that a few children have emotional problems of such significance as to preclude their remaining in a regular classroom. These children are not ill enough to require residential treatment. They often come from homes where the emotional problems of the child are receiving attention through psychiatric treatment or family counseling.

A small unit for emotionally disturbed children was set up in Ottawa in the fall of 1962. Two years later, five children returned to their regular school classrooms, and two others moved out of the special unit into an ordinary classroom setting. In four years, twenty-two children have been in the class for varying periods of time.

The purpose of this small class is primarily educational, with the responsibility for selection of children in the hands of the psychology department of the school. Children receiving psychiatric help are provided this outside of school—most often by the Child Guidance Clinic of the Ontario Mental Health Clinic.

Children considered appropriate for placement in the class are those who have no evidence of neurological impairment and average or better intellectual potential. Preference is given to younger pupils, and placements are made in consideration of the composition of the class at any one time. Diagnostic categories

Reprinted from *Exceptional Children*, Vol. 33 (1967), pp. 653-655. By permission of the authors and publisher.

are disregarded. The maximum number of children at any one time is eight, and both boys and girls are placed.

When a child is placed in this special adjustment class, the school psychologist consults with the psychiatrist who has seen and evaluated the problem. Parents are advised of the opportunity and invited to visit the class. Each child is introduced gradually, with the parent remaining for a time if necessary.

The Classroom

The physical setting of the room makes an important contribution to the smooth running of the program. Arrangements help reduce distractions and provide for flexible and individual programing.

Structural alterations (see Figure 1) include partitions eight feet high to provide individual cubicles or offices for each child. Each is equipped with an individual bulletin board, blackboard, and lamp. The room is further subdivided into an observation and quiet room and a play room. A one way glass makes it possible for visitors to observe both areas.

The room is furnished to provide for a variety of simultaneous activities. The observation room, where the children enter, is equipped with benches for them to sit on until they have quieted or settled sufficiently to go into the larger room. This room has a couch for a child who needs to rest. The teacher's desk is in the quiet room. The play room has a long table and chairs, and toys are kept on shelves above the sink.

In addition to desks in each office, there is a desk for each child in the front of the room near the blackboard, which is covered when not in use. A large sand table can be covered, and two movable shelves provide a quiet corner for individual teaching. The lower parts of the windows are covered with paper.

Program And Method

Because the focus of the class is academic, emphasis is placed on the academic achievement of each child up to his intellectual potential. Most children who come to the class have had discouraging and often unhappy school experiences. They have

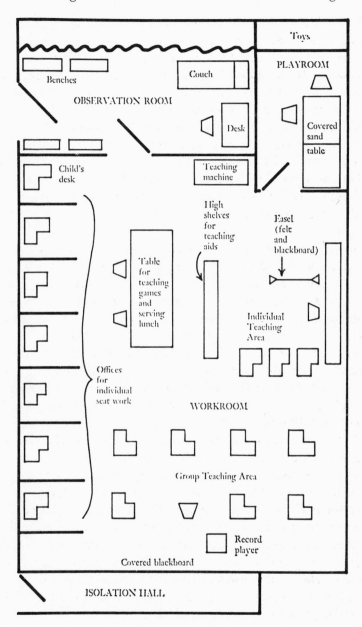

FIGURE 1. Adjustment Class, Hawthorne
School, Ottawa, Canada

little confidence in their ability and often use nonacceptable behavior to gain emotional satisfaction. It is important for them to learn to achieve satisfaction through academic success.

Assisting the children in learning to achieve academically involves close supervision of each child. In the beginning these children are actually receiving individual tutoring. Work is corrected immediately by the teacher and then redone by the pupil. Errors are erased at once. Children are usually started below their ability level to build up a pattern of successes. Much work is done on individual blackboards and plastic so that errors can be erased and the final result will be perfect. Good work is immediately rewarded by play periods, symbolic awards (stars), and praise.

Although academic achievement is highly prized, both for itself and because of its reinforcing properties, we are also interested in the whole child. Efforts are made to alter maladaptive behavior by focusing on one area of behavior at a time and using an intensive program of reinforcement for appropriate behavior. Unacceptable behavior is prevented and stopped rather than punished. As one level of improved behavior is reached, expectations are increased, but not all children are expected to behave at the same level at the same time. Children presenting bizarre symptoms are helped to eliminate these through conditioning techniques.

While children are in the adjustment class, an effort is made to give them experience in the regular classroom. Initially, they spend one period a week (usually gym, art, or music) in a classroom at an appropriate grade level. This is extended as they prove themselves able to manage. When behavior and academic achievement are considered acceptable, they are gradually integrated into a regular classroom within the same school. Their program and problems are interpreted to the regular class teacher by the teacher of the adjustment class. The move is usually made when the child's academic skills are better than required for the particular grade in which he is placed.

Ultimate success with problem children depends not only on classroom behavior but on how successfully they can handle the times out of the classroom, such as recess, lunch hour, and bus trips. When children come to the class, they are initially segregated to prevent difficulties and to break off old, inappropriate behaviors. They arrive later than the other children, have a shorter lunch hour, and leave earlier. They rest instead of having an afternoon recess, and if the behavior during morning recess is unacceptable, the child remains in the class working. Children exhibiting withdrawn behavior are introduced to groups with the teacher and required to go out for play at recess and after lunch. Playmates for these children are provided from other classes.

The entire school staff plays a part in the rehabilitation of these children. After a variable time—between four months and two years in the adjustment class—each child is moved to an appropriate grade in the same school for one year. At the end of this time, he is transferred to his home school or an adjacent one in the home community. Records of his previously disturbed behavior are not routinely forwarded. However, it is noted on his O.S.R. card that he is a graduate of the adjustment class and the consulting psychologist does a followup during the year.

Chapter 21

Teacher-Moms Help Emotionally Disturbed Pupils

GEORGE T. DONAHUE AND VICTOR A. REING

$\mathbf{M}$OST school district efforts to help severely emotionally disturbed children lead to dead ends. But they don't have to. The teacher-mom program at Elmont, N.Y., offers at least a partial answer to how these children can be provided with an appropriate method of instruction that is carefully integrated into the public school system.

Basically, it represents adaptive education in the extreme: completely individualized education in a therapeutic setting. Success of Elmont's program for elementary pupils can be measured not only by the number of children who have been rehabilitated, but also by the fact that other districts—New Rochelle, N.Y., New York City, Superior, Wisconsin, to name some—have built workable programs using Elmont's basic approach as a pattern.

Elmont has its share of headaches, the same as any other district. It needs more money to operate adequately; it has 6,000 pupils enrolled in buildings with a rated capacity of 4,800; it has emotionally disturbed children who disrupt normal classroom routine and, in some cases, tax teachers' patience beyond endurance.

Faced with the problem of these seriously disturbed children and convinced that special classes weren't the answer, Elmont's staff decided on a program, established within the educational framework of the community, with a one-to-one relationship be-

Reprinted from *Nations Schools*, Vol. 78 (1966), pp. 50-52. By permission of the authors and publisher.

tween pupils and volunteer teaching mothers. Ultimate goal was individualized training and final reintroduction of the child into the regular classroom setting without totally separating the youngster from his family or community structure.

Here's how the plan was put into action and administered:

Recruiting teacher-moms: Biggest hurdle was finding enough of the right kind of women in the community who would volunteer their services without pay. They had to be warm, empathic, mature, emotionally stable women who had done a good job raising their own children. Elmont has them; every community has them, but it takes time to seek them out. To avoid refusing those unsuited for the work, no broad appeal was made. Instead the women were recruited through personal contact by school officials.

Arranging facilities: With facilities already overburdened, school administrators took a look at other buildings in the community not used during regular school hours: church halls and basements, meeting halls, and the like. The Elmont Jewish Center, housing ten classrooms, an arts and crafts room, kitchen and playground, provided the answer. Arrangements were made to use six classrooms there during the morning and any of the other facilities the program needed. The board of education allocated funds for transportation, a teacher supervisor, psychological and psychiatric consultant services, and books and supplies.

Elmont's Kiwanis Club sponsored the project and provided some financial support. It paid the premiums to insure the center and staff from lawsuits should a child be injured and his parents sue. The club also provided six-hundred dollars for special equipment, such as two-sided easels, flannel boards, electric answer boards, storage cabinets, and milk and cookies for each child during daily snack time.

Scheduling assignments: Starting with twelve mothers assigned to six children, the program got under way with two teacher-moms teamed and each assigned to one child twice a week. This came close to the desired ratio of one-to-one and provided four mornings a week of instruction.

Treating teacher-moms like professionals: Teacher-moms are given professional status equal to the rest of the staff and are treated as the fourth member of the team. An elementary teacher is assigned to the project to supervise and coordinate details of supply, transportation and such, while an elementary principal assists when behavior and adjustment problems pop up. The district physician, psychiatric consultant, and psychologists work closely with the volunteers.

The teacher-in-charge keeps close watch over the project at all times, working with teacher-moms individually and in small groups, advising and coaching them. She helps them evaluate what their assigned children are doing and how they're doing it. She's often the bridge between the volunteer, the psychologist, and psychiatrist. Group meetings among teacher-moms, teacher-in-charge, psychologists, psychiatrist, and school administrator are scheduled twice yearly. But this isn't a fixed schedule because school officials believe meetings should be held whenever the need arises. Psychologists are on hand for a half day every two weeks, and the psychiatrist visits three or four times a year.

Choosing instructional materials: It was found that emotionally disturbed children can use the same educational materials, including new innovations such as programed reading, as can their normal contemporaries. Their academic achievement is not necessarily hampered by the handicap of emotional imbalance.

Here's A Teacher-Mom's Typical Day

The teacher-mom meets her project child as he leaves the station wagon, escorts him to his assigned room, and helps him put away his coat. She then takes him to the "good morning" room, where the professional teacher-in-charge is waiting to conduct the opening group exercises consisting of the salute to the flag and a short reading and discussion period. The reading and discussion evolves from what the teacher-in-charge has written on the chalkboard, or from "show-and-tell." She tries to include sentences at the reading level of each of the children which, when put together, make a paragraph about the day's weather, a holiday or an event, or something with which the children are familiar. Discussion is encouraged. The opening exercises may last a very few minutes or as long as fifteen, contingent upon the manageability of the group that day.

During this discussion the teacher-mom rounds up the books, games, and equipment she plans to use that morning and is in her assigned room ready to receive her child when he returns from the opening exercises. She sits next to, and close to, the child as the day's work begins.

She may begin with reading, usually using the reading series and supplementary materials available to the professional teachers of the district. She is encouraged to follow the teacher's manual more closely than a professional teacher, because the manuals are well-developed guides and provide comprehensive directions on how to teach the series with which she is working. From reading she moves to other subject areas, such as arithmetic, spelling, language skills, social studies, science. These activities, interspersed at her discretion with games, talk, a walk, or listening to records, go forward until the 10:30 snack break. She takes her child to a large room with a long table and benches. One of the children and his teacher-mom have laid out the cookies and milk beforehand. This preparation is done on a rotating basis. All the children as a group sit down and have their snacks under the supervision of the professional teacher-in-charge.

While the children are having their snacks, the teacher-moms usually assemble in the kitchen for coffee and cookies. Here there is much discussion of the project children. Following this fifteen or twenty minute break, the teacher-mom returns to her room to continue work with her child, adhering to the plan for the day as agreed upon with the teacher-in-charge. If other group activities are scheduled they usually occur during the time between the end of snacks and the end of the morning. These activities usually include arts and crafts, music education, physical education, or story time.

At 11:45 the teacher-mom begins to get her child ready to go home. At this point, she completes her log of what transpired with the child that day and leaves it with the teacher-in-charge, who gives it to the teammate teacher-mom scheduled to work with the child next time.

In the course of the morning she has probably been visited by the teacher-in-charge, who provides on-the-spot direction and suggestions for furthering the child's educational program.

This is a reasonable normal morning. There are some mornings that are not normal, however, because these children vary in their behavior and responses from day to day, hour to hour, and sometimes minute to minute.

Phasing back to the regular classroom: Children usually remain in the program two years. One was kept only six months; another five years. The psychiatrist, psychologist, and teacher-in-charge are the ones who decide when a child has progressed to the point where he is ready to assume regular classroom routine. He must be able to sustain himself in group activities, work as independently as some other children in his normal age-grade group, and be able to compete academically with others in the normal group.

This transition is a critical point in the total success of the child's adjustment, and the regular classroom teacher is one of the crucial factors. The psychologist and building principal decide to whose classroom the student will be assigned on the basis of which of the available teachers at the child's age-grade level is best suited to his personality. If none of the teachers in the child's neighborhood school has the appropriate temperament, disposition, and method of teaching for working with the child, the youngster is transferred to another school in the district where there is such a teacher. This scrutiny is not intended as criticism of any teacher, but is done solely with the knowledge that it takes a certain kind of person with necessary insights and an appropriate tolerance level to work with a disturbed child— even after he has undergone intensive rehabilitation and reorientation through the teacher-mom program.

Easing-in on a back-to-school schedule typically starts with a half day a week, such as a Friday afternoon when assembly program or other special activity might be scheduled. Thereafter the time is built up as rapidly as the child can take it. Sometimes a youngster will remain in the project part-time and in regular school part-time. Often the teacher-mom will stand by in the school building as the child starts back to regular class so that if he's released from the classroom for some reason a familiar face will be on hand to look after him. The child's schedule has to be structured so that, temporarily at least, he has some time at school with a supplementary teacher on a one-to-one or small-group basis. Or he may get extra time with an art, physical education, or music teacher.

Although discouraged at times, seven of the original twelve teacher-mom volunteers are still in the program. Most of those who dropped out did so for reasons over which they had no control. Since the 1959-60 school year, when the program began, their number has increased to thirty-eight, while pupil enrollment has climbed to eleven. These mothers have gained not only personal satisfactions but community recognition as well.

Professional educators are undergoing a subtle improvement of attitude, probably the result of greater knowledge that has led to understanding of children, acceptance of them as they are, and, as a result, adaptation to their needs. Teachers are developing not only awareness of but also skill in identifying children who need specialized help at an early age.

With more than a half million emotionally disturbed school-age children in the country today, public schools must adopt an enlightened attitude and positive action because

1. America's school system is the only social institution in this culture that's big enough to begin to come to grips in terms of the scope of the problem.

2. It has the advantage of staffs of professionals who are oriented in part, at least, to some of a child's developmental problems.

3. It is believed by professional educators that an emotionally disturbed child should not be separated from his normal environment.

Someone must start helping these children balance their social, emotional, physical and intellectual patterns so that they can enter into normal group situations in a way that the group will accept them. This requires a structure for early identification of disturbed children and a program for working with them, and is, according to many educators, the proper and appropriate job of public education.

Case Studies Tell Success Story

Not all emotionally disturbed children display all the following characteristics, but they usually exhibit some. They're normally intelligent, although their I.Q. measurements may vary along with their performance from day to day or from hour to hour.

Case studies cited here show how several Elmont youngsters were helped back to a normal school environment through the teacher-mom program:

C. A.—Female: 8 years, 1 month. She was an aphasic child (verbal and written communication defect) with organic involvement and extensive emotional problems. Known to many clinics in New York City as well as some local mental health authorities, the girl was considered hopeless, and it was advised that she be totally exempted from school. Completely withdrawn at the beginning she now enjoys physical contact. She has improved impulse control and, in appearance is a happy, normal, attractive little girl who plays with others and occasionally assumes a leadership role. She was phased into second grade, in the middle group in reading in her class, and is now in sixth grade where she is reading on the sixth grade level, she's anxious to learn, and writes and spells adequately for her age. Most important, she speaks, in fact at times is a chatterbox. She is not always easy to understand, but has a sizable vocabulary and is anxious to communicate.

J. B.—Male: 8 years, 8 months. His diagnosis was schizophrenic reaction of childhood with the severe regressive symptom of soiling. He was hyperactive, harmful to others, and so disruptive that he could not be contained in the regular classroom. There was considerable family pathology. His parents would not cooperate with the therapeutic proposals offered by the local mental health center. When placed in the educational-therapeutic millieu, this child progressed rapidly—both academically and socially. His soiling ceased. His relationships at home improved. He began to relate well to the other children in the program. He was phased into a regular third grade on a half-time program and is now functioning well in sixth grade.

C. D.—Male: 8 years, 9 months. Here was a schizophrenic child who, on the surface, appeared to be a severe behavior problem. He demonstrated gross distortions in conceptualization, visual-motor perceptualization, and extreme unevenness of performance. His deficits inhibited his adjustment in all areas. When entered in the special program, it was necessary to start his academic program at the beginning. He needed much repetition and variety of approach. He progressed to fourth grade level and is now functioning with competence in a regular seventh grade—this despite a family with much pathology.

SECTION F

OTHER TECHNIQUES

Chapter 22

The "Crisis Teacher" Public School Provision For The Disturbed Pupil

WILLIAM C. MORSE

O<small>NE</small> of the most encouraging aspects of recent Michigan public school planning for emotionally disturbed pupils is the flexibility which is anticipated.* Suggestions include special classes, consultant teachers, and individually designed experimental programs. It is recognized that these new programs are supplemental to efforts for overall school mental health and the services of visiting teachers, psychologists, school nurses, and guidance workers.

A few school districts have already been operating small classes for the emotionally disturbed: in several instances evaluative efforts have been incorporated. The whole role of therapeutic education is being explored. An outpatient school program has been in operation at Hawthorn Center for several years and the Children's Psychiatric Hospital is ready to start an outpatient school as soon as finances are available. In addition to this interest on the part of the inpatient psychiatric institutions, the child guidance clinics are studying the feasibility of school-oriented day care programs as a part of their effort. In short, Michigan is in the vanguard of a growing national interest in school programs for children too disturbed to be helped in the regular classroom.

Reprinted from the *University of Michigan School of Education Bulletin,* Vol. 37 (1962), pp. 101-104. By permission of the author and publisher.

* As described in *The Michigan Program for the Education of Emotionally Disturbed Children.* Bulletin 365 (preliminary draft). Lansing: Department of Public Instruction, 1961.

The plan presented in this new report is not a substitute for any of the present services or their anticipated legitimate expansion. Nor is it proposed that the school become a psychiatric institution. Rather, the plan is an immediate school rescue operation designed for the point of problem origin through the use of a new educational device, the crisis teacher. If the regular school is to function, it is mandatory that we keep the classrooms as free from teacher-exhausting, group-disrupting pupils as is possible. Conversely, the school has recognized the responsibility to offer additional assistance to these pupils when they cannot benefit from a well modulated classroom learning situation. The small but appreciable educational "fall out" presents a difficult situation: Authoritative handling seldom resolves the problem, and many cases go year after year until a negative school adjustment becomes fixed.

What are some of the school conditions which are necessary to keep a reasonably constant learning flow in classroom? First, there must be an immediate resource for the teacher when there is significant deterioration in the classroom group learning process. Help must be available without stigma or recrimination or even the implication of overburdening the administrator. The truth is, so many duties now devolve on the principal that his availability is limited. A new hand is required, but of a special type. Not only must the new person help the school at large, but he must provide immediate succor to the pupil as well. It is easy to forget that the pupil is in real need at his time of stress. And he needs help with two things: his school work and the feelings which distort his efforts at the moment. Of course, this is true for the acting-out child who disrupts the class. But it is also true for the withdrawn, unhappy, quiet underachiever.

The "crisis teacher" is the school resource designed to meet this situation. This teacher must really know curriculum at the school level served, must be steeped in remedial teaching techniques and must be skilled in life-space interviewing, a style of interviewing essential for the teacher who must handle diverse types of behavior problems. The space provided may include a small classroom with a pleasant anteroom. Books and materials of all sorts are at hand.

Since each school is unique, *modus operandi* are derived from the specific needs of a given school. There are several observations, however, which may serve as guides.*

1. *The crisis teacher can be effective only to the degree that the whole staff is concerned about understanding and helping the deviant child.* Case conference and strategy planning meetings involve all the teachers. Some planning for particular children can be done on a subgroup basis. The general principle is, that all the adults who deal with the pupil take part in devising the plan and evolving the strategy. Many failures in school relations are due to faulty communication among teachers who do not work together on their common problems. Merely providing another specialist will not make the necessary impact on the school environment. Also, regardless of what is accomplished in the special work, its real purpose is to help the child to get along properly in the regular classroom. The classroom teacher continues to spend more time with the pupil than any specialist does, and plans for assistance will have to consider her work as well as the time the child spends with the crisis teacher. Since many pupils are skillful manipulators, little will be gained unless all adults are aware of the case dynamics and have thought through the most appropriate management procedures. Frequently, after an encouraging start, an improvement plateau is reached and new plans must be evolved on the basis of a more complete understanding of the pupil and how he reacts.

2. *Referral procedures are the responsibility of the total staff.* When a teacher feels that a pupil cannot be helped in the classroom alone, this pupil becomes a potential candidate for the crisis teacher. It is important to note that this does not await a complicated diagnosis or parental permission, because the pupil is not in the usual sense a special case. His behavior *in situ* makes the referral. If possible, plans for assistance are worked out in advance; but the regular teacher may take the pupil directly to the crisis teacher and present the situation in a nonrejecting nonmoralistic but frank manner. This special service is not a

---

* Derived from the experience of the staff at Mack School, Ann Arbor, which is experimenting with a crisis teacher program with the author as consultant.

dumping ground or a discard heap. Rather, the two teachers discuss sympathetically the educational complexity at hand. Cues relative to the pupil's attitude about the referral are faced directly and the crisis teacher goes over possible goals. Afterward the pupil returns to the classroom only when he is considered ready to resume his progress in that setting.

Thus, the crisis teacher does not have a regular class or group. Pupils may come and go, sometimes on a more or less regular basis as seems advisable, but often on an episodic basis when specific pressure accumulates. Of course, at particular times, the special teacher may be working with more than one pupil. As crisis demands decrease or vacillate there are always underachieving children to be given individual help.

3. *The work which goes on in the special setting is determined by the pupil's problem.* Children seldom compartmentalize their relationships or their quandaries. Home, school, and play are all intermixed. General attitudes and schoolwork motivation are a confused combination. Consequently, the teacher has to take a broad humanistic approach in crisis teaching. The interaction may take on characteristics of a "man to man" talk, a parental surrogate, or a counselor, besides involving the general teacher role. Free of large group responsibilities, immediate achievement goals and time restrictions, the able teacher can operate with a new flexibility. Perhaps it will be individualized tutoring, an informal talk, a diversionary activity, or an intensive life-space interview session around the feelings and tension evinced in the pupil. In short, what is done is what any teacher would want to do were it possible to determine action by the needs of the child rather than the large group learning process in a classroom. At times several children may be involved, and group work is called into play. The difficulty may turn out to be a learning frustration, an interpersonal conflict, or an internal feeling. As the crisis teacher sizes up the situation, plans are made for immediate and long-term steps. This teacher may get the outpouring of the child's inner conflict and must be prepared to handle whatever the child brings, as well as to refer special problems to other services. It is particularly important for the child to learn that he will be listened to and that his problem will be considered,

even to the point of initiating joint sessions with his regular teacher to discuss conditions as he sees them. There are few of the secrets and confidences which some professional school workers make much of at the expense of exchanging information needed to solve the pupil's school problem. While it is obvious that this work takes utmost skill and sensitivity, it should also be clear that co-equal members of a staff can be open with the child, and no professional worker is "handling" another. All too soon we are faced with the fact that the total staff, with all the insight we can muster, will still not be able to influence the lives of some of these children at any better than a surface level. On the other hand, if we can help a pupil meet what are for him reasonable social and academic school expectations, this is itself a worthwhile goal, though other problems remain.

4. *While a child does not have to be certified as any type of a special pupil for this service, some of the clientele will already have been studied intensively in the normal course of events.* Other pupils will present baffling difficulties to the crisis teacher and staff. Here psychological study, visiting teacher investigation, or material from a psychiatric examination may be in order. Perhaps it becomes evident that the pupil's needs are for individual casework or family contact which can best be done by the visiting teacher or counselor. Since these specialists participate in the planning meetings, trial decisions are the product of mutual discussion. The sharing of cases becomes the sharing of a problem-solving venture. In this way, the school principal, specialists, crisis teacher, and classroom teacher work as a team: Possessiveness and contention are a luxury schools cannot afford.

With adequate research it may eventually be possible to predict which pupils will respond to such a program. At present the value is in the improved learning climate provided for the whole school, as well as helping the particular child.

Chapter 23

Resource Programing For
Emotionally Disturbed Teenagers

Eileen M. Connor and John F. Muldoon

ONE of the seriously puzzling problems in contemporary education is that of involving the emotionally disturbed person in the formal learning process. Home tutoring or special class teaching, the usual public school provision for those with learning disabilities, can be offered to the student whose aggression, withdrawal, or disorientation precludes the satisfactory classroom management needed to implement his learning. However, these solutions have built-in limitations, because they can restrict where the child needs freedom to correct his own errors; they can protect where he needs to assume responsibility for the task at hand, his education. Neither tutoring nor the special class use the social aspect of the total community, the community within which the child can meet, recognize, and be involved in natural interactions at all levels, and in the process of these interactions master the developmental steps necessary for involvement in the learning process.

If learning—both process and product—is to be considered a valid goal for the disturbed teenager, then a comprehensive approach to the problem is indicated, an approach that would retain the strengths of both regular and special handling, and program around their inadequacies. Resource programming is an exploratory step in this direction.

Reprinted from *Exceptional Children*, Vol. 34 (1967), pp. 261-265. By permission of the authors and publisher.

History

Technoma Workshop moved into resource programming in February, 1965, in an effort to meet the developmental needs of its clients. It is an agency that was established in August, 1961, to provide a day care program for severely disturbed teenagers who for practical purposes had been dropped from the regular therapeutic and education programs in the community. These young people had been too openly aggressive or withdrawn to be maintained in public schools or were "too unmotivated" or "too impulsive" to be offered regular agency services.

The basic agency goal for these young people, adequate functioning in the community, required provision of extensive educational and vocational services. As these teenagers improved in their ability to learn and in their ability to meet the educational and social demands of the agency's classroom, the day care staff faced the need to return them to regular public school classes. This move gave the staff a way to maintain the child's educational level and provided the child with a halfway step for resuming community living. (Technoma also recognized the needs of the marginally functioning student in the public schools whose disorganization could lead to a break with his education unless extensive supportive measures were readily available. It was felt that such a break with accepted peer group goals unnecessarily compounded the student's basic problems.)

To implement this plan, Technoma sought the help of the Pittsburgh Public Schools. There, the agency director obtained permission from the superintendent of schools to explore means of educating disturbed teenagers in a joint agency public school program. Technoma's educators worked out the procedures with the department of pupil services and the principal of the high school involved. A plan was agreed upon whereby the high school would accept the agency's students at their grade or achievement levels on a full or part time basis, and it would consider the agency's offer of special help for the troubled teenagers already enrolled in the school if some provision could be made for offering support to the school, teacher, and student, in both general educational planning and in the event of crisis.

The day care center agreed to provide a qualified teacher to develop and staff this public school based program for disturbed teenagers and to give the teacher continued support in the form of consultation and supervision. The school, Schenley High School, provided classroom space, gave the agency teacher the freedom to operate as a regular staff member in the school, and offered administrative guidance and protection for the program. The board of education offered appropriate consultation through the available services in administration, school social work, psychology, and psychiatry. The teacher and representatives of these services formed a committee dedicated to making the program work at all levels. Meeting weekly, the committee became a resource to the disturbed teenager, the classroom teacher, and the school, both for crisis situations and for ongoing programing.

In the first two years of its exploratory existence, resource programing has shown two positive results: (a) Adolescents use the program, and (b) school administrations accept it. The extent to which this programing serves modification of the learning difficulties of disorganized teenagers is yet to be determined, but it has shown demonstrable success as a method for helping the adolescent to maintain himself in the physical space and emotional climate where learning can take place.

Problem

Involving the student in the learning process through the use of public education is a multilevel problem requiring consideration of the following needs:

Why the student needs to be involved: The disorganization of the disturbed adolescent is reflected in obscure and unrealistic goals, in an inability to see the continuous relationship between goal and steady effort, and in resistance to assuming responsibility for determining goals or maintaining purposeful action. Learning provides the goal of education, which leads toward a primary life goal of work. This educational goal is rational, oriented to a teenager's peers. The goal is also personal enough to motivate, yet general and impersonal enough for the student to "hide in." The disturbed student needs goals that "fit." The student's task of seeing and assuming responsibility for cause and effect—the continuous effort that results in education—requires a degree of organization and self-control not readily at his command. Outside controls, which can be supplied by public education, are required to aid him in developing learning skills and gathering content.

How the needs of administrator, teacher, and student conflict: The solution to this problem is more complex. First, the administrator must keep the contagion of disorder to a minimum in the total school and protect the teachers from excessively disruptive or demanding children.

Secondly, the teacher must maintain a balance between educating a group of students and using evaluation and remediation to meet the specific needs of the individual student whose previous emotional stresses prevented him from learning subject content. The teacher must personally offer to motivate this student, to keep him coming to school, and to help him in class when his anxiety spills over into the acting out or withdrawn behavior that commands the adult's total attention.

Third, the disturbed teenager himself must be able to use the supportive measures which are offered. He is not consistent; his needs are in a state of flux. The burden of meeting and allowing for these needs falls on both teacher and administrator, who must operate within a well defined educational structure. The difference between the extremely wide range of the student's needs and the limited range of active responses allowed to personnel by the structure of school sometimes leaves a gap, a gray area, through which the teenager cannot grope and into which the school cannot reach. The adolescent who does not have the inner controls with which to work through his own problems or wait out such periods is often forced to break with his educational goal because he lacks the capacity to use the educational vehicle, the public school classroom.

Education in a public school setting is a practical goal for many disturbed adolescents. When the paradoxical quality of their needs is recognized, public school education is also a possibility. The task of the resource programer and program is to meet these excessive, inconsistent, and uncontrolled needs in such a way that the disturbed adolescent can achieve the necessary balance to make progress toward education and the mental health goals in education.

Description

The best way to describe resource programing is to study the resource person and the tools he has at his command. This person is both one and many individuals. The "one" is a teacher, because he can use education, the natural product of the school system, as the entree to solving the multiple problems of the disturbed teenager. This teacher's goal is to involve the student in learning within the structure of the regular class, to help the student to maintain himself within this structure, and to enable the student to profit from it. The resource teacher's methods are as varied as the changing needs of the child, the capacity of the regular class teachers, and the resourcefulness of the administration. The "many" are the people within the school who symbolize the reality of school functioning and who in any way touch the lives of these students, from friend to counselor, from janitor to principal.

The resource teacher meets the disturbed teenager as a teacher counselor. The adolescent comes to the resource teacher for help by way of the school social worker's office for being truant; by way of the vice principal's office for being a hall walker; by way of the counselor's office as an underachiever; and by way of the regular class as a noncommunicating daydreamer. And sometimes he comes by himself. He comes in search of "something" to which he cannot assign realistic dimensions. He comes because his behavior impresses school personnel who come in contact with him as disoriented, as expressing need.

He is received at the level of the help he seeks. He comes to explain that he cuts class due to a home problem; his father is angry with him and therefore he cannot do school work. He wants to talk; he is listened to. He comes blaming academic failure for his inability to read; he begins a diagnostic reading evaluation. He comes saying nothing is wrong, he just didn't have any place to go; he looks out the window. Initially the student asks for and is given this personal support. He may never ask or, or be able to accept, anything more, but a student coming to the resource person is usually in need of extensive care if his goal, participation in public education, is to be realized.

The tools the resource teacher has at his command are evaluation procedures, educational techniques, personal counseling, the resource space itself, and programing.

Evaluation can be both behavioral and academic. A behavioral reading is gained from the combined personal observations of regular school staff and resource teacher, plus, where indicated, an optional psychiatric interview and psychological testing. (A child may receive full benefits of resource programing without psychiatric evaluation, if it is felt that such inquiry might create unnecessary anxiety in child or parent.) To predict and help prevent the self-destructive behavior that can result in separation from school, the following questions are asked: At what level might the student see normal school group pressure as a personal attack? How does this student defend himself? What type of caring response will he accept from the adult? Academic evaluation, both informal (teachers' records and resource teacher observations) and formal (achievement and diagnostic records) provides the base for the diagnosis of skill and content deficits and for the remedial help fundamental to the student's capacity in acquiring new content and skills.

Education is directed toward helping the adolescent acquire the learning essential to survival in the classroom. The resource teacher does not replace the regular class teacher, but cooperates with him. He assists students whose emotional problems are manifested in learning difficulties by modifying these difficulties. He may reteach subject content which the student has missed or which the student has been unable to absorb. For the student whose anxiety severely limits his attention span in a particular class, the teacher may help him to structure study time so that subject continuity is not lost. The teacher may also use specific techniques, such as self-teaching devices, to implement the learning of a student whose negative reactions prevent him from accepting direct help when tutoring is indicated. The unmotivated student may be encouraged to attend to the assignments of the regular teacher by being involved in learning through the use of creative projects in which he feels interest and sees value.

The purpose of counseling is to assist the adolescent in meeting the demands of responsible interaction with adults and peers who are encountered in daily life. How can a student go back into a class he has walked out of? How can he ask a teacher for a makeup test? How can he go to lunch, when there is no one to sit with? How can he walk down a hall when everybody is looking at him? The caring, burden-sharing, aspect of group discussions carries many; others need a personal listener. The aim of personal counseling is to provide the tools, in this case the social tools, needed to relate to the school group in such a way that spending the day in their company is a possible and often gainful experience.

The resource space is a classroom complete with chalkboards, texts, and desks, readily accessible, located in the mainstream of student traffic away from the school discipline and counseling areas to reinforce its identification with education. It is orthodox in appearance and essentially mobile. The student uses this physical space supportively, sometimes at the request of and in cooperation with the resource teacher and sometimes in lieu of personal contact. A young person whose anger threatens to overwhelm him in the classroom can escape to the room, pace, and slam his books on the floor. The frightened person can push chairs into a corner and hide; the hurt one can stare out of a window; the anxious one in need of activity can rearrange the furniture in the room. The student who has mentally played truant from an emotionally stressful class can study, use self-teaching devices, or be tutored without interference; the student who temporarily cannot tolerate the physical presence of another person while writing an assignment can pull a screen around a desk and isolate himself. The student who cannot respond to peers in open halls and classrooms can put out tentative smiles and conversation feelers or can get angry within the protection of a familiar space and in the presence of friends. And the student who cannot or should not use this space is met in his own "space"—the halls, cafeteria, or locker area, where he is offered the degree of supportive care he can accept.

The student is taught to take responsibility for using this room and its teacher as a support, a crutch, that can be deliberately used and set aside when the needs that precipitated use of this crutch can be met in the regular school setting. The student is asked to commit himself to staying in school and make the effort to do so.

Programing is both a tool and minor goal. The adolescent who uses the skills of the resource teacher and the space provided for him in the resource room finds the arrangement comfortable. An ongoing, goal-directed procedure is to gradually transfer the young person to full participation in the regular school program and to plan for meaningful experiences with other skilled adults, peer groups, and other areas of space, thus giving support at a reality level. The resource teacher becomes a programer: he sells the quality of a student, his skills, deficiencies, and needs, to the teacher and administrator most competent to handle him. He counsels the student on approaching these adults regarding the kind of support to be expected, how to ask for it, and how it use it. He supports both adolescent and adult in their initial attempts to relate to one another. He teaches the student to use the space provided within the school—that the library is a quiet room, that the cafeteria line is a place to try a conversation, and that the gymnasium is an area in which it is possible to work off anger. He asks that the student be held responsible to the administration for his actions, and supports both child and administration in the task of carrying out disciplinary controls.

In the process of taking the care, control, and responsibility of transferring the disturbed teenager into the regular school programs, the resource teacher comes in contact with school personnel and becomes a source of help to them in handling other problem adolescents who have not been considered for programing. This concern for mental health and the general mental health climate is greatly extended and results in more thoughtful handling of troubled students. The possibility of preventing crises becomes appreciably greater, and so do the child's chances of profiting from his school experiences.

Chapter 24

A Modification In The Sequential Tutoring Of Emotionally Disturbed Children

L. K. BRENDTRO AND PHYLLIS R. STERN

Iₙ their study of public school classes for the emotionally disturbed, Morse, Cutler, and Fink (1964) found that the primary intervention technique by special teachers was the provision of a great deal of individual attention, with the teacher rotating from student to student. This "taking turns process tended to become a continual, nagging, competitive focus. The sight of children receiving the teacher's response while others were denied it, except for a periodic turn, upset many youngsters in this feast or famine arrangement" (p. 76). In a subsequent article, Morse (1965) has labeled this intervention technique "sequential tutoring" and argues convincingly that "in the individualization . . . there must be a counterbalance, since we are involved in teaching groups" (p. 31). Morse then suggests several nontutorial interventions which might serve to minimize the necessity for excessive use of sequential tutoring.

The widely acknowledged heterogeneity in the educational functioning of almost any group of emotionally disturbed children continues to present an irrefutable case for individualization. The only question is how this individualization process should be structured. Some argue that teaching machines provide the most effective means of meeting individual needs (Quay, 1963) or that self-sustaining programs (Haring, 1964) or multilevel group projects (Morse, 1958; Rhodes, 1963) would

Reprinted from *Exceptional Children*, Vol. 33 (1967), pp. 517-521. By permission of the authors and publisher.

best serve this end. While each of these approaches has much to offer, it is likely that some form of sequential tutoring will continue to be necessary in classes for the emotionally disturbed. The purpose of this paper is to (a) examine the rationale for and limitations of sequential tutoring as typically structured in classes for the disturbed, and (b) suggest an alternate way of structuring sequential tutoring designed to minimize these problems. Each section of the discussion will begin with an observer's recording of the classroom interaction characteristic of the particular approach to sequential tutoring.

Typical Interactions In Sequential Tutoring

Classroom A:

Each of the eight students in this class for the emotionally disturbed is seated at his desk with a workbook or worksheet before him. The teacher is leaning over the desk of one child, helping him with a particular question. She then walks from one child to the other, observing each child's progress, occasionally interrupting a working child to point out an error. As she is tutoring one individual, the hands of other children are raised; for several minutes she "gets behind" so that there are always at least two or three children waving their hands to get her attention. Two boys, seemingly tired of waiting their turn, begin to throw pieces of an eraser at one another. The teacher moves in their direction. . . .

The observation cited above is so typical that most teachers will question the purpose of its inclusion. Although sequential tutoring of emotionally disturbed children presents certain problems, are not these some of the unavoidable byproducts of assembling a group of such youngsters in one classroom? Since it cannot be disputed that disturbed children need much individualization, would not the logical role of the teacher be to go from child to child giving the needed assistance?

There seem to be several reasons why this style of sequential tutoring is so widely practiced. It allows the teacher to exert the central role in the classroom, as she assumes a dominant position by standing over the children or moving among them. She is in the best possible position for surveillance activities; she can note behavior problems in the early stages and is in a better position to deal with them. She can readily employ the important control technique of proximity (Redl, 1952), since simply moving in the direction of trouble often eliminates the disturbance.

Less obviously, such an approach may give the teacher the feeling that she is exerting maximum energy to benefit the child; were she to sit at her desk in the corner, she would feel that she was withdrawing from the group and perhaps even cheating the children of the benefit of her central presence. Furthermore, the very activity of moving about the room may serve to reduce anxiety in the teacher. In certain cultures, adults carry around a string of beads which serves the purpose of keeping their hands busy in potential anxiety arousing situations; in any culture, cigarette smokers have a readily available technique for motoric discharge at times of tension. Likewise, many teachers of the disturbed have developed ways of "being busy" when classroom interactions become tense; this enables them to conceal their anxiety beneath a veneer of calmness.

In contrast to the foregoing, there are several rather serious problems which emerge in this practice of sequential tutoring. The first and most obvious is that the teacher may provide distracting and disruptive stimuli to the individual child who is trying to attend to a learning task. The advocates of stimulus reduction theories (Strauss and Lehtinen, 1947; Cruickshank, Bentzen, Ratzeburg, and Tannhauser, 1961) have suggested that bright clothing or even the jewelry of the teacher may distract many hyperactive children; if this is true, then most certainly a mobile, five-foot-tall, noisemaking stimuli complex (viz. a special education teacher) would interrupt the attention of such children. In our universities we often provide graduate students with private carrels located in the silent recesses of the library, yet we expect distractible children to function with a teacher wandering in and out of the rows, pausing frequently here and there for a spell of all too audible conversation with a particular child. The teacher's almost continual movement and verbal communication provide a readily available program of stimuli which is often much more novel and interesting to the child than the task at hand.

As Morse (1965) stated, "One could hardly imagine conducting a series of individual interviews in a social setting, yet we assume we can teach this way" (p. 31). Usual procedures in sequential tutoring force the child to reveal his inadequacies to the peers who surround him. No matter how much effort is made to individualize each child's program, the tendency of children to assess their progress according to the achievements of their classmates cannot be totally eliminated. Thus, a common problem in sequential tutoring is that a neighboring child will interrupt with a comment such as "I know that—that's simple!" or he may even blurt out the answer, compelling the teacher to remind him to attend to his own business.

Certain disturbed children do not respond well to being watched and the intensity of surveillance inherent in sequential tutoring may have a detrimental effect upon their classroom learning or performance. Furthermore, the teacher often finds herself in the role of imposing assistance upon a highly reluctant client, with the result that further negativism and resistance are encountered.

Analyzing the behavior in the sequential tutoring situation from the viewpoint of operant conditioning, it would appear that the children are frequently engaged in attention-seeking behavior. At its best this behavior is ostensibly appropriate, as when the child raises his hand to obtain socially reinforcing interaction with the teacher; on the other hand, much behavior is inappropriate and maladaptive, as the child engages in various troublemaking efforts, which then secure for him the attention of the teacher. Those children who do not know the answer to a problem are sure to receive potentially reinforcing social attention from the teacher. In contrast, the more diligent students who complete their work quickly and correctly may get very little of the teacher's attention. Thus, social reinforcement, a most efficient and significant reward for many disturbed children, may frequently serve to maintain undesirable behavior.

Modifying The Interaction In Sequential Tutoring

Classroom B:

The students are seated at trapezoidal tables arranged in a circular pattern. The teacher's desk is situated in a corner of the room designated as the "helping corner." During periods of individual work, each child brings his paper to the helping corner as he completes a specific assignment. The teacher and the child then go over the work and the child is assigned either remedial work or is given another task. The teacher sometimes uses this time to give instruction in a particular skill or to explain a new task to the child. The interaction of teacher and child is relatively private, and the teacher often engages in a brief moment of pleasant or supportive conversation with the child prior to his resuming individual work.

It is readily apparent that the teacher-child interactions in Classroom B are quite unlike those in Classroom A. The two styles of sequential tutoring can be differentiated on the basis of (a) the initiator of the interaction, (b) the locus of the interaction, and (c) the focus of the interaction. These comparisons are summarized in Table I.

TABLE I

A Comparison of Styles of Teacher Child Interaction
in Two Classes of Emotionally Disturbed Children

	Classroom A	*Classroom B*
Initiator of Interaction	Teacher	Child
Locus of Interaction	At child's desk in the group	At teacher's desk marginal to group
Focus of Interaction	Teacher engaging in surveillance of child	Child engaging in evaluation with teacher

In Classroom A, the teacher generally initiates the interaction, which takes place at the child's desk, central to the activity of the group; the basic focus of the interaction might be conceptualized as surveillance, and the child may or may not be requesting teacher assistance. On the other hand, in Classroom B the child generally initiates the interaction by coming to the teacher's desk, usually to show a completed piece of work and then to receive his next task.

What are the advantages of child-initiated sequential tutoring structured in the manner of Classroom B as contrasted with the teacher-initiated style in Classroom A? There seem to be at least eight distinct advantages to the former approach.

1. Assuming that the group is under control, the children's work area is relatively quiet and is not disturbed by the wanderings of the teacher.

2. The privacy of the tutorial exchange is much greater; it is almost impossible for peers to monitor the conversation since it is carried out on the margin of the group. This gives the teacher and child more freedom in what they choose to discuss.

3. When the child comes to the teacher rather than the teacher to the child, there is probably less resistance to receiving help. This expectation is compatible with the frequent observation of psychotherapists that success is most likely when the client seeks help rather than having it imposed upon him.

4. The child is not forced to work under excessively close surveillance, but rather works somewhat independently in a manner more closely approximating the regular classroom.

5. The teacher can evaluate the performance of each child upon completion of a given task and provide the necessary corrective measures or appropriate subsequent task. Her location at her own desk, rather than in the middle of the room, provides ready access to the file of available materials.

6. Each child is provided with systematic feedback upon the completion of a logical unit of work.

7. The child is allowed a brief period of motor activity upon the completion of each task: he brings his work up to the teacher and then walks back to his seat with a new assignment. It is probable that this activity reinforces task completion behavior, according to Premack's (1959) principle. A response (i.e. task completion) will be strengthened if followed by a response with a higher independent rate of occurrence (i.e. motor activity).

8. Finally, and perhaps most important, social reinforcement becomes most readily obtainable, not by competition with peers for teacher attention, but by completion of an assigned task and bringing it to the teacher. By association with social reinforcement, the completed task itself should eventually acquire reinforcement value: in Classroom B this generally appears to be the case, since the children soon come to take great pride in the quality and quantity of their work.

Some Practical Concerns

The foregoing discussion has compared the styles of sequential tutoring used in two different classes for disturbed children. A number of reasons have been suggested as to why the child-initiated approach (Classroom B) might be more therapeutic and educationally sound than the adult-initiated approach (Classroom A). There still remain, however, several practical concerns about the implementation and operation of a child initiated system of sequential tutoring; four of the most frequently raised questions are considered below.

How does one assign tasks to the children? The teacher must prepare in advance a series of appropriate tasks (worksheets, pages from workbooks, etc.) for each child, usually having a tentative collection of materials sufficient to keep each child involved for one school day. Each child has his own in-out box where he receives new tasks and deposits completed and checked tasks. Exactly how the teacher decides on appropriate tasks depends to some extent upon the child's stage in the program: (a) initially, the teacher may have to rely primarily upon tests and previous teachers' reports of achievement; she should determine his apparent level of functioning, and then develop tasks below this level to insure initial success; (b) subsequently, the child's performance on the daily tasks will determine where he needs more work, what areas he might be able to skip over, what specific remedial tasks or tutoring he might require; (c) finally, academic materials used in the regular class to which he will presumably be transferred will serve as the basis for task determination.

What about the child who demands help, claiming he doesn't know how to do his work? With exceptions of course, the response would probably be, "I think you are able to do that problem, please look at it again." This tends eventually to cut down the incidence of "educational malingering" and encourages the child to get into the habit of first using his own problem-solving skills before turning for help. On the other hand, it may very well be that the child is right: He doesn't know how to solve the problem or is not capable of facing the frustration which seems imminent in the task at hand. In this case, the plea of the child signals the teacher that she has made a tactical error in assigning this particular task to this child at this time, and she must modify the length or complexity of the task, or substitute a different task. Some children need frequent support from the teacher if they are to remain busy and satisfied. However, rather than constantly going by this child to keep him working, the teacher can select tasks which are much shorter; this gives the particular child legitimate access to the teacher upon completion of each short task. It is then possible to extend the length of the task gradually and decrease the amount of teacher attention required.

What can one do if a child refuses to do any work? Since the entire emphasis of this approach is upon the value of work, the most consistent response is to agree with the child, take away all of his work, and tell him that work is special, and if and when he is ready he may ask for it. If he becomes disruptive, he may be isolated from the mainstream of the group (without his work or other entertainment) and told that he may get his work when he can behave. Most children will usually ask for work after only a brief period of idleness. Furthermore, contrary to some teachers' expectations, it has not been found to be true that other children will also refuse work just to get out of it.

How does one keep several children from wanting their work checked at the same time? This problem is really one of logistics. By a certain amount of preplanning, the teacher can gear the length of assignments so that she is usually able to handle all of the children. Yet, it is not possible to predict just when children will complete tasks, so one of two procedures may be employed when a pile up occurs: (a) The children are told that when the teacher is busy they may, if they desire, go to their boxes and get another sheet to begin working on. Since the teacher has preplanned, each child has several available work sheets which he is able to do independently. (b) Some teachers have found it helpful, particularly with adolescents who are less inclined to do extra work, to designate a waiting chair for the pupil who is next in line. This assures him that he will indeed get to see the teacher, and it removes him physically from the group (where he might create a disturbance) and the tutoring situation (where he might eavesdrop or interfere.)

References

Cruickshank, W. M.; Bentzen, F. A.; Ratzeburg, F. H., and Tannhauser, M. T.: *A Teaching Method For Brain-injured And Hyperactive Children.* Syracuse, Syracuse, 1961.

Haring, N. G.: Educational research with emotionally disturbed children. Paper presented at the University of Michigan Colloquium on Special Education, Ann Arbor, December, 1964.

Morse, W. C.: Education of maladjusted and disturbed children. In W. M. Cruickshank and G. O. Johnson (Eds.): *Education Of Exceptional Children And Youth.* Englewood Cliffs, N.J., Prentice-Hall, 1958, pp. 507-608.

Morse, W. C.: Intervention techniques for the classroom teacher of the emotionally disturbed. In P. Knoblock (Ed.): *Educational Programming For Emotionally Disturbed Children: The Decade Ahead.* Syracuse, Syracuse, 1965, pp. 29-41.

Morse, W. C.; Cutler, R. L.; and Fink, A. H.: *Public School Classes For The Emotionally Handicapped: A Research Analysis.* Washington, D.C., Council for Exceptional Children, 1964.

Premack, D.: Toward empirical behavior laws: I. positive reinforcement. *Psychol Rev, 66:* 219-233, 1959.

Quay, H. C.: Some basic considerations in the education of emotionally disturbed children. *Exceptional Child, 30:* 27-31, 1963.

Redl, F., and Wattenberg, W. W.: *Mental Hygiene In Teaching.* New York, Harcourt, 1959.

Rhodes, W. C.: Curriculum and disordered behavior. *Exceptional Child, 30:* 61-66, 1963.

Strauss, A. A., and Lehtinen, Laura E.: *Psychopathology And Education Of The Brain-injured Child.* New York, Grune, 1947.

Chapter 25

Toward A Broader Concept Of The Role Of The Special Class For Emotionally Disturbed Children

PETER KNOBLOCK AND RALPH A. GARCEA

T HIS REPORT describes recent attempts by a group of professional workers affiliated with a special class program to broaden the scope of their efforts. This included the influencing of educational practices as applied to disturbed children in regular classrooms by directing efforts to professional workers responsible for the education of these children.

It is believed that the uniqueness of the proposal described in this paper lies in the utilization of specific special class program personnel for the express purpose of disseminating their skills and experiences to others in the school who were facing the same problems of educating disturbed children, but on a larger scale. In essence, the approach used was a form of mental health consultation directed toward the needs of the participating schools and their personnel.

After three years of experimentation in the developing of a special class program for emotionally disturbed children, the Syracuse Scholastic Rehabilitation Program, hereafter referred to as the SSRP, reached the following conclusions: First, that the program personnel had acquired through trial and error, experimentation, and testing of hypotheses, a number of techniques and theories which needed further testing in order to validate their efficacy for larger groups of disturbed children in educational programs; second, that there are certain kinds of

Reprinted from *Exceptional Chilldren*, Vol. 31 (1965), pp. 329-335. By permission of the authors and publisher.

children and problems that could be dealt with in the regular classroom, provided some program modification is made; third, that as the program became known and accepted by the community and public school personnel the number of children referred for admission into the special program far outweighed available openings.

It would not be accurate to conceptualize the need for a broader concept of intervention only from the standpoint of the needs of the children involved. It is patently clear to those professional workers who deal with disturbed children that the interaction process is such that strong needs and feelings on the part of the adult are aroused. These feelings may operate to impede or hasten the development and maintenance of a relationship (Katz, 1963). The SSRP personnel in their contacts with teachers and administrators began to focus on the needs of other school personnel in relation to programing for emotionally disturbed children. For example, it became clear that many teachers and administrators were simply in need of factual information. Closely related was the inability of many professional workers in the schools to effectively utilize the information in their possession. More importantly, many others desired ways in which they could conceptualize the educational needs of such children. Along with supplying of factual information, it became apparent that once such efforts were made to change or modify attitudes it was necessary to offer support to the school personnel involved. In still other instances, the nature of the school population in certain areas of the city was changing so rapidly that the public school personnel involved were under considerable pressure to effect certain changes in curriculum and management for great numbers of children, including those children with emotional handicaps.

Related Literature

The proposal and ideas presented in this article reflect the influence of two sources. The first is found in the substantial writings of Caplan (1959) and his colleagues who have attempted to employ public health concepts in an effort to design preventive approaches to mental health. In the conceptualization of their program they have advocated mental health consultation as one method to achieve their goal. Kazanjian, Stein, and Weinberg (1962) quote Caplan's definition of mental health consultation as follows:

> Mental health consultation may be defined as an interaction process taking place between two professional workers, the consultant and the consultee. In the interaction an attempt is made to help the consultee solve the mental health problem of his client or clients within the framework of his usual professional functioning. The process is designed so that while help is being given to the consultee in dealing with the presenting problem, he is also being educated to handle similar problems in an effective manner (p. 1).

The second source influencing our approach is the technical assistance to public school personnel described by Newman, Redl, and Kitchener (1962). Similar to our concerns, they began by focusing on the problems of effectively dealing with disturbed children in the public schools. Their sensitivity to this need developed in the residential treatment of disturbed boys when it became apparent that the teachers needed definite skills and understandings in order to maximize their functioning as professional workers. In their monograph they described the expansion of their efforts to the public schools once they had begun to systematize their supervising and interstaff communication methods in the residential center. Thus we see in their approach a much closer rapprochement between the consultant and the public school, with the original plan stemming from the practical problems arising in the management and education of disturbed children in a residential center.

Cutler and McNeil (1960) viewed with skepticism the utilization of specialists employed by the school as seen in the following statement:

> To some degree the teacher attempted to turn to the mental health specialists in her school for the solution of these practical problems. But here, she met obstacles in the short supply of specialists, and the limited clinical orientation which had been transplanted in the schools and which flourished in the hearts of the specialists themselves. Further, the specialists, as employees of the school system were placed in a difficult position when it came to "training" colleagues who, in theory at least, were responsible professionals in their own right (p. 19).

Again, it is felt that the approach outlined in this article negates several of the concerns discussed in the quotation. First, personnel directly involved with disturbed children are deployed for consultation purposes, thus drawing from a ready source of specialists, who were also dynamically oriented. Second, the training approach utilized by the consultants was essentially one of enabling school personnel to capitalize on their existing skills along with aiding them to mobilize their school and staff to program for disturbed children. It is felt that by the implementation of such an approach, the high degree of resistance referred to by Cutler and McNeil is considerably reduced.

Planning Phase

The plan involved an attempt to influence administrative and teaching personnel in elementary schools so that their perceptions and attitudes of disturbed children could be positively modified. The authors firmly believe that such changes in attitude can lead to more adequate educational programing for these children and further that much of this programing can be accomplished within a regular classroom setting.

Two clinical psychologists and one psychiatric social worker who were working regularly with the SSRP attempted to offer consultative services in regard to these problem children who were not in the special program. It was felt that the authors' identification with the SSRP would offer certain advantages. It was presumed that they would be perceived by the school personnel as having particular training and interest as well as concurrent experience which would qualify them to discuss problems meaningfully and appropriately.

The initial focus was the large number of children referred to the special class program who could not be accepted, usually because of the small size of the special program. Based on the authors' growing conviction that much of their experience in a special class program would possibly have wide applicability, they decided to employ a form of mental health consultation. Such an approach was designed to focus on school personnel who were responsible for programing for disturbed children in general, and did not deal only with those children on the waiting list.

With this in mind, the authors faced their next strategic question; that is, which schools should be approached with these ideas. The plan was given no advance publicity and therefore no one was in a position to request this aid. There were three factors taken into consideration in this selection: (a) a school which showed a high density of emotionally disturbed children; (b) a visiting teacher assigned to that school who showed better than average ability to profit from the experience so that she could perpetuate and refine the procedures developed; and (c) a building principal who had shown an interest in dealing with this kind of problem. With this combination of factors in mind, three schools were selected as possible sites, one for each consultant.

With this rationale, the director of special projects was approached and the plan was presented to him. He felt the magnitude of the problem of programing for disturbed children called for a special effort and that this plan was feasible. He agreed to meet with the three principals involved along with the chairman of the special class program who would eventually serve as a consultant. The purpose of the meeting was to give as much administrative encouragement as possible to the implementation of the plan.

There was mutual agreement that all planning would begin with the building principal. The authors believe, as do Newman, Redl, and Kitchener (1962) that no plan can be effective without this key person's endorsement and support. During these conferences, the principals raised questions as to how an attempt would be made to deal with these children, for all agreed that they were a problem in school. In reply, it was noted that the help given would be in terms of the services of one consultant, one-half day per week for the remainder of the school year. Also, that this consultant's activities would depend on what was mutually agreed upon by both the principal and the consultant. It was made clear that any ensuing plan would be based on the principal's estimation of where the emphasis should be placed. In short, the initial step was to design a plan with the principal using the services of the consultant which would help to meet the needs of the staff and of the emotionally disturbed children in that elementary school.

On this basis each of the three principals agreed to become involved in the project. A consultant was then assigned to each school. He, in turn, contacted the principal and together each of the three teams began its planning.

The initial stages were very difficult for everyone. One question which had to be faced by all was: What could one person working one-half day per week accomplish? The needs were so many and so great yet the means offered toward their accomplishment seemed so insufficient. With this recognition more traditional services such as individual therapy with children, counseling with problem families, more psychological testing service, and group counseling with children, were discarded. An awareness grew that something else which would have a broader impact on the problem needed to be developed.

The Consultation Process In One School

Initially, the consultant found that the school had made certain manipulations in class grouping which enabled the staff to better handle a certain percentage of the problems. It was felt by the principal that such procedures were effective where tried, but that attempts were limited. The limitations came from faculty members who had strong reservations about such planning. It was felt that these reservations often resulted from lack of both information and personal involvement in further planning. This, in turn, resulted in insufficient interest which prevented school personnel from experimenting with these difficult problems. Many of the school personnel including the principal felt the need for new information and understanding which would involve the faculty in a meaningful manner. By joint agreement of the consultant and principal it was decided to focus initial efforts on the teachers of younger children.

The plan involved a meeting of the consultants with all of the first and second grade teachers. The purpose of the meetings was to discuss the effective handling of emotionally disturbed children by the classroom teacher. It was decided that such meetings would be offered to the teachers on a voluntary basis and that they would take place on a once a week basis, during the teacher's lunch hour. It was further decided that the principal would not attend such meetings, since it was felt that the teachers should feel as free as possible to express any feelings in regard to school routine or practices which affected programing for children. It was made clear to the participating teachers that the meetings would in no way be used to evaluate teacher performance and further, that no individual teacher would be discussed by the consultant and the principal.

A procedure was worked out so that the consultant would visit one classroom each week, usually for one or two hours. During this time he would observe the group at large and focus particularly on the disturbed children who were earlier identified by the teacher. During the lunch period, which followed the classroom observation, the consultant and the teacher would share their morning observations with others.

The focus of the group was directed by the consultant into two main areas: First, by using classroom observation, what could the teacher learn about disturbed children? second, once the behavior was understood what intervention techniques were available to classroom teachers? The discussions revealed, among other things, that all of the teachers demonstrated a sincere interest in more effectively coping with these children. Also, that many had more ability to understand the meaning of behavior than they believed themselves capable although symptomatic behavior was frequently accepted without an appreciation of underlying dynamics. The group as a whole seemed to feel that they could deal with the behavior, but they felt generally pessimistic about the ultimate effects of their intervention on the status of the child. This feeling was somewhat modified as the group consciously dealt with one little girl who was recognized by all as a problem. The change in the girl's behavior as a result of teacher understanding and altered techniques, was both exciting and rewarding to them. All such problems were discussed by the group of teachers with the consultant's role being that of resource person. He also served the purpose of keeping the discussion centered on two main areas as agreed upon by the group.

The teachers' evaluation of the project indicated that they, as a group, became more interested and involved in the problem-solving process as it related to planning for emotionally disturbed children. This was indicated in their general acceptance of the meetings and in their critical appraisal of their own practices. They did feel, however, that they could benefit further from more group sessions, and that the consultant should have more direct contact with the children with whom they were concerned. They also felt that more of the traditional mental health services should be made available for the schools.

Discussion

It is hoped that the approach described in this article will be replicated and improved upon by other school systems facing the same educational planning problems related to emotionally disturbed children. It is with this purpose in mind that several facets of the approach have been spelled out in considerable detail. As a case in point, what transpired during the planning phase, and even prior, had a great bearing on the form and content of the plan which evolved in a school. To illustrate this point a description of the planning phase in a second school is described in detail.

In the following discussion of the consultation procedures at the second school, it should be pointed out that the consultant had, on prior occasions, spent several very brief periods of time in the school. The consultant felt that this previous contact made the initial phases of the consultation process smoother.

Several meetings were held during the early stage of the consultation process. It was mutually agreed upon by the principal and consultant that perhaps the school social worker should be involved in this early planning phase. The initial question was one of determining how and in what ways the consultant would be of service to the school. The initial suggestion was one of allocating time for the evaluation of individual children who presented the greatest management and planning problems. It is of interest to note that the earlier contact with the school had followed the procedure of evaluating individual children. The principal spent a considerable portion of time discussing such children, and this proved to be of great benefit in regard to the initial question of where to focus time and energy. By discussing individual children, the consultant was provided with an opportunity to familiarize himself with the kind of child with whom the school was concerned and to gain a clearer picture of the operating philosophy of the school as it was directed to the management of difficult children. In contrast to procedures adopted at the first school, it was agreed that in this instance it would be of benefit to have the principal participate in the group meeting. Those familiar with the scheduling problems confronting the public schools will acknowledge the difficulty experienced in finding a meeting time that was mutually convenient for the teachers, principal, visiting teacher, school psychologist and consultant. The principal informed each of the kindergarten and first grade teachers of the proposed plan and gained some expression of their interest in participating and in accepting a meeting during their lunch hour.

It is of interest now to chart the differences between what occurred in the first school described in the previous section, and in the second school just discussed. In the second school, much less emphasis was placed on discussing individual children but rather the group focused on the development of a comprehensive school plan. This plan was drawn up by the group and included curriculum and school programing modifications which were finally put in written form and submitted to administrative officials in the school system.

Needless to say, it is difficult to pinpoint the precise reasons for the variation in process and outcome between the two schools. Careful analysis revealed, however, that several factors differed from school to school: (a) The principal, school social worker, and school psychologist were present at the second school's group meeting; (b) that unlike the situation faced in the first school, the consultant did not come into a school which had done any appreciable preplanning; and (c) the orientation of the teachers involved seemed to focus directly on the need for long-range plans. Closely related to this was their strong belief in the therapeutic advantages which could be realized by the curriculum and administrative changes in the schools.

From the very outset, the consultants pondered what the effect would be of going into the schools without, so to speak, being invited. It was felt, at least initially, that this factor had a great deal to do with the structuring of the relationship beween the consultants and the school principals. Support of this perception is seen in Caplan's (1964) statement: "In many cases where contact is initiated from higher levels of administration, as by a directive of the superintendent of schools, the consultant is asked by the school principal to consult with the newest and least experienced teacher on the staff" (p. 234). At least in one of the schools the consultant was asked to deal with teachers in the early grades not primarily because of any firm belief in prevention, but rather because the personnel was experiencing a great amount of difficulty coping with the behavior. Caplan goes on to say: "From experience we have learned that, although initial entry into an institution may be a result of an invitation by a peripheral member of the system, it is essential to understand the authority pattern and quickly contact all key figures" (p. 234). It has already been described as to how much valence was initially placed on the evaluation of individual children. Once relationships and ground rules were worked out, the consultant was drawn into larger problems and came in contact with more key school personnel.

What looked like fortuitous circumstances at the time eventually turned out to greatly enhance the relationship and process of consultation. For example, early in the consultation process both consultants offered support, suggestions, and techniques to the groups in terms of dealing with specific problem children. Much to everyone's delight the children improved, seemingly in ways directly related to the new intervention techniques employed. Such incidents gave credence to the group's sometimes wavering belief that changes could be effected. The adage, "Nothing succeeds like success," seemed to apply in these instances.

It is the authors' belief that this modest and relatively short-term experiment has justified itself on the basis of the following outcomes:

1. A small number of mental health specialists were able in a

short period of time to effect changes in the attitudes, techniques, and programing approaches of public school personnel in three separate schools.

2. Others in leadership positions in the schools, including the teachers themselves, were afforded an opportunity to consolidate their skills and to continue such school planning on an all school basis or in their individual classrooms.

3. A form of advance screening of youngsters in need of special class placement was accomplished. By spending time in these schools the consultants became familiar, either directly or indirectly, with many such children. No attempt has been made to suggest that this particular approach is a panacea for the problems confronting schools in planning for disturbed children. Rather, it should be considered as just one of many potential plans which judiciously uses existing school personnel.

As with any intervention technique, it will be necessary for those interested in continuing or refining such an approach to conceptualize in clear terms what their role as consultants will resemble. For example, Caplan (1964) points out that the consultant's role may take many forms such as inspection, supervision, manipulation, collaboration, psychotherapy, liaison, to name just a few. He stated, "I believe that we will attain a higher level of professional functioning when the specialist is able to differentiate these various activities and employ each of them consistently in relation to his assignment, his professional goals, and his understanding of the demands of each situation" (p. 213). In conjunction with being able to differentiate the procedures of mental health consultation, it is equally important to focus on the stages or progression through which such procedures pass.

References

Caplan, G.: *Concepts Of Mental Health And Consultation.* U.S. Depart. of HEW, Office of Education, Publication No. 373. Washington, D.C., Gov. Print. Office, 1959.

Caplan, G.: *Principles Of Preventive Psychiatry.* New York, Basic Books, 1964.

Cutler, R. L., and McNeil, E. B.: *Mental Health Consultation In Schools: A Research Analysis.* Ann Arbor, U. of Mich, 1963.

Katz, R. L.: *Empathy: Its Nature And Uses.* Glencoe, Illinois, Free Press, 1963.

Kazanjian, V.; Stein, S., and Weinberg, W. L.: *An Introduction To Mental Health Consultation.* U.S. Depart. of HEW, Public Health Service Monograph No. 69. Washington, D.C., Gov. Print. Office, 1962.

Newman, Ruth G.; Redl, F., and Kitchener, H.: *Technical Assistance In A Public School System.* Washington, D.C., Washington School of Psychiatry, School Research Program, 1962.

SECTION G

MANAGEMENT AND DISCIPLINE

Chapter 26

Psychoeducational Aspects Of Classroom Management

GASTON F. BLOM

THIS PRESENTATION deals with certain aspects of classroom management from the psychoeducational viewpoint. Principles and experience developed in a special education and treatment setting for emotionally disturbed children may have implications for public programs for both normal and disturbed children of elementary school age. The education of these children should make use of structure, management skills, program planning, and teaching styles in the classroom.

A Clinical Episode

Fourteen children in a classroom in Denver are watching a live television broadcast of the inauguration ceremony for the President of the United States. Walt, age 11, "buzzes" his neighbor, Don, age 10, with remarks that Johnson is a crook, he shouldn't be there, we don't have to watch this; and some provocative sexual curse words are interspersed. Teacher One remains in her seat and looks to another teacher at the opposite end of the classroom. They signal agreement that the first teacher will deal with this and do it quickly. The ripple of this type of behavior through the classroom can bring disorganization in a short time. The other twelve children are beginning to look on and wait to see what will happen. Teacher One obtains Walt's gaze and tries to control him with a stern look.

Teacher Two directs herself to the rest of the class to main-

---

Reprinted from *Exceptional Children*, Vol. 32 (1966), pp. 377-383. By permission of the author and publisher.

251

tain attention to the television program. The look of Teacher One does not help Walt, but it does seem to split off Don, who is more responsive to disapproval. Teacher One then moves in Walt's direction. She doesn't do this very often, for teachers moving about frequently become distracting to the children. Also, children wonder who will get attention in the form of punishment or in the form of special help. It is now clear that the teacher will control Walt's behavior since that is to be expected when she moves. She takes Walt away from his seat to the side of the room; and because of his continuous buzzing, she calls on the intercommunication speaker to the front office for the standby officer.

The standby officer this day is Miss B, a social worker who is one of the full-time staff and is acting as the principal for the day. Miss B comes to the classroom and takes Walt out of the class. Teacher One accompanies them into the hall to explain what took place and that Walt can come back to see the program as soon as he can control himself. Teacher One goes back into the classroom and takes her former position. All of these events have taken place in the space of five minutes. The class continues to watch the TV broadcast with Don attending to the task.

Walt accompanies Miss B to her office, switching off the lights a few times as he goes along the hall. Sometimes it is more effective not to interact with Walt, but to be quiet and offer him the silence of the office. Other times, a discussion of the issue that led to behavioral disruption is more helpful. Miss B considers the alternatives, realizing that getting back to class to learn is important. Although Walt and his family were strong adherents of the opposite presidential candidate in the campaign, he now needs to accept the decision. She offers quiet, and Walt settles down. About ten minutes later, she decides he is ready to return.

Walt returns to the class and buzzes slightly. As he enters the room, Teacher One tells him to sit in a seat other than the one next to Don, and the class continues undisturbed. Walt gradually settles into an acceptance pattern. Later on that day, Teacher One follows through on the incident with Walt. She clarifies that he was sent to standby so that he can be helped to differentiate disapproval from rejection.

There is further follow through that continues for a number of days. The incident is reported and discussed two days later during the morning conference which all staff attend. It was discovered that the physical education teacher, a man, had been discussing good and bad world leaders with Walt and his friend Reggie on the way to the tennis court, covering Hitler, Mussolini, Roosevelt, and Churchill. Walt's therapist and the social worker for the parents contributed to the discussion and spoke about the parents' having disappointed him another time by not coming for a visit. The parents live in a town some 125 miles away from Denver, and Walt lives in a group placement home. Other staff members continued the discussion informally at various times during the next few days.

It is clear that the incident reported here has interesting and significant psychological dynamics. It helps a teacher and other staff to obtain this understanding from the child's therapist. Yet, without diminishing the importance of clinical understanding, there are many other issues to be considered such as management and control, values which need presentation, clearly communicating that deviant behaviors are not condoned, and that the central significance of the learning in school is not forgotten.

The Psychoeducational Setting

Walt is an emotionally handicapped boy, and the setting described is a special psychoeducational facility. He and his thirteen classmates have problems which are typical headaches in elementary classes in our schools. In a sense, they are selected for this special class with this idea in mind, i.e. a representative sample of headaches. The setting is the Day Care Center of the University of Colorado Medical Center. Together with other academic departments on the Boulder campus, a laboratory school with demonstration, training, and research functions is being developed for emotionally handicapped children of elementary school age.

It is hoped that through the collaboration of clinical and educational staff, new knowledge and experience can be obtained to deal more effectively with the management, treatment, and education of emotionally handicapped children. Since such children represent a significant percentage of elementary school populations (estimates range from 7 to 12 percent [American Psychiatric Association, 1964]), the communication of such experiences and principles as they develop may be useful to the regular school setting. It is possible that psychoeducational techniques developed for emotionally handicapped children may be applied to normal child populations.

In the clinical episode of Walt, one should consider the many issues other than clinical understanding that were involved. These considerations can be grouped under the general heading of psychoeducational approach. The term psychoeducational is used by the staff of the Day Care Center to connote the integration of clinical and educational viewpoints. The educational viewpoint stresses academic progress and achievement for the child, even though handicapped in his learning, but also emphasizes presenting reality and moral demands to the child and his family within their capacities to meet them.

The clinical viewpoint includes both empathic and intellectual understanding with the objective of discovering patterns, sequences, relationships, and dynamics in the wide range of verbal, motor, perceptual, social, and cognitive behaviors. From such discoveries it becomes possible to program and plan for the child individually and in groups. This fosters academic and social progress, which strengthens and enhances the ego. Success experiences and the development of skills in real life are needed by such children just as much as psychotherapeutic assistance.

Program Planning

In order to accomplish these many facets of the psychoeducational approach, time for observing and pooling ideas and for planning attitudes, approaches, and specific lesson plans is essential. It is incredible that one can expect a teacher of a class of 35 to 40 children to develop lesson plans, managerial styles, and special materials without time being provided for this. Would we not teach more effectively and students learn more in elementary education if there were time for planning new activities and comparing notes with colleagues? Could not teaching commitments be so arranged to make this essential time available?

An essential aspect of classroom management is time to observe, evaluate, and plan for the experiences which can bring success and pleasure in learning. Furthermore, it can encourage the wish to be more like the adults from whom the child learns. Success and pleasure with learning materials are probably the most significant aspects of Montessori teaching methods. Not only do emotionally disturbed children require such experiences but all children do, and it need not be only with Montessori materials.

In the case of Walt, the staff of the Center capitalized initially on some of his neurotic patterns to achieve success and pleasure in learning. He would use novel and nonconformance approaches to achieve, and this was initially exploited. Walt, for example, did not know his six, seven, and eight times tables for numbers over five and less than nine; but he could do the 13, 14, 16, and 17 times tables with speed. The teacher used Roman numeral multiplication for the six, seven, and eight tables and also some modern math approaches, the distributive principle in particular. Eventually he mastered the six, seven, and eight tables in a direct conformance manner. However, when division followed multiplication he had difficulty again.

It was the teacher's opinion that Walt was encountering the general problem of not being able to use reversal. An example is his response to the presidential inauguration ceremony. Walt could not reverse in the sense that Johnson was opposed as a candidate but supported as a president. In his own family experiences, he was exposed to reversals that were inappropriate or situations where reversals should have been used but were not. His family presented an oppositional attitude to the world, and Walt was caught up in his family's opposition.

A number of other teacher management and control principles are involved in the clinical episode initially described. One of these is the phenomenon of ripple effect in which a deviant behavior interaction can spread to other children and lead to group disorganization. The teacher can often spot such beginnings and nip them in the bud before they become flowering weeds. Dealing with deviant behavior in one child is far easier than dealing with many. One would generally uphold the principle that one child should not defeat the educational experience of an entire class.

Another principle is concerned with task orientation. It is conceivable that a teacher might spend the entire classroom day responding to and dealing with deviant behaviors and in that respect manage. Here the means to an end can become an end in itself, for what good is management if learning is not its consequence or goal? Task orientation means getting something done or accomplished. The task, however, must be within realistic limits of the child's potential for accomplishment. One could use such adjectives as determination, persistence, doggedness, and with-it-ness (Kounin, Personal communication, 1965) to describe the approach of the teacher who is task oriented.

The Classroom Situation

How does a teacher further behave in a classroom? The clinical example presented a team teaching situation with two teachers, one at either end of the class, communicating with each other nonverbally. This situation provides the teacher with eyes both in front and in back of the head. It has been staff experience that structuring the classroom according to functional areas and expectant behaviors of teachers has many advantages. It provides predictability, uniformity, and defined purposes. Communication of intent and meaning also tends to become clear.

We have defined three areas of the classroom as (a) a project area on one side of the classroom where a child may put models together, make dioramas, and work with clay; (b) an independent work area which is the central part of the room and consists of the children's desks; (c) two centers of learning at polar opposites of the room where each teacher sits at a table around which four or five children can comfortably sit, with instructional materials and chalkboard easily accessible. Group and individual teaching take place at this table with each child coming to the teacher for instruction, direction, clarification, and support (Blom, in press). Since classrooms at the Center have children of various age ranges and markedly different achievement levels within and across subject areas, this arrangement provides a structured environment within which to operate. It has been the staff experience that emotionally disturbed children greatly need such structure.

Staff observations indicate that an environment where the child moves to the teacher, who remains relatively fixed in her position, offers many advantages. The child who walks appropriately to the desk takes an aggressive and active attitude toward learning, rather than sitting at his desk waiting to be fed by the teacher coming to him. When the Day Care Center program first began, it was decided to have table-desks having two seats where the teacher could occasionally sit next to the child to offer assistance. The concept was a mobile teacher and a stationary student.

Because of subsequent experiences and different orientation, the desks are being altered to three-fourths size with one seat. Another advantage of this arrangement is that the passive position may not be well tolerated by children and may encourage fantasy production with consequent distractibility and loss of task orientation in reality. An adult, in contrast, has greater capacities for accepting and being comfortable with the passive position.

The impressions are that the mobile teacher stimulates distractibility in a number of ways. The child has to search and look for her presence, a situation which introduces uncertainty; a stationary object easily found offers security. The teacher moving around the class mobilizes opposite and varied expectations: (a) Will she offer assistance and give, or is she going to help someone else? (b) Will she criticize or punish, rather than be giving?

One can see that such a situation could accentuate sibling rivalries and jealousies with which emotionally disturbed children frequently have difficulties and which all children experience to greater or lesser extent. The teacher as an authority figure represents a potential threat or punishing agent, and these children have much about which to feel guilty and anxious in both reality and fantasy. The teacher sitting next to the child can create a closeness which may accentuate conflict, both in her being there and in her leaving. The child's coming to the teacher offers a greater opportunity for the child to regulate distance and closeness, comings and goings, and sharing with others.

The teachers tend to remain stationary in the classes at the Day Care Center. While they work with small groups of children at the table, they are able to supervise the rest of the class in the independent work area. The teachers also communicate with each other through nonverbal methods. When a teacher moves out from her center (this is not done very often), it is usually for the purpose of control through stronger measures than a look, nod, hand signal, or occasional verbal thrust from the stationary position. Occasionally the student may be requested by a signal to come to the table for control. Sometimes the teacher goes to the child at the desk when he needs support and encouragement, but the relatively stationary teacher position still holds as most typical.

The atmosphere of the classroom is one of respect for learning, accomplishment, and pleasure and reward in knowing. Lesson plans are designed to utilize materials of particular interest to the child. Though there is considerable structure, this is not applied rigidly since modifications and alterations are used when needed. There is adaptability of teaching style and learning materials to fit learning styles and patterns of students. As in the case of Walt, one may exploit a neurotic learning style such as nonconformance learning with the eventual goal of developing more conformance patterns.

If a boy such as Walt can experience success, he can better look at and admit his failures. By being able to accept the fact that he does not know and that he does things the wrong way, he can learn and change. The denial and avoidance reactions on the part of children at the Day Care Center to defend against failure which has been associated with pain and humiliation are very striking. Such defensive operations interfere with the learning process; one way in which to overcome them is through the experience of success.

Although the classroom situation is described as a task-oriented one within the capacities of individual children and the group to achieve them, alternate lesson plans are sometimes used when the original plan is not working or if conditions are not considered suitable for their execution. Some children who are undergoing intrapsychic or situational stress in their lives may be given familiar or review exercises until the crisis has lessened or abated. There are also breaks and changes in the daily schedule: a midmorning snack and free period of fifteen minutes; lunch and play period of forty minutes; physical education in the latter part of the morning every day; music in the afternoon; less demanding academic work in the afternoon; a project period of twenty minutes; afternoon snacks, and an activity program at the end of the school day.

Behavioral Management—Standby

Children at the Center usually view the classroom situation with respect, interest, and pleasure. To be out of the classroom is usually viewed as a deprivation of all activities except the therapy sessions. While the children profess on the surface to dislike school and to delight in weekends and vacations, their behavior does not correspond to this. They more often than not arrive early and leave late, give the staff a difficult time after separation breaks, and have good attendance records. Therefore, to be in standby represents a deprivation which the child dislikes.

There are occasions when the management and discipline techniques used by the teacher are not successful. Under such circumstances, the individual child does not benefit from the classroom situation and may be in need of further individual help. He may also disrupt the classroom for others. Therefore, a standby officer is available who is equivalent to principal of the day. Five members of the staff rotate this function, and each arranges his schedule so that he can be quickly available on short notice. The standby officer may be called to the classroom, lunch area, gym, playground, or crafts area to provide help with an individual child. The child returns to the office of the standby, sometimes called the quiet room by the children.

Discussion of the event is often beneficial along lines similar to but modified from the life-space interview approach (Redl,

1959); however, mere quiet with no further stimulating interaction with others is sometimes more helpful. The main objective
of the standby is to return the child to the school area or program
as quickly as possible and feasible. However, important issues,
conflicts, and anxieties may be further clarified through discussion. Stabilization in behavior may result. The standby is not
used very often by children to escape from situations and avoid
tasks.

Walt is a more frequent attender of standby than other children, with a frequency of about three to five times a week. On
another occasion than the episode mentioned, he was sent from
lunch because of his provocative and loud use of crude sexual
language. This was disapproved by the lunch supervisor, and
the standby officer that day talked about his use of language as
a reflection of sexual behavior. Walt began to talk about his
involvement with other boys at the group placement home in
masturbatory activities about which he felt guilty and anxious.
In fifteen minutes he returned to the lunch area considerably
calmed down.

In the example of Walt's derogation of the President and
provocation in the classroom, the event was reported and discussed at the next morning rounds. The standby officer wrote
up the event on a report form which serves as a daily log.
"Rounds" is a half-hour meeting held three times a week from
8:00 to 8:30, and all the full time staff attend regularly. Part-
time staff attend at least one meeting a week. Rounds give the
staff the opportunity to pool observations, clarify the meaning of
events that take place, and develop methods for dealing with
individual and group behaviors.

Other Psychoeducational Contributions

The contributions and suggestions of a number of workers
interested in psychoeducational problems have been used in the
operations of the Day Care Center. Meaningful dimensions of
teacher style have been developed through direct study of live
classrooms (Kounin, Gump, and Ryan, 1961). These dimensions
have been used in understanding and training staff teachers in
effective role functioning. Sarason's interests have offered sug-

gestions in the preservice training of teachers, the more adequate training of mental health consultants to schools, the development of live, vital, direct, and practical suggestions to teachers in classroom situations, and the effectiveness of direct help to the child in the school setting (Sarason, Davidson, and Blatt, 1962; Sarason, personal communication, 1964).

Methods have been developed for teaching hyperactive children through reducing stimulation in the classroom, providing carefully structured lesson plans, encouraging appropriate academic regression, and exploiting inadequate learning styles (Cruickshank, Bentzen, Ratzeburg, and Tannhauser, 1961). The influence of teaching style on learning responses and the effect of cognitive training in the classroom have also been studied (Sigel, Personal communication, 1964). The life-space interview has been adapted to the school situation as a method of dealing with deviant behavior (Morse, 1963). Approaches in Montessori teaching methods (Standing, 1962) and the discussions of Ashton-Warner (1963) offer general attitude suggestions in the teaching of elementary school children.

There are, of course, a wide variety of specific teaching approaches to reading, arithmetic, and other subject areas. In addition, special motivational materials become increasingly available. The task here is to have some familiarity with these offerings but not to become too enamoured by their being the easy answer to all situations or to be fooled into the position of attributing success to a specific approach or materials when it was the influence of enthusiasm, the appeal of gadgetry, or something else. Unfortunately, there is insufficient knowledge about the learning process in general and specifically with particular children, and there is probably less knowledge about the rationale for teaching styles and procedures. These two areas are currently some of the most exciting ones for experimentation, evaluation, and psychoeducational research.

Individual Program Planning

One of the most difficult yet interesting aspects of classroom management involves programing for individual children. At the Day Care Center in Denver there is a population of handicapped children who require this type of program. It is possible to make individual decisions because of available time, smaller numbers of children, a rich supply of information and observations from a sufficient staff of teachers, psychiatrists, psychologists, social workers, pediatricians, and others, and the legitimized goals of training and research.

Gwenn, age seven, initially showed marked immaturity and primitiveness in her behavior, though she is not a psychotic child. She operated mainly on the readiness level in her school work and progressed primarily in one-to-one teaching situations where concrete, simple, and repetitive tasks were offered. Her emotionally limited parents provided little stimulation and awareness of the environment (its tools, opportunities, and resources) and of social skills in relating to others. Initially, it was considered advisable to place major emphasis in our setting on socialization, such as learning good table manners, having rules made explicit, saying please and thank you, covering her mouth when she coughed, taking turns, saying hello and goodbye, learning to wait, raising her hand for attention, and taking part in games.

The teacher would also spend some time in culture enrichment in connection with reading readiness materials, showing her ice skates and how they are used, a basketball and a hoop, letters, stamps and the postoffice, record players and how they work, and a trip to the airport with other children. If all aspects of the program focused on socialization and acculturation, i.e. classroom, gym, lunch, play activities, and therapy, progress might be more rapid.

Other kinds of programing have included a variety of attitudinal and specific procedures:

1. Reducing the level of anxiety which leads to disorganized behavior through the use of medication.

2. Cutting down on stimulation in the classroom by using a shield board.

3. Allowing a phobic child who became anxious when new learning material was introduced to return momentarily to familiar material and then move ahead.

4. Providing appropriate age reading interests for an eleven-year-old boy who was reading at the second grade level.

5. Responding to correct and wrong answers to questions in a neutral, mechanical way, since correct and wrong had strong connotations of good-bad and love-reject, which in turn provoked strong emotional responses.

6. Helping a child accept "I don't know" and failure as a part of learning.

7. Using academic regression introduced by the teacher to further strengthen basic skills in such a manner that self-esteem is not injured.

8. Substituting competition with oneself for intense competition with others that usually resulted in painful hurt.

9. Programing instructions and things to do for a boy with thirty seconds' attention span.

10. Giving short paragraphs to read to an obsessive boy who had difficulty in scanning and would get caught up in checking and rechecking what he had previously read.

These examples represent types of specific procedures that can be used to facilitate learning progress on an experimental, trial basis. The procedures are not always successful. Sometimes it is difficult to know whether one should modify an approach or continue with the same one for a longer period of time when change does not result.

References

American Psychiatric Association: *Planning Psychiatric Services For Children In The Community Mental Health Program.* Washington, D.C., Author, 1964.

Ashton-Warner, S.: *Teacher.* New York, S. and S., 1963.

Blom, G. E.; Rudnick, M., and Searles, J.: Some principles and practices in the psychoeducational treatment of emotionally disturbed children. In *Psychology In The Schools.* In press.

Cruickshank, W. M.; Bentzen, F. A.; Ratzeburg, F. H., and Tannhauser, M. T.: *A Teaching Method For Brain-injured And Hyperactive Children.* Syracuse, Syracuse, 1961.

Kounin, J.; Gump, P., and Ryan, J.: Explorations in classroom management. *J Teacher Education, 12:* 235-246, 1961.

Morse, W. C.: Training teachers in life-space interviewing. *Amer J Orthopsychiat, 33:* 727-730, 1963.

Redl, F.: Strategy and techniques of the life-space interview. *Amer J Orthopsychiat, 29:* 1-18, 1959.

Sarason, S.; Davidson, K., and Blatt, B.: *The Preparation Of Teachers.* New York, Wiley, 1962.

Standing, E. M.: *Maria Montessori: Her Life And Work.* New York, New Am. Lib., 1962.

Chapter 27

Neutralization: A Tool For The Teacher Of Disturbed Children

STANLEY JACOBSON AND CHRISTOPHER FAEGRE

W HAT EDUCATIONAL TECHNIQUES are appropriate for the seriously disturbed child? Prescriptions for teaching disturbed children have focused largely on class size, teacher-pupil relationship, and child study. Very little has been said about appropriate methods and materials. As a result, there has been a tendency to apply the same methods in the special class that have been found so productive for children at large. Lecturing is avoided, coloring books give way to mobiles and montages, and drills are de-emphasized in favor of learning games. The curriculum is spiced with "experience," "problem solving," and "free expression."

In planning a lesson, teachers ask: Will the child participate in directing his activity? Is he asked to think creatively? Will the material and the procedure be stimulating?

In classroom planning for *most* children, questions like these may be the vital ones to ask, but for *some* children, for emotionally disturbed children and perhaps for some other atypical children as well, a different kind of question ought to be given priority, namely, How neutral is it?

By neutral we mean free of significance to the child's area of problem, unlikely to irritate his sore spots or to depend on those personality characteristics in which he happens to be weakest. Experienced teachers intuitively use something like neutraliza-

Reprinted from *Exceptional Children*, Vol. 25 (1959), pp. 243-246. By permission of the authors and publisher.

tion when they work with children with obvious physical handicaps; for example, a child with a game leg is discouraged from competing in the hundred-yard dash. Something akin to our idea of neutralization, the sharp reduction of distracting visual and auditory stimuli in the classroom, is also becoming widely used with the brain-injured child.

Neutralization takes different specific forms because emotional disturbances differ from each other as much as the brain-injured boy differs from the child with the game leg. Some disturbed children lag behind in important areas of development, like the ability to delay the gratification of impulses. Others are immobilized by a fear of growing up. Still others are so afraid of disapproval that they cannot risk being wrong. And of course, there are many other kinds and degrees and mixtures of problems.

But disturbed children are alike in their tendency to distort the events of the classroom in terms of their personal problems. Given an opportunity, they fall easily into behavior which interferes with growth and learning. They may cling to the teacher like the infants they feel themselves to be or they may *unconsciously* look for an excuse to hate the teacher, then insist on letting the class know it. Some may refuse to read or count or fingerpaint, for example, because of the special meaning the activity has for them. A few will slide into the daydreams and day-nightmares which give them that faraway look, or break up a productive session because serenity makes them anxious; and others will act as if their life depends on success in learning.

Schools are planning for disturbed children by providing special counseling and referral services, by manipulating class size, group composition, and the length of the school day. We are suggesting *neutralization* as an additional classroom tool, an approach to planning classroom activities to minimize the influence of personality problems on the learning process.

How Does Neutralization Work?

Our own experience with this approach has been in a school program for extremely disturbed, aggressive boys whose chief problem is in the area of self-control. In the classroom they tend to become easily frustrated, overexcited, and explosively hyper-critical of the teacher, their classmates, and themselves. Although they are seriously retarded in at least one basic academic skill, their dominant problem is the sudden violence of their impulsive reactions. We have taught them in very small groups and in short school sessions, and we have learned to control the content and procedures of the classroom so that it is possible for them to have productive educational experiences.

For our boys, neutralizing methods and materials has meant controlling the ability of the materials to arouse multiple associations and distracting fantasies, minimizing the demand for creative thought and action, and discouraging individuality. In many ways, the neutral program for these boys has been the opposite of the multifaceted and stimulating curriculum that is considered most meaningful by ordinary standards. Careful management of the form of activities has been as vital as the control of their content. Here, because of limitations of space, we want to describe only the latter—the neutralizaiton of materials.

Some Materials Are Not Neutral

Like every other school, we have depended on published literature, texts, workbooks, games, and classroom aids in building a part of our program. From the mountain of available materials, we have chosen those which are neutral in their own right or can be neutralized by the way we use them. The following passage, paraphrased from a firstgrade reader, is an example of a kind of story we would avoid:

THE RABBIT AND THE BLOCKS

One day a rabbit went for a walk,
He came to a house.
"Oh" he said, "The door is open."
He went in.
"What do I see?" he said.
He saw toys and toys and toys.
He saw a big red ball.
He saw a little blue boat.
He saw many blocks.

"I will play with the blocks," he said.
"I will make a house."
"I will make a house with the blocks."
"I will put one block on top," he said.
Bang! The blocks fell down.
Down and down they fell!
The rabbit ran.
He ran up and he ran down.
He looked down and he looked up.
"I want to go home," he said.
"I want to get out."
"Help me! Help!" he cried.
"Oh! Oh! Help me go home!"

In the end, of course, the rabbit is rescued or manages to escape, but perhaps not before the hypersensitive young reader is sharing the animal's panic. The theme of curiosity leading to destruction and disorganizing fear is a powerfully innocuous theme, but it is built around characters and relationships which exemplify precisely what our boys are *not* and what they fear to become. In many cases a whole series of readers will follow typical children like Jim and Joan and their parents and siblings and friends through the varied adventures of everyday life. Picnics and parties, trips to the zoo, visits to the doctor or to Daddy's office; through all these and more the authors take a happy, unified family, a family whose home is clean, whose meals are regular, who like each other and the world around them.

For most children, idealized pictures of middle-class life do offer the chance for close psychological identification between reader and story that the authors intend. But there are children who have experienced the opposite of consistent warmth and pleasure in living. Their close relationships have been painful and damaging to their growth, so much so in some cases that they try to reject the notion that they are children dependent on adults and they insist that warmth between people is for "sissies" only. By emphasizing the very closeness of relationship that these children fear, reading material can be a serious block to learning. Innocent enough on the face of it, it can nevertheless unleash anxiety and develop enough resistance to bring the child to a standstill as far as learning to read is concerned.

Neutralization Techniques

We would *neutralize* reading materials by unloading them of their ability to arouse disturbing feelings and fantasies. Where the material has high potential for distracting children of a particular age or problem group, we would replace it with more neutral material. Fortunately, most stories for children have more or less neutral themes and a potentially upsetting piece in an otherwise good book can be omitted without difficulty. A graded science series which emphasizes science facts and experiments without dramatizing the characters in the book can substitute for the family-story series.

The majority of available material is appropriate but for single scenes or passages. In screening it for classroom use we would note its potential dangers and be prepared to neutralize it by explanation as the need arises. On some occasions a potential issue can be unloaded in advance by remarking casually, "Remember as we read this that it is not something that really happened but is only a made-up story." When a particularly touchy passage appears, the teacher can digress and explain, "This sort of thing might happen in the jungle, but it couldn't happen around here." Even after a distracting section has been read it is possible to neutralize it so that children can move on to other class business, as the following selection from a school report illustrates:

> . . . As part of the Daniel Boone project we have been reading an excellent set of materials on Boone. In today's session we hit a passage about Daniel being bathed by squaws "to take all his white blood out." I knew we were going to hit that part and decided to keep the lid on possible excitement by reading that whole page aloud myself. Sure enough, Bernie wanted to know, "Did they really take out his blood?" and Jack's expression showed that Bernie was speaking for him, too. I reassured them that it was only a ceremony and make-believe as far as the blood went—a way of giving Boone a fresh start among the Indians. Soon as that was handled, Joe said—and I could see the giggle rising in him: "Did he have his clothes off when the squaws washed him?" I said that Indians are used to nakedness and thought little of it and added gently that "they didn't get excited about it any more than you need to." That settled it very quickly, and we went on with the reading. . . .

Here the teacher removed the sting from an exciting piece of material, first, by reading it aloud himself so that the inherent possibilities for trouble would not be embellished by a keyed-up child and second, by handling questions in matter-of-fact manner, without allowing himself to be drawn into irrelevant discussion or byplay. His gentle and self-assured recognition of Joe's precarious excitement level gave Joe a clue to his internal state of affairs, and Joe was able to respond by calming down.

"Casual," "gentle," "matter-of-fact," "self-assured"—there are keys to successful on-the-spot neutralization of a touchy issue. If the teacher is uncomfortable about a question, if he implies blame or ridicule, if he shows curiosity about the child's feelings, he risks increasing the child's anxiety and inner agitation. It goes without saying that the severely disturbed child will not always be able to use the teacher's help to remain task-oriented or to regain his composure once it has been lost. This raises the issue of limit setting, an aspect of the management of behavior which is important but not pertinent here.

Selecting Themes

In addition to themes of inner turmoil and the happy-family story, we have had to be selective about many kinds of situations and phrasing, not only in reading material, but also in arithmetic problems, in songs, and in choice of social studies topics. Scenes involving bodily damage, even to a doll or a pet, and pseudo-magical situations, for example, a snowman who runs into a house and melts, are bound to produce anxiety. Object lessons, like the value of listening to mother, the importance of taking care of possessions, or of 'virtue rewarded" in any form are too familiarly distressing to be anything but an interference.

Besides carefully screening the kind of content *we* provide, we have had to become alert to the opportunities we give the child to furnish disruptive content of his own by inference or distortion. Sex, obscenity, and violence are powerful magnets for the attention of the kind of boy we have worked with. Seemingly innocent words and phrases can be distorted into obscenities or excuses for wild excitement by making a pun or a rhyme or by giving free rein to associations. It is strategic, therefore, to avoid subject matter which lends itself easily to corruption and to be prepared to handle with casual and self-assured directness comments which may really insult the teacher's sensibilities.

We have already noted some of the materials that can be used successfully with our kind of child. We can also suggest several rules of thumb which guide us in selecting material.

"Far away" and "long ago" subject matter is generally more neutral than contemporary characters and situations. Violence among medieval knights or dinosaurs is ordinarily not as disruptive as the same degree of violence among contemporary soldiers or deer in the North Woods, for example.

Struggles against nature, like Indians or frontiersmen fighting hardship, and legitimate forms of physical aggression, like the necessary killing of animals for food, are usually more neutral than aggression based on hostility.

Facts and experiments about nature and technology can be comparatively neutral because they can be separated from people and their interests and strivings.

The active, adventurous heroes of history and explorers of faraway places are good subjects on all counts. They are remote enough in space or time to discourage close personal comparison; they are physically aggressive enough to be interesting to action-oriented children, and their aggression is directed into productive channels.

We Learn What We Do

The idea of neutralization hinges, at least in part, on the concept *we learn what we do*. When we want a child to be learning reading skills, then our material and method ought to help him focus his attention on the task at hand. If the material or method leads a crippled child or a slow child or an emotionally disturbed child to ruminate about his problems, he will be learning to ruminate, not to read. Neutralization is a means of withdrawing extraneous, possibly troubling meanings from material and method so that there will be little provocation for a child to *do* anything other than what we want him to *learn*.

It goes without saying that no one can predict a child's reactions so well that he can eliminate all dangerous stimuli, even in an ideal classroom. But a perceptive teacher can screen out the most obvious dangers; he can be sensitive to some of the possibilities for disruption in the materials and methods he uses; and he can handle some of the issues that arise. When a teacher has thirty children for six hours a day, his ability to apply the technique will be sharply limited.

We are suggesting *neutralization* as a tool to be used along with tools like grouping, timing, and limit setting. In selecting and using materials, neutrality to a child's problems would have equal status wth factors like reading level, interest level, and legibility. The specific forms that neutralization takes will vary from setting to setting and from group to group. As a principle, however, we feel neutralization can be useful in planning work with many kinds of atypical children.

SECTION H

BEHAVIOR MODIFICATION

Chapter 28

Modification And Maintenance Of Behavior
Through Systematic Application Of Consequences

RICHARD WHELAN AND NORRIS G. HARING

IT HAS OFTEN been asserted that a fifty-year gap exists between knowledge gained in basic research laboratories and application of that knowledge to problems which exist in classrooms. Educators are confronted with an ever-growing fund of scientific knowledge from the learning laboratories. The assignment for educators is as follows: Reliable scientific knowledge must be applied to classroom situations; it is only through such applications that information concerning behavioral principles discovered in laboratories can be validated. Educators should no longer have to answer or defend themselves against the indictment of not utilizing known discoveries in classroom settings.

The Educational Challenge

Ferster (1964) completed a study concerned with teaching the meaning and use of mathematical symbols to very young subjects. The results of this study are cited to emphasize the importance of applying laboratory data directly to classroom settings. Two subjects, Dennis, age three and one-half, and Margie, age three, were selected for the study. Ferster chose the language of arithmetic because it describes environmental relationships in a clear, systematic, and consistent manner. The symbol three describes a set of objects which exhibits the quality of

Reprinted from *Exceptional Children*, Vol. 32 (1966), pp. 281-289. By permission of the authors and publisher.

"threeness," and it does this precisely. Arithmetic symbols also provide the experimenter with simple, distinct stimuli which can be reliably presented and controlled. "Moreover, the language of numbers gets around the obstacle of vocal limitations" (Ferster, 1964, p. 98).

Using a binary number system, the subjects learned to write or say numbers by pushing buttons which turned lights on or off. The binary system was chosen because its two digit base, zero and one, was most amenable to presenting symbolic material in a light-on, light-off fashion. Also, by presenting problem-solving tasks in this way, verbal communication between subject and experimenter was totally curtailed. Presentation of learning tasks and recording of responses were fully automated; the learner and the environment interacted without the variable of experimenter presence.

Behavioral responses which constitute an understanding of mathematical fundamentals are a very complex process. Therefore, the subjects were presented tasks which were sequential, ordered, and reduced to very small steps. The subjects first learned to match colors accurately and subsequently learned to match binary numbers. From that point, Dennis and Margie learned to match binary numbers to correct numbers of objects, i.e., three triangles were matched to appropriate light-on, light-off sequences. To ensure that the subjects were attending to numerosity concepts and not making matching responses because of consistent stimuli arrangements, the experimenter substituted other objects for triangles, and rearranged size and location of objects on the stimuli presentation panel. When the subjects could match binary numbers to objects correctly, the experiment moved into the final phase. The subjects learned to respond to objects by writing, in lights, a symbol which represented numbers.

Each phase of the experiment was mastered before the subjects moved on to the next step. Correct responses resulted in a subsequent consequence which increased such responses; in this experiment, food was the consequence. Food was delivered to the subject as a consequence for making a correct response. This consequence acted as an environmental event which increased the frequency of correct responses in comparison to the frequency of error responses. For the subjects in this study it was determined prior to the initiation of the experiment that the consequence (food) would increase the frequency of behavior occurring immediately prior to the delivery of the consequence.

The consequence of an error was a time out period; all of the lights on the stimuli presentation panel were darkened. Responses which the subjects wrote during the time out resulted in subsequent consequences which decreased the frequency of error responses. Under time out conditions, or after an error response had been made, the subjects could not receive the consequence (food) because it was provided only after correct responses were made. An error response removed the subjects from conditions where only correct responses received consequences which served to increase the frequency of these correct responses. Any response, then, which removed the presentation of the consequence (food) was virtually eliminated from the subject's behavior. After a lapse of time, the panel was relighted and the subjects were again in a position to receive consequences for correct responses. Increasing correct responses, small learning sequences, and eliminating incorrect responses resulted in practically errorless learning (Ferster, 1964).

What is the significance of this experiment? The results are not too surprising even though the subjects were quite young. Bruner (1963) believes that highly abstract concepts can be learned at a very early age if they are presented simply and with materials appropriate for subjects being taught. If Bruner is correct, the type of learned behavior illustrated by Ferster's experiment should be considered as well within the behavior repertory of most young children. This is highly significant information, but of even more importance is the introduction of Ferster's subjects. Dennis and Margie were chimpanzees. Ferster stated: "We have developed in these animals forms of behavior that bear a much more complex relation to the environment than chimpanzees normally show" (Ferster, 1964, p. 106).

Learning through verbal interaction is often emphasized in classrooms. That is, the children are expected to receive auditory stimuli, interpret them with understanding, process them, and then respond in the manner dictated by the verbal stimuli. Normal children who have, over a period of years, learned to control their behavior as a result of consequences contingent upon verbal emissions, usually function adequately in such classroom situations. Stated another way, their behavior is under the control of environmental consequences.

What relevance does the preceding discussion have to the behavioral management of an emotionally disturbed child? What possible connection can animal research and verbal interactions between pupil and teacher have with behavioral management methods? If a teacher were asked to teach mathematical concepts similar to those in Ferster's experiment to a severely disorganized child, the comments to that request might be as follows:

1. That is impossible; the child could not possibly understand what he is to do.

2. The child would only be confused if he were presented with such material.

3. He just would not understand a word said about the task.

4. Because the child would be confused, he would be unable to respond appropriately.

The teacher may also assert that the child is too disturbed to learn such information; when he becomes more amenable to verbal instruction, work may begin on such topics.

What is the explanation for this discrepancy between educators' perception of the learning process and reported results of well designed learning experiments? Michael stated, "The basis of this misunderstanding seems to involve the assumption that most learning takes place by processes requiring an ability to verbalize the requirements of the learning situation, or to profit from verbal instructions" (Michael, 1963, p. 4). If this condition is accurate, then non-verbal organisms would not learn at all. Of course, this is not a true state of affairs; non-verbal organisms do learn. Behavioral principles apply to the management of children as well as to lower animals. Even severely emotionally disturbed children possess more complex behavior repertories than chimpanzees, rats, or dogs. The challenge for educators is to utilize behavioral principles to modify undesirable and maintain desirable behavior in emotionally disturbed children, and also to apply these principles to prevent children from becoming candidates for special education classes.

Behavioral Principles

There is a small but rapidly expanding accumulation of data which indicate that behavioral principles, reliably demonstrated in learning laboratories, are also applicable to managing, modifying, building, and maintaining the behavior of children who function in special education classrooms (Haring and Phillips, 1962; Bijou, 1964). The fundamental concept upon which these principles rest is that behavior, abnormal as well as normal, is learned.

Educators are interested in the behavior of children, or more specifically, the effects of behavior upon the environment. Furthermore, educators study "the connection between a response and its consequences" (Skinner, 1963, p. 505). Analysis of these connections has demonstrated behavioral principles which account for a major portion of human activity. Behavior is maintained by its effect on the environment, and it consists of those activities which change the external environment, which in turn changes the subsequent state and behavior of the individual (Nurnberger, Ferster, and Brady, 1963).

There are some environmental consequences which increase the frequency or rate of behavior. These environmental events may be defined as accelerating consequences since their effect is to increase the emission frequency of behavioral responses (Lindsley, O., Personal communication, April, 1965). If accelerating consequences are provided only after the occurrence of a correct response, then that behavior will increase in frequency. For example, in our society an accelerating consequence for increasing work rate may be additional salary. Increasing the salary as a consequence of higher work rate may result in even higher work rate.

There are also some environmental consequences which decrease the frequency or rate of behavior. Such environmental changes may be defined as decelerating consequences. The presentation of a decelerating consequence subsequent to a behavioral response will decrease the frequency of that response. If, in our example cited above, work rate is below minimal standards, a decelerating consequence may be less salary. Decreasing salary because of low work rate may decrease the emission or occurrence of such a low rate.

These two examples are highly simplified in order to convey the meaning of some behavioral principles. Actual application of these principles to children in a classroom is a very complex process. Additional examples concerned with the precise and systematic applications of behavioral principles are discussed in subsequent sections of this paper. A comprehensive presentation of behavioral principles (Holland and Skinner, 1961), application to behavioral modification (Eysenck, 1960; Ayllon and Haughton, 1962; Barrett, 1962), and utilization of these principles in academic learning situations (Hewett, 1964; Staats, Minke, Finley, Wolf, and Brooks, 1964) are beyond the scope of this paper. The reader will experience positive consequences for exploring procedures used in the functional analysis of behavior.

Behavioral Modification Techniques

Of particular importance to educators is Lindsley's statement regarding behavioral modification. It is as follows: "There is a great tendency today to confuse the acquisition of behavior with its maintenance" (Lindsley, 1964, p. 65). For example, a teacher may wish to change the behavior of a child from running to her desk with questions, to holding up his hand and remaining at his desk until the teacher can come to him. The teacher, through discovery of effective consequences, may use these to accelerate remaining in the seat and holding up a hand. At first, consequences would be applied after every correct response. Such a procedure is utilized to assist the child in the acquisition of appropriate behavior. Along with this, the teacher would apply decelerating consequences for getting out of the chair and running to the teacher's desk; that is, the teacher may not verbally interact with the child or give him attention until he remains seated. For this example, the assumption is made that the teacher's attention is meaningful to the child, and this is certainly not true in every case.

After the child has acquired the desired behavior, the teacher need not apply accelerating consequences to him for each and every response; she may only need to do so for every fifth or tenth correct response. By using aperiodic consequences, the teacher maintains the desired behavior. At this point of the behavior management program, maintenance procedures would be utilized to strengthen appropriate behavior which had already been acquired.

One goal of education is to enable children to work and learn independently in the classroom. The teacher's task is to arrange the environment in such a way that when children interact with it, learning is maximized. When a child has acquired a behavior, and that behavior is being maintained, the teacher can devote more time and skills to other children who need to acquire specific behaviors. Many teachers, because they experience gratification for helping children grow and learn, often find it difficult to use maintenance techniques, or to allow children to learn independently. Teachers may use techniques which are vitally important for the acquisition of behavior, but these techniques are not necessary for ensuring a continuous maintenance of positive behavior.

When behavior needs to be maintained, then it is no longer necessary to provide accelerating consequences to each behavioral response. Maintaining behavior requires that the teacher reduce considerably the number of accelerating consequences provided; indeed, it is a necessity if a child is to develop independent learning skills and self-control. It is during this maintenance process that appropriate behavior is accelerated by consequences which are intrinsic to completion of tasks, social approval, feelings of self-worth, and the satisfaction of assuming self-responsibility. Therefore, dependence upon numerous teacher applied consequences gradually loses significance to a child.

Zimmerman and Zimmerman (1962) demonstrated the use of behavioral modification techniques to alter specific behavior in a classroom situation. One subject, when asked to spell a word which he had previously studied, would make faces, mumble, and pause for a few seconds. Because of this behavior, the teacher spent considerable time in helping the boy sound out the word, and gave other cues until the word was spelled correctly. Even though the teacher was making extra time and effort available to the boy, spelling behavior did not improve. It was postulated that teacher attention might actually be maintaining this undesirable behavior, since over a period of several class sessions it required increasing amounts of time to elicit the correct response.

To check the accuracy of the postulate, the teacher asked the child to go to the blackboard to take a quiz over ten spelling words. The boy misspelled the first word ten times, but the teacher ignored this behavior by attending to other work at her desk. Each time the boy misspelled the word, he would look at the teacher. However, the teacher did not respond to this behavior. This procedure was followed for the rest of the spelling test. With the presentation of each word, the boy exhibited fewer incorrect responses, and the time required to write the word correctly was decreased. Teacher attention immediately followed each correct response; inappropriate responses did not receive teacher attention. When the ten words were spelled correctly, the boy received an A grade and social attention from the teacher. After a month of exposure to this technique, the frequency of undesirable responses decreased to near zero, and the boy continued to make academic progress.

A similar procedure was utilized in working with a child who received staff attention whenever he displayed tantrum behavior. The tantrums were ignored, and staff attention was made dependent upon appropriate behavior. In several weeks, tantrum behavior disappeared (Zimmerman and Zimmerman, 1962).

Equally successful results were obtained when crying, emitted or maintained, depending upon its effects on the environment, was brought under control of social consequences. Teachers ignored children's crying and gave social attention and approval for non-crying behavior. To prove that the crying was a function of adult social consequences, the teachers reversed procedures and gave added attention to crying episodes. The results indicated that when adult attention was given to crying, crying increased in frequency. When such crying was ignored, episodes decreased from ten times a morning to zero or one. It was further noted that the children, when their crying did not receive teacher attention, became absorbed in constructive activity (Hart, Allen, Buell, Harris, and Wolf, 1964).

Baer (1962) used movie cartoons to bring thumbsucking under the control of environmental consequences. When the child put his thumb in his mouth, the cartoon was turned off; withdrawal of thumb from mouth resulted in continued presentation of the cartoon. During initial learning sessions thumbsucking decreased in frequency, but it recovered quickly upon termination of experimenter controlled consequences. After further sessions, thumbsucking decreased in areas other than the experimental room. This study readily demonstrates one application of behavioral modification techniques to the alteration of specific behaviors. However, it must not be concluded that cartoons would be equally effective with all thumbsuckers.

Application Of Behavioral Modification Techniques

The Children's Rehabilitation Unit, University of Kansas Medical Center, is a training, demonstration, and research center housed in a medical center complex. The schools of education, medicine, and related disciplines join to provide comprehensive behavioral modification programs for most categories of exceptional children. Unit staff are currently investigating the results emanating from the application of behavioral modification techniques to a wide variety of behavioral deviations and learning disabilities.

Staff members are investigating and demonstrating the efficiency of utilizing behavioral modification techniques with individuals, small class groups, and classes of 15 to 20 children. Validity of these techniques will be achieved only if they can be practically applied to groups of children by one teacher. It is most unreasonable to expect school districts to staff special classrooms with a teacher, assistants, and expensive automated equipment. Instead, the concept of staging seems to offer a more efficient approach.

Staging refers to adding children one at a time to groups until the class size reaches a point where the teacher can still comfortably plan task assignments, schedule appropriate consequences, record and measure behavior, and evaluate behavioral progress. Staging is closely related to the acquisition and maintenance phases of behavioral modification. Given appropriate materials and knowledge of behavioral modification techniques, there may be no reason why one teacher could not plan remediation programs for ten to fifteen children with emotional problems. When one child's behavior has been brought under the control of environmental consequences (his behavior is being maintained), then another child could be added to the class. The adding of children one by one could be continued until the maximum size for efficient programing is reached.

A specific example selected from our collection of data illustrates the effectiveness of correctly applying behavioral modification techniques. Bob is in a class for boys with emotional problems. He has a history of yelling, running about the room, tearing up his work, and not accomplishing assigned tasks. The teacher assigned Bob fifteen arithmetic problems to complete within thirty minutes, which was the time lapse before another task was to be initiated. Bob spent fifteen minutes of that time looking around the room, tapping his feet, and playing with his pencil. The teacher had noted that Bob consistently tried to get her to stand by his desk and watch him work. Taking this cue, the teacher instituted a systematic schedule of consequences. That is, Bob did one problem without the teacher being present; then the teacher watched him do one. Within fifteen minutes Bob had his work completed, and the teacher in that space of time had successfully raised the number of problems done independently, compared to those completed with teacher present, to a ratio of three to one. Bob completed three problems without the teacher observing his work and then worked a problem with the teacher observing the process.

For this example, an accelerating consequence (teacher presence) was used to aid Bob in acquiring a specific behavior. However, in a very brief time lapse, the teacher assisted Bob in maintaining the behavior by reducing the number of accelerating consequences provided for the completion of problems. In this case, teacher presence was an effective consequence for

Bob. Precise scheduling of consequences, systematic application of behavioral modification techniques, and environmental manipulation have combined to bring Bob's behavior under better control. The goal with Bob is to modify his behavior to the extent that it can be maintained by the environmental consequences present in regular classes; when he reaches that stage he will return to a regular class placement.

A statement of caution is certainly indicated at this juncture. Teacher's presence and verbal praise served as accelerating consequences for Bob. Teachers who work with such youngsters know that praise is not effective in all cases. Levin and Simmons (1962a, 1962b) demonstrated that praise was actually aversive for some emotionally disturbed children; it did not serve as an accelerating consequence. When given verbal praise for responses, the frequency of responding decreased rapidly and dramatically. Of course, using praise as an accelerating consequence is a goal; teachers must attempt to modify children's behavior so that it will come under the control of normal social consequences.

The best planned classrooms for children with behavior problems experience episodes when children become obstreperous. On occasion, these episodes may reach proportions which necessitate physical restraint. Unit staff have demonstrated that an effective technique for decreasing this type of behavior is to provide time out contingent upon the emission of this behavior. Time out is simply removing a child from a situation in which he has been receiving accelerating consequences for appropriate behavior. The child is placed in a small room next to the classroom until the deviant behavior subsides. When this occurs, the child may leave the time out area and return to the classrooms. However, the technique of time out is effective only when the classroom provides so many accelerating consequences for the child that he would rather spend his time there than in the time out room.

Premack (1959) has added a relevant dimension to the task of formulating empirical behavior modification techniques. Stressing the importance of behavioral consequences, Premack stated the following principle:

Any response A will [accelerate] any other response B, if and only if the independent rate of A is greater than that of B (Premack, 1959, p. 220).

Briefly intepreted, the Premack principle simply states that any behavior is strengthened or accelerated when followed by behavior which occurs at a high frequency or rate. (Homme and de Baca, 1964).

This principle has been effectively utilized in one experimental study (Haring and Phillips, 1962) and is presently being demonstrated at the Unit. Once the teacher has observed any child for a period of time, she is able to list high frequency behaviors and low frequency behaviors; for one child, reading a paragraph may be low frequency behavior, but making a model airplane may be high frequency behavior. It becomes relatively easy for the teacher to plan a reading lesson immediately before the child builds the model. Building the model becomes the consequence for engaging in reading behavior.

Task assignments, such as in reading or arithmetic, are arranged on a ratio basis, while engaging in high frequency behavior is scheduled on an interval basis. For example, the child may have to complete a ratio of five problems before he can engage in five minutes of model building. The ratio of problems completed is gradually increased, but the time interval devoted to model building can remain relatively constant. It may be discerned that larger and larger ratios of work can be required until more time is spent on what was originally low frequency behavior than on high frequency behavior. In fact, a reversal is often noted; arithmetic or reading may become high frequency behavior because the successes accumulated in such activity may be self-maintaining. Expressed in another manner, the child has learned self-control.

The possibilities for utilization of these techniques in classrooms are practically limitless. Again, caution must be mentioned. What is high frequency behavior for one child may not be true for another. The teacher must discover this information for each individual and apply it correctly. Evaluation of application must be demonstrated by subsequent behavior modification; that is, did the child's responses closely approximate the responses necessary for the successful completion of a task or a specific behavioral movement? These procedures make it possible to refrain from making value judgments about the child. When a planned program does not bring about desired changes of behavior, the teacher revises or modifies the program, instead of saying that the child cannot learn because he is emotionally disturbed. Successful modification of deviant behavior depends upon the refined applications of these techniques. This approach negates the necessity of labeling behavior; and even more important, it avoids the possibility that a label can be used to explain behavior, such as stating that the reason a child cannot learn is because he is schizophrenic.

Discussion

Initial responses to the presentation of behavioral principles and behavioral modification techniques might be as follows: I use these procedures in my classroom everyday; they are not new at all. Homme and Tosti (1964) have the most adequate reply to this response.

> If it is not the lack of [consequences] which makes behavioral control difficult, one might reason, it must be the lack of knowledge of the principles of behavioral control. If one attempts to verify this, he will find that this, too, is incorrect. If given a test on the principles so far discussed, most people would score very high. It is not a lack of [consequences] or a lack of knowledge about how to use them. The difficulty can be primarily traced to a failure to *systematically* apply what is known. It is not only that [behavior] principles are not systematically applied, they are, if applied at all, only sporadically applied. (Homme and Tosti, 1964, p. 4).

This quote and the prior cautions concerning applications of behavioral modification techniques are vitally important. It is only through correct, efficient application that children's behavior can be changed to the extent that they can subsequently contribute to the real world in which they live.

There are advantages inherent in using behavioral modification techniques in classroom situations. Teachers have traditionally been assigned to change or modify the behavior of children entrusted to them for several hours a day. Causes of deviant behavior, while important for some disciplines, are not of primary concern for educators. Educators must work with exhibited, overt behavior, and not with general, dynamic causes of that behavior. Behavioral responses can be measured and analyzed quantitatively. Precise, observable measurements are directly related to the application of appropriate behavioral modification techniques. Behavior can be observed; postulating unobservable causes that attempt to explain behavior leaves educators with esoteric concepts which cannot be arranged or manipulated in classrooms designed to modify behavior.

Educators often express concern about motivating children. Motivation is often referred to as drive, need, and such other terms which imply that motivation is internally based. Perhaps a more practical explanation of motivation is in asking what consequences are available to control behavior. High rates of responding in problem-solving situations, such as in working arithmetic problems, because such responses have accelerating consequences, is in reality what many label motivation when they view occurrence of that behavior. When one states that a child is motivated, what is really being observed is a child who is responding under the control of environmental consequences.

Behavioral modification techniques may possibly provide precise aids which the teacher can utilize in assisting children to learn the desirable consequences of organized, appropriate behavior. Children who exhibit deviant behavior cause pain to themselves and also to others who interact with them. Teachers must not only modify or remove specific deviant behaviors, but must also develop socially acceptable behavior patterns in children. Behavioral modification techniques provide teachers with systematic skills which can be utilized to modify children's behavior to the extent that when it is emitted in a variety of situations, it is consistently more appropriate than inappropriate.

While behavioral modification is not antagonistic to any professional concerned with such problems, an individual more concerned with unconscious behavioral determinants might claim that removing inappropriate behaviors is merely changing the surface signs of emotional disorders. This individual might also assert that the underlying conflicts which caused the behavior have not been resolved; therefore, the individual will merely substitute other, and possibly more, deviant behaviors. A review of cases where behavioral modification techniques have been applied to removal of deviant behaviors indicates that effort "directed at elimination of maladapted behavior ('symptoms') is successful and long lasting" (Grossberg, 1964, p. 83). Knowledge concerning behavioral principles "has clarified the nature of the relation between behavior and its consequences and has devised techniques which apply the methods of a natural science to its investigation" (Skinner, 1963, p. 515).

Information presented in this paper reviews behavioral modification techniques which have been practically and efficiently applied with individuals and groups of children; the results of such application have been reported. Whether these techniques achieve satisfactory results when compared to behavioral systems that have different orientations can only be known by observing and recording behavioral changes in children. The proof of which system is the most efficient for solving behavioral problems will be discerned only when such problems are solved.

Behavioral modification techniques provide systematic procedures and tools which teachers may implement to change or modify deviant behavior and encourage more acceptable, appropriate growth behavior. Skeptical, cautious acceptance and application of behavioral modification techniques are certainly indicated. Data reported from laboratory experiments and a few studies with small groups of children have demonstrated a high degree of reliability. However, these data must be validated in regular and special classroom situations. This validation may or may not be forthcoming; it has yet to be demonstrated.

References

Ayllon, T., and Haughton, E.: Control of the behavior of schizophrenic patients by food. *J Exp Anal Behav,* 5: 343-352, 1962.

Baer, D.: Laboratory control of thumbsucking by withdrawal and representation of reinforcement. *J Exp Anal Behav,* 5: 525-528, 1962.

Barrett, B.: Reduction in rate of multiple tics by free operant conditioning methods. *J Nerv Ment Dis, 135:* 187-195, 1962.

Bijou, S.: Application of behavioral principles to normal and deviant young children. Paper read at American Psychological Association, Los Angeles, September, 1964.

Bruner, J.: *The Process Of Education*. Cambridge, Harvard, 1963.

Eysenck, H.: *Behavior Therapy And The Neuroses*. New York, Pergamon, 1960.

Ferster, C.: Arithmetic behavior in chimpanzees. *Sci Amer, 210:* 98-106, 1964.

Grossberg, J.: Behavior therapy: a review. *Psychol Bull, 62:* 73-88, 1964.

Haring, N., and Phillips, L:. *Educating Emotionally Disturbed Children*. New York, McGraw, 1962.

Hart, B.; Allen, E.; Buell, J.; Harris, Florence R., and Wolf, M.: Effects of social reinforcement on operant crying. *J Exp Child Psychol, 1:* 145-153, 1964.

Hewett, F.: Teaching reading to an autistic boy through operant conditioning. *Reading Teacher, 17:* 613-618, 1964.

Holland, J., and Skinner, B.: *The Analysis Of Behavior*. New York, McGraw, 1961.

Homme, L., and de Baca, P.: Contingency management on the psychiatric ward. Unpublished manuscript. Behavioral Technology Department, Westinghouse Research Lab., Albuquerque, 1964.

Homme, L., and Tosti, D.: Some consideration of contingency management and motivation. Unpublished manuscript. Behavioral Technology Department, Westinghouse Research Lab., Albuquerque, 1964.

Levin, G., and Simmons, J.: Response to praise by emotionally disturbed boys. *Psychol Rep, 11:* 10 (a), 1962.

Levin, G., and Simmons, J.: Response to food and praise by emotionally disturbed boys. *Psychol Rep, 11:* 539-546 (b), 1962.

Lindsley, O.: Direct measurement and prothesis of retarded behavior. *J Education, 147:* 62-81, 1964.

Michael, J.: Relevance of animal research. In R. Schiefelbusch and J. Smith (Eds.): *Research In Speech And Hearing For Mentally Retarded Children*. Conference report, Bureau of Child Research, U. of Kansas, 1963.

Nurnberger, J.; Ferster, C., and Brady, J.: *An Introduction To The Science Of Human Behavior*. New York, Appleton, 1963.

Premack, D.: Toward empirical behavior laws: I. positive reinforcement. *Psychol Rev, 66:* 219-233, 1959.

Skinner, B.: Operant behavior. *Amer Psychol, 18:* 503-515, 1963.

Staats, A.; Minke, K.; Finley, J.; Wolf, M., and Brooks, L.: A reinforcer system and experimental procedure for the laboratory study of reading acquisition. *Child Develop, 35:* 209-231, 1964.

Zimmerman, E., and Zimmerman, J.: The alteration of behavior in a special classroom situation. *J Exp Anal Behav, 5:* 59-60, 1962.

Chapter 29

Behavior Modification Of An Adjustment Class:
A Token Reinforcement Program

DANIEL K. O'LEARY AND WESLEY C. BECKER

P RAISE, teacher attention, stars, and grades provide adequate incentive for most pupils to behave in a socially approved way. However, for some students, notably school dropouts, aggressive children, and some retarded children, these methods are relatively ineffective. Where the usual methods of social approval have failed, token reinforcement systems have proven effective (Birnbrauer, Bijou, Wolf, and Kidder, 1965; Birnbrauer and Lawler, 1964; Birnbrauer, Wolf, Kidder, and Tague, 1965; Quay, Werry, McQueen, and Sprague, 1966). Token reinforcers are tangible objects or symbols which attain reinforcing power by being exchanged for a variety of other objects such as candy and trinkets which are back-up reinforcers. Tokens acquire generalized reinforcing properties when they are paired with many different reinforcers. The generalized reinforcer is especially useful since it is effective regardless of the momentary condition of the organism.

For the children in this study, generalized reinforcers such as verbal responses ("That's right" or "Good!") and token reinforcers such as grades had not maintained appropriate behavior. In fact, their teacher noted that prior to the introduction of the token system, being called "bad" increased the children's inappropriate behavior. "They had the attitude that it was smart to be called bad. . . . When I tried to compliment them or tell them

Reprinted from *Exceptional Children*, Vol. 33 (1967), pp. 637-642. By permission of the authors and publisher.

that they had done something well, they would look around the room and make faces at each other." It is a moot question whether the poor academic performance of these children was caused by their disruptive social behavior or vice versa. It was obvious, however, that the disruptive behaviors had to be eliminated before an academic program could proceed.

Although classroom token reinforcement programs have proved effective in modifying behavior, the pupil teacher ratio has usually been small. In the study by Birnbrauer, Wolf, et al. (1965), a classroom of seventeen retarded pupils had four teachers in the classroom at all times. Quay (1966) had one teacher in a behavior modification classroom of five children. One purpose of this project was to devise a token reinforcement program which could be used by one teacher in an average classroom; a second purpose was to see if a token system could be withdrawn gradually without an increase in disruptive behavior by transferring control to teacher attention, praise, and grades, with less frequent exchange of back-up reinforcers.

Subjects

The subjects for this study were 17 nine-year-old children described as emotionally disturbed. They had I.Q. scores (Kuhlmann-Anderson) ranging from 80 to 107. They had been placed in the adjustment class primarily because they exhibited undesirable classroom behaviors such as temper tantrums, crying, uncontrolled laughter, and fighting. The children were in the classroom throughout the day with the exception of some remedial speech and reading work. Although the token reinforcement system was in effect for the whole class, the study focused on the eight most disruptive children.

Method

The children's deviant behaviors were observed by two students in the classroom from 12:30 to 2:10 three days a week. A third student made reliability checks two days a week. Among the behaviors recorded as deviant were the following: pushing, answering without raising one's hand, chewing gum, eating, name calling, making disruptive noise, and talking. Each student observed four children in random order for twenty-two minutes each session. Observations were made on a 20 second observe/10 second record basis. Deviant behaviors were recorded on observation sheets. During the observations, the children had three structured activities: listening to records or stories, arithmetic, and group reading. During these activities, instruction was directed to the whole class, and the children were expected to be quiet and in their seats.

Base Period

The teacher was asked to handle the children as she normally did. To obtain data which reflected the frequency of deviant pupil behavior under usual classroom procedures, a base period was used. The observers were in the classroom for three weeks before any baseline data were recorded. At first the children walked up to the observers and tried to initiate conversation with them. As the observers consistently ignored the children, the children's approach behaviors diminished. Thus, it is likely that initial show-off behavior was reduced before baseline measures were obtained.

The average interobserver reliability for individual children during the four-week base period, calculated on the basis of exact agreement for time interval and category of behavior, ranged from 75 to 100 percent agreement (Table I). A perfect

TABLE I

AVERAGE INTEROBSERVER RELIABILITIES DURING BASE
AND TOKEN REINFORCEMENT PERIODS

	Base Period		Token Reinforcement Period	
Subject	Percentage of Perfect Agreement	Number of Reliability Checks	Percentage of Perfect Agreement	Number of Reliability Checks
1	85	3	88	9
2	82	2	94	9
3	92	3	96	9
4	100	1	93	5
5	77	3	87	9
6	75	4	87	9
7	80	4	80	8
8	75	3	88	8

agreement was scored if both observers recorded the same behavior within a twenty-second interval. The reliabilities were
calculated by dividing the number of perfect agreements by the
number of different responses observed. The percentage of each
child's deviant behavior for any one day was calculated by
dividing the number of intervals in which one or more deviant
behaviors occurred by the number of observed intervals for that
day. As can be seen from Figure 1, there was a fairly stable base
rate of deviant behavior with a slight increasing trend.

FIGURE 1
Average Percentages of Deviant Behavior
during the Base and Token Periods

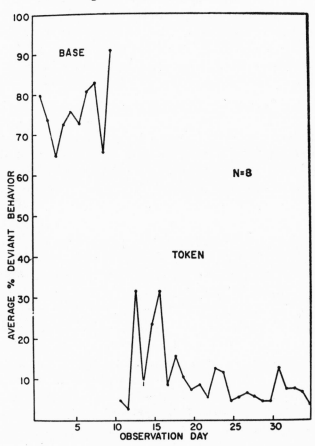

Token Reinforcement Period

On the first day of the token period the experimenter placed the following instructions on the blackboard: In Seat, Face Front, Raise Hand, Working, Pay Attention, and Desk Clear. The experimenter then explained the token procedure to the children. The tokens were ratings placed in small booklets on each child's desk. The children were told that they would receive ratings from 1 to 10 and that the ratings would reflect the extent to which they followed the instructions. The points or ratings could be exchanged for a variety of back-up reinforcers. The reinforcers consisted of small prizes ranging in value from one to twenty-nine cents, such as candy, pennants, comics, perfume, and kites. The total cost of the reinforcers used during the two months was $80.76. All the pupils received reinforcers in the same manner during class, but individual preferences were considered by providing a variety of items, thus maximizing the probability that at least one of the items would be a reinforcer for a given child at a given time.

The experimenter repeated the instructions at the beginning of the token period each day for one week and rated the children to provide a norm for the teacher. It was the teacher, however, who placed the ratings in the children's booklets during the short pause at the end of a lesson period. The ratings reflected the extent to which the child exhibited the appropriate behaviors listed on the blackboard. Where possible, these ratings also reflected the accuracy of the child's arithmetic work.

The number of ratings made each day was gradually decreased from five to three, and the number of points required to obtain a prize gradually increased. For the first three days, the tokens were exchanged for reinforcers at the end of the token period. For the next four days, points were accumulated for two days and exchanged at the end of the token period on the second day. Then, for the next fifteen days, a three day delay between token and reinforcers was used. Four day delays were employed for the remaining twenty-four school days. During the three and four day delay periods, tokens were exchanged for reinforcers at the end of the school day. By requiring more appropriate behavior to receive a prize and increasing the delay of reinforcement it was hoped that transfer of control from the token reinforcers to the more traditional methods of teacher praise and attention would occur.

After the first week, the teacher made the ratings and executed the token system without aid. Procedures were never discussed when the children were present.

The children also received group points based on total class behavior, and these points could be exchanged for popsicles at the end of each week. The group points ranged from 1 to 10 and reflected the extent to which the children were quiet during the time the ratings were placed in the booklets. The number of group ratings made each day were gradually decreased from five to three as were the individual ratings. However, since the children were usually very quiet, the number of points required to obtain a popsicle was not increased. The points were accumulated on a thermometer chart on the blackboard, and the children received popsicles on seven of the eight possible occasions.

At first the teacher was reluctant to accept the token procedure because of the time the ratings might take. However, the ratings took at most three minutes. As the teacher noted, "The class is very quiet and usually I give them a story to read from the board while I give the ratings. One model student acts as the teacher and he calls on the students who are well-behaved to read. . . . This is one of the better parts of the day. It gave me a chance to go around and say something to each child as I gave him his rating. . . ."

The rating procedure was especially effective because the teacher reinforced each child for approximations to the desired final response. Instead of demanding perfection from the start, the teacher reinforced evidence of progress.

In addition to the token procedure, the teacher was instructed to make comments, when appropriate, such as: "Pat, I like the way you are working. That will help your rating." "I am glad to see everyone turned around in their seats. That will help all of you get the prize you want." "Good, Gerald. I like the way you raised your hand to ask a question."

A technique used by the teacher to extinguish the deviant behavior of one child was to ignore him, while at the same time reinforcing the appropriate behavior of another child. This enabled the teacher to refrain from using social censure and to rely almost solely on positive reinforcement techniques, as she had been instructed.

The investigators also were prepared to use time out from positive reinforcement (Wolf, Risley, and Mees, 1964) to deal with those behaviors which were especially disruptive. The time out procedure involves isolating the child for deviant behavior for a specified period of time. This procedure was not used, however, since the frequency of the disruptive behavior was very low at the end of the year.

The average interobserver reliability for individual children during the token period ranged from 80 to 96 percent. As indicated in Table I, the reliabilities were recorded separately for the base and token periods because reliabilities were higher during the token period when the frequency of deviant behavior was low.

Results

As can be seen from Figure 1, the average percentage of deviant behavior at the end of the year was very low. The daily mean of deviant behavior during the token procedure ranged from 3 to 32 percent, while the daily mean of deviant behavior during the base period ranged from 66 to 91 percent. The average of deviant behavior for all children during the base period was 76 percent as contrasted with 10 percent during the token procedure. As can be seen from the F ratio (Table II), the change from the base period to the token period was highly significant ($p < .001$). Using an omega squared, it was estimated that the treatment accounted for 96 percent of the variance of the observed deviant behavior.

TABLE II

ANALYSIS OF VARIANCE ON DEVIANT BEHAVIOR SCORES (N=8)

Source	df	MS	F
Between Subjects	7	72.86	
Within Subjects	8	2203.00	
Treatment	1	17424.00	609.87*
Residual	7	28.57	

* $p < .001$

An examination of the individual records (Figure 2) shows the small degree of individual variation and differences in deviant behavior from the base to the token period. Although subjects 2 and 7 exhibited more deviant behavior than others during the token period, the percentage of deviant behavior was obviously less than during the base period. The percentage of deviant behavior declined for all pupils from the base to the token period.

FIGURE 2

Percentages of Deviant Behavior for Individual
Children during Base and Token Periods

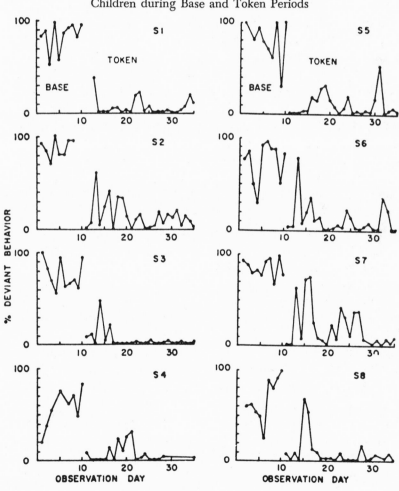

Discussion

At least two variables in addition to the token procedure and social reinforcement possibly contributed to the change in the children's behavior. First, during the baseline and token phases of this demonstration, the teacher was enrolled in a psychology class which emphasized operant and social learning principles. The influence of this class cannot be assessed, although the dramatic and abrupt change from the base to the token phase of the demonstration makes it seem highly implausible that the psychology class was the major variable accounting for the change. However, in a replication of this study now being planned, the teacher will receive only a short introduction to the basic principles and subsequent instruction by the experimenter throughout the procedure.

Secondly, the reduction in deviant behavior enabled the teacher to spend more time giving children individual attention during the token phase of the experiment. She had time to correct and return the children's work promptly, thus giving them immediate feedback. She was also able to use teaching materials not previously used. Some children who had not completed a paper for two years repeatedly received perfect scores. The immediate feedback and new materials probably contributed to the maintenance of appropriate behavior.

An experiment within the Skinnerian paradigm involves the establishment of a stable base rate of behavior; next, environmental contingencies are applied and the maladaptive behavior is reduced. The contingencies are then withdrawn and there is a return to base conditions. Finally, the environmental contingencies are again instituted and the maladaptive behavior decreased. This procedure of operant decrease, increase, and finally decrease of maladaptive behavior in association with specific environmental conditions demonstrates the degree of stimulus control obtained by the technique.

A return to base conditions early in the treatment period of this study was not carried out because of a concern that the enthusiasm and cooperation generated by the program throughout the school system might be severely reduced. There is little doubt that a return to base conditions following three or four weeks of the token procedure would have resulted in an increase in disruptive behavior. When a reversal was used by Birnbrauer, Wolf, *et al.* (1965), a number of children showed a decline in the amount of studying and an increase in disruptive behavior. As an alternative, it was planned to return gradually to baseline conditions during the following fall, but radical changes in pupil population prevented this reversal.

Without a reversal or a return to baseline conditions it cannot be stated that the token system and not other factors, such as the changes that ordinarily occur during the school year, accounted for the observed reduction of deviant behavior. To demonstrate clearly the crucial significance of the token procedure itself, a systematic replication with different children and a different teacher is planned. As Sidman (1960) noted, "An investigator may, on the basis of experience, have great confidence in the adequacy of his methodology, but other experimenters cannot be expected to share his confidence without convincing evidence (p. 75)."

Two interesting implications of this study are the effects of delay of reinforcement and generalization. The use of tokens provides a procedure which is intermediate between immediate and delayed tangible reinforcement. In Birnbrauer, Wolf, *et al.*'s (1965) class of severely retarded children this delay was extended from a few seconds to over an hour. Some educable children studied for many days for checkmarks only and, presumably, the knowledge that they were approaching a goal. All the children in the present study worked for four days without receiving a back-up reinforcer. In addition, more than one child made the comment toward the end of school that next year they would be old enough to behave and work well without the prizes.

Anecdotal records indicate that after the token procedure was put into effect, the children behaved better during the morning session, music, and library periods. These reports suggest that a transfer to normal classroom control using social reinforcement and grades would not be very difficult. Also, the gang behavior of frowning upon "doing well" disappeared. Some children even helped enforce the token system by going to the blackboard just before class began and reading the instructions to the class.

References

Birnbrauer, J. S.; Bijou, S. W.; Wolf, M. M., and Kidder, J. D.: Programmed instruction in the classroom. In L. P. Ullman and L. Krasner (Eds.): Case Studies In Behavior Modification. New York, Holt, 1965, pp. 358-363.

Birnbrauer, J. S., and Lawler, Julia: Token reinforcement for learning. Ment Retard, 2: 275-279, 1964.

Birnbrauer, J. S.; Wolf, M. M.; Kidder, J. D., and Tague, Cecilia E.: Classroom behavior of retarded pupils with token reinforcement. J Exp Child Psychol, 2: 219-235, 1965.

Quay, H. C.; Werry, J. S.; McQueen, Marjorie, and Sprague, R. L.: Remediation of the conduct problem child in the special class setting. Exceptional Child, 32: 509-515, 1966.

Sidman, M.: Tactics Of Scientific Research. New York, Basic Books, 1960.

Wolf, M. M.; Risley, T. R., and Mees, H. L.: Application of operant conditioning procedures to the behavioral problems of an autistic child. Behav Res Ther, 1: 305-312, 1964.

Chapter 30

Remediation Of The Conduct Problem Child
In The Special Class Setting

HERBERT C. QUAY, JOHN S. WERRY, MARJORIE McQUEEN,
AND ROBERT L. SPRAGUE

A SPECIAL CLASS program within the public school system for children with behavior problems should have two basic guidelines. First, direction should be obtained from knowledge of the nature of behavior disorders in children and the methods whereby such disorders can best be remediated. Second, the program should be guided by knowledge of the nature of the public schools as a setting for such remediational attempts. The experimental class described in this paper is a cooperative effort of the Urbana public schools and the University of Illinois Children's Research Center.

Nature Of Children's Behavior Disorders

On the basis of present evidence, it appears that children's behavior disorders can be viewed most profitably, both in diagnosis and remediation, in terms of the problem behavior itself, rather than in terms of deviant personality types or disease entities. It is further assumed that it is most useful to attempt to conceive of problem behavior in terms of external observable events rather than internalized hypothetical constructs like the unconscious, the ego, and so on, even though such concepts may

This research was supported by grant MH-07346 from the National Institutes of Health, U.S. Department of Health, Education, and Welfare. Reprinted from *Exceptional Children*, Vol. 32 (1966), pp. 509-515. By permission of the authors and publisher.

serve heuristic functions. The goal in treatment is the elimination of the problem behaviors, and when this is achieved, the child is viewed as no longer exhibiting any disorder. Thus, the authors' philosophy can be described as pragmatic and practical.

As regards etiology, the problem behavior is seen to be the end product of an interaction between environmental experiences and predispositional factors, such as heredity and status of the central nervous system. This interactional process is called learning, and it is this process which is of primary concern to the authors. Predispositional factors are seen as limiting the ultimate complexity of possible behaviors, increasing the probability of emission of certain classes of behavior, and influencing the rate at which learning may occur. The environment, through discriminative stimuli and through response-reinforcement contingencies, is seen as the major influence determining the precise behavior repertoire of an individual child. Thus the child with a cerebral dysfunction might be prone to the excessive emission of motor responses (hyperactivity), but it would be the environment which, through patterns of reinfocement, would determine the precise nature of the behaviors observed in the child and would serve to increase or decrease their frequency in various situations.

Even though the primary focus of attention is on discrete, observable problem behaviors of the individual child or is, in short, ideographic, the nomothetic approach is nevertheless assumed to be of definite, though limited, value. A wide range of discrete problem behaviors has been shown by factor analytic techniques (Peterson, 1961; Quay and Quay, 1965; Quay, Morse, and Cutler, 1966) to represent four underlying dimensions of behavior along which all children will vary. The child who comes to be known clinically as emotionally disturbed is one whose behavior has come to be extreme on one or more of the dimensions. Certain specific problem behaviors cluster along the different dimensions and have thus given rise to descriptive labels for each dimension. Though different studies have used different terminology in labeling the dimensions, the constituent specific behaviors are essentially similar.

One such dimensional cluster of behaviors is called unsocialized aggression, psychopathy, or conduct disorder and is composed of such behaviors as aggression, overactivity, defiance, irresponsibility, and other such disrupting behaviors. The neurotic or affective dimension includes such behaviors as self-consciousness, chronic fearfulness, shyness, and sadness. The immaturity-inadequacy dimension contains such behaviors as daydreaming, lethargy, suggestibility, and laziness. The dimension called socialized delinquency is made up of behaviors most closely associated with the young delinquent of the urban, deteriorated area where deviant, rather than deficient, socialization is characteristic.

Dimensional assessment, as opposed to individual problem or target symptom assessment, has two main functions: First, because there is some normative data for a variety of populations (Peterson, 1961; Quay, 1964; Quay and Quay, 1965), it is possible to quantify the degree to which an individual child departs from various population means on the dimensions and thus to estimate the degree of maladjustment. This information is, of course, helpful in arriving at decisions as to whether or not a child should be placed in a special class. Second, the dimensional profile of a given child has some general predictive value for response to particular treatment approaches and for prognosis which, though rather limited at the moment, is likely to increase with further validation studies.

Though theoretically the number of individual dimensional profiles is practically unlimited, it is convenient to delineate certain typologies of children who have extreme loadings on one or another of the dimensions. Thus, one may speak of the aggressive, the neurotic, and the immature-inadequate child and the socialized delinquent. Such specifications, however, do not preclude children of mixed categories, nor do they carry any implications of etiological specificity.

While there is no denying the importance of programs for the neurotic, immature, and socialized delinquent child, the special class described in this paper is comprised of children who manifest behavior mainly associated with high loadings on the unsocialized aggressive dimension. This is partly through choice, but also partly because this is the type of child who is most obviously troublesome in the usual public school setting and therefore most likely to be referred to a special class. This is also the child who seems most predisposed to an entire life of maladaptive behavior (Robins and O'Neal, 1958; O'Neal and Robins, 1958; Morris, Escoll, and Wexler, 1956) and who is thus particularly deserving of energetic, secondary, preventive efforts.

General Concepts Of Remediation

Since the proper focus of attention in remediation is considered to be on the maladaptive behaviors which, as discussed above, are seen as learned responses, it follows that the key to remediation is seen in the application of both the basic principles of learning theory and the interaction of selected techniques with the behavioral characteristics of the child (Quay, 1963; Quay, in press). The aim is to bring about the elimination (extinction) of inappropriate behaviors, or the substitution of incompatible but adaptive alternative behaviors (counterconditioning), or the acquisition of personally and socially productive responses where none presently obtains (conditioning).

There is now considerable evidence from both laboratory studies (Bandura and Walters, 1963) and from field experiments (Zimmerman and Zimmerman, 1962; Azrin and Lindsley, 1956; Patterson, Jones, Whittier, and Wright, 1965) that maladaptive behavior can be modified in a variety of situations by the direct manipulation of response-reinforcement contingencies (that is, the *immediate* consequences of the behavior in terms of reward or punishment).

It is important that the nature of reinforcement be clearly understood. Positive reinforcement is any definable environmental event consequent upon or coincident with the termination of a response which can be *demonstrated* to increase the probability of that particular behavior. In general, reinforcement is according to the pleasure principle—the obtaining of reward and the avoiding or termination of pain. Punishment which has two forms (the application of a noxious or aversive stimulus and the withdrawal of reward or pleasure) also has powerful effects upon responses which immediately precede it, in general, the opposite to that of reinforcement.

There are two important principles in the use of reward and punishment in behavior modification. The first is that the reinforcement must follow immediately upon the behavior under study. This principle of immediate contingency is probably one of the most crucial factors in behavior modification and yet probably one of the least appreciated among those working with children. The second important principle is that in the complex human organism, reward and punishment may be at times quite idiosyncratic, and it may require considerable clinical skill to devise therapeutic programs which are meaningful to the child concerned.

In dealing with the aggressive outbursts so characteristic of conduct problem children who make up the experimental class under discussion here, it is the aim of all concerned to see that the environmental responses to these outbursts are not reinforcing or rewarding to the child. This does not mean that the child must be necessarily punished for his aggressiveness, but rather that a conscientious search must be made for less obvious forms of reinforcement which may be maintaining his aggressive behavior in order that they may be eliminated. Very often this hidden reinforcement will prove to be attention (even though the content of the attention is disapproving) from adults or peers. All too frequently, programs which are designed to remediate maladaptive behavior in children can be seen in practice to be rewarding that very behavior, particularly where the emphasis is on discussions relative to the "meaning" and the antecedent history of the problem behavior, rather than its here and now characteristics.

With the aggressive child, there is usually little difficulty in getting him to emit this maladaptive behavior. As Bandura and Walters (1963) have pointed out, it is more efficient to attempt to counter condition maladaptive behavior or replace it simultaneously with incompatible, adaptive alternatives than attempt merely to extinguish it without replacement. It is therefore important to find methods of facilitating the emission in the child of these adaptive alternatives which can then be promptly rewarded and thus rendered more probable.

The most obvious approach to this problem is to cue the child in through verbal instruction. The second technique is the use of modeling or imitation in which the child can observe appropriate models emitting the desired behaviors and preferably being subsequently rewarded for his efforts. The third principle is that of successive approximation whereby one rewards types of behavior which, while well below the desired standard, nevertheless are within easy reach of the child under treatment. When these initial adaptive behaviors have been well learned, the goal is then raised until the socially acceptable norm is achieved.

Special Characteristics Of The Conduct Disorder Child

In addition to the general remediational principles, there are certain characteristics of the unsocialized aggressive child which carry special implications for retraining in the special class setting. Aggressive behavior, using the term in its broadest sense, is obvious and therefore carries a high potential for modeling. Thus, it seems important as a practical point to increase the size of the class slowly to insure that the teacher can maintain control of the group situation. In this way, examples of acceptable behaviors are available for modeling by the incoming child as well as the maladaptive aggressive behaviors.

There is also research (Johns and Quay, 1962; Levin and Simmons, 1962) to suggest that social reinforcers, such as praise and other verbalizations, are relatively weaker in effect in individuals with conduct disorders. It therefore appears that in the early stages of retraining the aggressive, unsocialized child, it may be necessary to utilize reinforcers of a fairly concrete nature, such as candy, trinkets, and toys. However, the dispensing of more primary rewards ought to be paired deliberately with social reinforcers, such as praise and approving gestures, to facilitate the development of responsivity to more usual reinforcers. In short, then, the use of concrete reinforcers is not seen as an attempt to subvert the moral fiber of the American child, but rather as the first halting step on a long and difficult path of rehabilitating a child who is both rejecting of and rejected by normal society.

Another problem particularly characteristic of the conduct disorder child is the high probability that behavioral maladjustment is accompanied by significant academic retardation. This is not surprising since these children have histories of poor school attendance, frequent ejection from class, and rejection by their teachers; and they very often exhibit hyperactivity, distractability, short attention span, and specific cognitive deficits (Clements and Peters, 1962).

This academic retardation suggests that, at least in the initial stages, it is probably necessary and desirable to tailor the academic program individually to the requirements of each child (Haring and Phillips, 1962). Further, though it may seem somewhat heretical to so state, there seems no good reason that the learning of academic skills should be qualitatively different from the learning of socially acceptable behavior. Hence, the principles of remediation outlined above, principally maximizing the probability of successful behavior and the immediate reinforcement of desired or successful behavior utilizing primary or concrete reinforcers, should be applied, if necessary, to improving academic skills.

The authors have been impressed in their own class by the very poor attention and hyperactivity of the pupils as a serious impediment not only behaviorally, but also academically. Before they can be taught anything, whether it be social or academic, it is necessary to obtain their attention. In general, this problem can be minimized through individual tuition and individually programed courses of instruction. If, however, the ultimate goal of the special class, namely, to rehabilitate the child into the normal classroom (vide infra), is kept in view, there is merit in attempting systematically to train the children in attending to the teacher in group instructional situations.

Examples of Empirical Attempts To Deal With Specific Problems

Training Visual Orientation To Teacher In Group Setting

In an attempt to increase the attending behavior of the pupils in the experimental class, the authors devised a situation in which reinforcement could be silently and unobtrusively delivered to an individual child if he had kept his eyes, as instructed, on the teacher during that period. Each child was observed serially for a ten-second interval for a total of fifteen such intervals (total for the class of five pupils = 75). Observation was carried out at the same time each day and during the same activity (listening to a story). Prior to the instituting of reinforcement, observation was carried out over a period of twelve days to obtain a baseline. This showed that between and within subject variation was large and that the mean for the group was low at 6.18 of a possible total of 15 (41 percent success).

After the baseline period, a box containing a light which could be flashed on by the experimenter was placed on each child's desk. The children were told that if they were paying attention to the teacher, their light would go on from time to time and they would receive one piece of candy for each light flash at the end of the story. From a technical point of view, the reinforcement of the orienting behavior is on a fixed ratio schedule of 1 : 5. This would be predicted to result in greater resistance of the behavior to extinction after acquisition, but to require a much larger number of learning trials for acquisition. It is to be hoped that the advantage of the experimenter's being able to condition five (or more) children at once would outweigh the disadvantage of more trials resulting from the intermittent reinforcement schedule. Results accruing from fifty-two days' reinforcement suggest that this method is, indeed, having some effect. The group mean for the entire reinforcement period is 9.09; for the last twenty days of reinforcement, it is 11.43.

Individualized Remediation Of Retardation In Basic Academic Skills

The fact that most special classes for the emotionally disturbed necessarily contain children at various levels of academic achievement presents serious problems in group instruction. One way of mitigating this problem somewhat is to provide some individual instruction for those children so deficient in basic academic skills as to limit their participation in various phases of the group instruction. This has been done primarily with reading, using programed instructional methods coupled with immediate concrete reinforcement.

In one instance, a six-year-old child of average ability acquired the alphabet in approximately 12 ten-minute sessions spread over about two weeks. In the course of this procedure, it was also possible to shift from primary reinforcers (candy), delivered immediately and on a continuous or one-to-one basis, to a symbolic reward (poker chips) to be traded for a concrete reward (candy) at a later time (lunch hour) on a ratio of 4 correct responses for 1 reward. Thus, at the same time that reading was being taught, the child was also being taught (a) to work for symbolic rewards, (b) to delay gratification, and (c) to work on an intermittent reinforcement schedule—three characteristics which must be developed if the emotionally disturbed child is to participate ultimately in a regular school program.

Teaching Social Skills

Rejection by the peer group, so common of the child in the special class, seems in some instances due to the failure of the emotionally disturbed child to acquire the basic social skills necessary for successful peer interaction. Its is hard to see how such a rejected child can acquire these skills on his own or from the rejecting peer group, and it seems that some kind of active instruction must be inaugurated. Such a process of education presupposes some knowledge of the technology of peer interaction, such as acceptable verbalizations and recreational activities, and of the learning process.

To this end, a recreational specialist has been working with one child, teaching him how to approach the children, how to greet them, and how to initiate and engage in acceptable activity. The adult model first demonstrates the behavior which the child then imitates. If the subject does so successfully, he is then reinforced with a token which he may subsequently exchange for candy. In the next stage of instruction, the adult plays the role of a second child and, when in this simulated interaction the subject emits socially appropriate behavior, he is reinforced or corrected as necessary.

In the third stage another child participates in the practice sessions who is not in the special class and who has been selected for his high probability of reinforcing, rather than rejecting, the subject's overtures. This still takes place under the surveillance and reinforcement of the experimenter. The fourth stage involves the subject's finding himself a playmate on the playground while he is still under adult supervision, which lasts until he has acquired sufficient skill to ensure some minimal acceptance by the peer group. Hopefully then, peer group reinforcement will serve to maintain and improve the socially adaptive behaviors, permitting the withdrawal of the experimenter.

Remediation Of Behavior Disorders In Public School Setting

Group Versus Individual Techniques

The economics of public schools obviously require the development of techniques that will allow children to be handled in a group situation by as few adults as possible. Most of the techniques of behavioral remediation have been developed for use on an individual basis and its seems crucial at this stage to attempt to extend these techniques to group situations. This is a problem to which the authors are most seriously addressing themselves, since even if the techniques of behavior remediation should prove to be very highly effective when applied on an individual basis, they are nevertheless likely to remain economically unfeasible, unless they can be adapted for use in a group setting such as the classroom.

Role Of The Mental Health Professional

It seems clear that because of their scarcity and their high costs, mental health professionals such as psychiatrists, psychologists, and social workers should give careful attention to defining their roles so as to maximize their usefulness in special settings. Obviously, they will have to continue to make the behavioral diagnoses that are so vital for the initial placement and the planning of therapeutic programs. However, it seems essential that such therapeutic recommendations be couched in such terms that they can be readily implemented by the teacher and be of demonstrable effectiveness.

The authors consider that the present effort by clinicians to help teachers understand their pupils is less likely to be success-ful than the problem-oriented approach in which attention is focused on overt problem behavior as exhibited in the classroom, rather than on its remote historical antecedents. Clinicians should provide the teacher with information on how to elicit adaptive behaviors, which reinforcers are most likely to promote these adaptive behaviors and extinguish the problem behaviors, how to schedule these reinforcers in terms of immediacy and con-sistency during the course of remediation, and how to plot a course of priorities to program the acquisition of social and aca-demic skills for a given child.

Treatment Outside The Classroom

If one were to arrange a hierarchy of treatments for children according to their social acceptance in the present thinking of many mental health professionals, it likely that individual psy-chotherapy would head the list and the special class would be found near the bottom. Such an attitude, of course, weights pro-fessional training much more highly than the length of time to which the child is exposed to the particular treatment. It fails to take into account the unique possibilities of the special class, and it could be argued that a more realistic view, especially in light of the scarcity and expense of mental health professionals, would be a complete reversal of the therapeutic hierarchy.

The child has three quantitatively major learning situations: the family, the peer group, and the school. It is obvious, there-fore, that the ideal therapeutic program would attempt to op-erate in these three areas, but this is something which will be only rarely attained. Although some kind of parental counseling aimed at generalizing the adaptive behavior outside the class-room situation is highly desirable, it seems nevertheless apparent that society would be derelict if it neglected these unique op-portunities to remediate problem behavior in children, even where parental counseling is either impracticable because of a shortage in professionals or is rejected by the parents.

Hence, concurrent individual psychotherapy or parental counseling should not be prerequisite for placement in the spe-cial class setting unless the number of candidates greatly exceeds the facilities available. Even in this latter case, it is possible to argue that the children who cannot obtain other kinds of therapy should actually receive priority for placement in the special class.

Goal Of The Special Class

While it is probably unrealistic in the case of every child, the goal of the special class should be to rehabilitate its pupils into the regular class system. Partly as a result of legal restrictions, special classes tend to be better staffed and often better equipped than regular classes. This can easily lead to the development of what can be called "hot house" techniques and standards of behavior. This is probably both necessary and useful initially in shaping the child's behavior to approximate the norm; but real life procedures such as group, rather than individual, instruction and less tolerance for deviant behavior must ultimately be instituted, preferably by successive approximation. This is the principle of instituting rather than assuming generalization of behavior.

Role Of The Techniques Of The Special Class
In The Regular Class

A final but certainly no less important point is that techniques developed in the special class setting should ideally have some general applicability in the regular classroom. In the last analysis, the aim should be that of prevention, rather than that of remediation, of preventing children from becoming discordant enough in their behavior to warrant special class placement, rather than simply attempting to modify disturbing behavior once the situation has become intolerable. The special class should see itself not only as a treatment setting, but also as a laboratory in which techniques for teaching adaptive behavior in a group setting can be developed and then communicated to teachers in the regular class system, possibly through behavior remediation specialists drawn from the teaching profession itself or from special education officers.

References

Azrin, N. H., and Lindsley, O. R.: The reinforcement of cooperation between children. *J Abnorm Soc Psychol, 52:* 100-102, 1956.

Bandura, A., and Walters, R. L.: *Social Learning And Personality Development.* New York, Holt, 1963.

Clements, S. D., and Peters, J. E.: Minimal brain dysfunctions in the school age child. *Arch Gen Psychiat, 6:* 185-197, 1962.

Haring, N. G., and Phillips, E. L.: *Educating Emotionally Disturbed Children.* New York, McGraw, 1962.

Johns, J. H., and Quay, H. C.: The effect of social reward on verbal conditioning in psychopathic and neurotic military offenders. *J Consult Psychol, 26:* 217-220, 1962.

Levin, G. R., and Simmons, J. J.: Response to food and praise by emotionally disturbed boys. *Psychol Rep, 11:* 539-546, 1962.

Morris, H. H.; Escoll, P. J., and Wexler, R.: Aggressive behavior disorders of childhood: a follow up study. *Amer J Psychiat, 112:* 991-997, 1956.

O'Neal, Patricia, and Robins, L. N.: The relation of childhood behavior problems to adult psychiatric status: a 30 year follow up study of 150 subjects. *Amer J Psychiat, 114:* 961-969, 1958.

Patterson, G. R.; Jones, R.; Whittier, J., and Wright, Mary A.: A behavior modification technique for the hyperactive child. *Behav Res Ther, 2:* 217-226, 1965.

Peterson, D. R.: Behavior problems of middle childhood. *J Consult Psychol, 25:* 205-209, 1961.

Quay, H. C.: Some basic considerations in the education of emotionally disturbed children. *Exceptional Child, 30:* 27-31, 1963.

Quay, H. C.: Personality dimensions in delinquent males as inferred from the factor analysis of behavior ratings. *J Res Crime Delinquency, 1:* 33-37, 1964.

Quay, H. C.: Dimensions of problem behavior in children and their interactions with approaches to behavior modification. *Kansas Studies.* In press.

Quay, H. C.; Morse, W. C., and Cutler, R. L.: Personality patterns of pupils in special classes for the emotionally disturbed. *Exceptional Child, 32:* 297-301, 1966.

Quay, H. C., and Quay, Lorene C.: Behavior problems in early adolescence. *Child Develop, 36:* 215-220, 1965.

Robins, L. N., and O'Neal, Patricia.: Mortality, mobility and crime: problem children 30 years later. *Amer Sociol Rev, 23:* 162-171, 1958.

Zimmerman, Elaine H., and Zimmerman, J.: The alteration of behavior in a special classroom situation. *J Exp Anal Behav, 5:* 59-60, 1962.

Chapter 31

Attention Span: An Operant Conditioning Analysis

GARRY L. MARTIN AND RICHARD B. POWERS

Contemporary literature suggests that the concept of attention span refers to two different phenomena. Under "span of attention," English and English (1958) list (a) the number of distinct objects that can be perceived in a single momentary presentation; and (b) the length of time a person can attend to one thing. The first of these two definitions has historical precedent over the second. It relates to one of the oldest questions in the field of experimental psychology, namely, How many things can we attend to in a single instant of time?

The second definition, the more recent and frequent usage of the concept, is the one with which this paper is concerned. The length of time a person can attend to one thing was initially referred to as voluntary attention (James, 1890; Angell, 1904). More recently, the length of time a subject concentrated on a task has been referred to variously as interest span (Herring and Koch, 1930), sustained attention (Schacter, 1933), occupation interest (Bridges, 1927), perseveration (Cushing, 1929), or, most usually, as attention span (Cockrell, 1935; Bott, 1928; Van Alstyne, 1932; Gutteridge, 1935; Moyer and von Haller Gilmer, 1955).

With respect to special populations, it was suggested as early as 1904 that, "alienists and specialists in nervous disorders inform us that mental disease is commonly accompanied by disturbance in the power of attention" (Angell, 1904, p. 80). The

---

Reprinted from *Exceptional Children*, Vol. 33 (1967), pp. 565-570. By permission of the authors and publisher.

concept of short attention span was suggested by Kuhlman (1904) as a way of accounting for the retardate's apparent difficulty in discrimination learning. Recently, Strauss and his associates (1947, 1955) have been influenced in stressing the difficulty of brain-injured children in attending to a task for any length of time, and references to the short attenion span of retardates are common in the contemporary literature (Blodgett and Warfield, 1959; Goldstein and Seigle, 1961; Cromwell, Baumeister, and Hawkins, 1963; Weber, 1964; Garton, 1964).

Although the attention span concept appears to be widely employed in psychological and educational literature on special populations, current usage of the term is not entirely consistent. Some of these inconsistencies will be discussed briefly in the following section.

Current Usage

The concept seems to be used currently in at least three major ways. First, empirical evidence indicates that "attention span" is task specific. Measurements with normal children have yielded values ranging from seconds to forty-five minutes (Moyer and von Haller Gilmer, 1955). Moyer and von Haller Gilmer concluded that to speak of the concept of a "mean attention span" for children was meaningless because its measure depended so much on selecting the right task for the right age child. They proposed the notion of attention span*s* to replace that of attention span. Their point is well taken and might profitably be applied to the concept of *a* short attention span for retardates. That is, it seems reasonable that attention span measures of retardates are also task and child specific, and not a characteristic of retardation per se.

Second, although several authors have talked as though short attention span, distractibility, and hyperactivity to different phenomena, differences among the behavioral referents of these concepts are often difficult to specify. For example, concerning the brain-injured child, Strauss and Kephart wrote

> He finds it impossible to engage in any activity in a concentrated fashion, but is always being led aside from the task at hand by stimuli which should remain extraneous but do not. . . . Under these conditions it would be expected that the individual would tend to

respond to a variety of extraneous stimuli and lose track of the task at hand. We would describe such behavior as "distractibility" (1955, p. 135).

In their report on research in activity level, Cromwell *et al.* (1963) stated

> Another paramount problem is that activity level, owing to its lack of clarity in definition, can be confused with other variables. For example, the subject with a short attention span who shifts quickly from one goal-directed activity to another may appear to the observer to have a higher rate of activity than a subject fixated at one task but exerting the same amount of activity (1963, p. 634).

In view of such statements, a reader might refer to a child who engages in a task for a brief period of time as having a short attention span, or being easily distractible, or showing superactivity. Yet the concepts are discussed as though they were distinct phenomena. For example, in their article on activity level, Cromwell *et al.* wrote

> According to their (Strauss' and his associates') conception of the brain-injured child, an environment of overstimulation should exaggerate the symptoms of distractible behavior, short attention span, and superactivity (1963, p. 641).

If these concepts do refer to different behavioral phenomena, the differences are not always obvious.

Third, attention span is sometimes discussed as though it were a faculty or process and the observed behaviors are considered as symptoms of the underlying short attention span. A consequence of this approach is the tendency to refer to short attention span as an absolute, unchanging characteristic of mental retardation. In some cases, a very short attention span is simply cited as a characteristic of the mentally retarded with no elaboration offered (Weber, 1964). In other cases, it is used as a diagnostic device to distinguish categories of mental retardation (Blodgett and Warfield, 1959).

A major consequence of these usages of short attention span is that they tend to impede the education of the retarded. A "rigid attention span" can be easily invoked as a way of accounting for poor attending behavior. But paying attention is a prerequisite in all classroom situations. Thus, as others have observed (Lewis, Strauss, and Lehtinen, 1960), various educational activities are often not attempted with a particular retarded child simply because his short atention span is thought to interfere with the necessary task attendance.

An Operant Conditioning Analysis Of Attention Span

An operant conditioning analysis of attention span suggests an alternative view. This approach offers powerful tools which can be used to manipulate the length of time a child attends to a particular task. The most important single principle of operant conditioning is the empirical principle of reinforcement. The principle refers to the observation that there are certain environmental events (commonly called rewards) that we will work to produce. We influence others with these events when we reward any behavior that we wish to make more frequent. These rewarding events are more technically referred to as reinforcers. A reinforcer is defined as a stimulus, the presentation of which, following a response, increases the probability of future occurrence of that response. The common sense notion of reward is certainly not new. What is new is the precise specification of several variables that are crucial to the success of the reinforcement procedure.

The first crucial variable is the contingent relationship between the response and the reinforcer. The contingency is a logical if-then relationship, which is to be distinguished from a simple pleasant or rewarding situation in which a person might find himself. A pleasant situation typically doesn't require the person to do anything. The reinforcement procedure, however, requires the occurrence of some specified response prior to the presentation of a reinforcer. The second crucial variable is the immediacy of reinforcement. To be most effective, the reinforcer must follow the response without delay. A more extensive discussion of operant conditioning techniques may be found in Sidman (1962) and Michael (1964).

In this framework, the term "attention span" refers to nothing more than the behavioral events to which the name is attached.

These behavioral events are explained in terms of environmental variables in the presence of which the behavior occurs. This interpretation places emphasis upon behavior that interferes with attending to a task, as well as the attending behavior itself. Thus, task perseverance, or a long attention span, is primarily a function of presenting reinforcement contingent upon attending behavior, and allowing incompatible behavior to go unreinforced. On the other hand, short attention span is observed when reinforcement is contingent upon behavior that is incompatible with attending to the task of interest, and attending behavior goes unreinforced. A similar analysis has been made by Michael (1963) in a discussion of the relevance of animal research to problems of learning in the retarded.

An experiment conducted by the authors supports this analysis. The purpose of the experiment was to study the effects of novel human stimuli upon an operant response in retarded children (Martin and Powers, 1965). The experimental chamber was divided into two cubicles separated by a plexiglass partition that allowed visual and auditory feedback. Each cubicle contained a lever mounted on a table. The children were conditioned individually to operate a lever; that is, when the child pressed the lever, a token fell into a token cup. The token could then be exchanged for either salty foods (popcorn, pretzels, peanuts, etc.) or juice immediately after its receipt. Gradually, the number of lever presses required was increased until the schedule of reinforcement was a fixed ratio 10 (every tenth response was reinforced). The subjects were exposed to this schedule until they achieved a stable performance for five consecutive sessions. Each daily session lasted twenty minutes or until the subject received fifty reinforcements.

At this point, a confederate was introduced into the opposing cubicle with instructions to do one of three things. A, sit quietly and read a book; B, operate the lever and receive food or juice on a fixed interval thirty second schedule of reinforcement (the first response after 30 seconds produced the reinforcement); C, operate the lever and receive a token for every thirtieth response (fixed ratio 30). The token was then exchanged for food or juice.

These three conditions of the confederate were introduced on the assumption that each varied with respect to the frequency and intensity of the auditory and visual stimuli they provided to the subject. Two subjects were exposed to condition C; one was given condition A and B in that order; and the other subject was exposed to the sequence A, B, C. When more than one condition was used, the subject was returned to the control condition (fixed ratio 10) for a session prior to the onset of each new test condition.

In all three test conditions, the introduction of the confederate produced a temporary disruption of the stable pattern of responding that was observed under the control conditions. However, this stable pattern of responding was recovered, indicating that adaptation to the stimuli presented by the confederate had occurred.

Observations made during the initial conditioning sessions and during the test sessions have direct relevance to the issue of attention span. During the first four conditioning sessions, no subject earned the fifty reinforcements within the allotted time of twenty minutes. Failure to earn all available reinforcements appeared to be due to the frequent occurrence of responses that were incompatible with lever pressing such as climbing, crouching, banging on the door, lying on the floor, and so on. In other words, the subjects might have been described as shifting quickly from one goal-directed activity to another, and many persons undoubtedly would have been willing to use the notion of a short attention span as an explanation for the subject's failure to respond in a consistent manner on the lever. Yet, by the fourth session, the subjects came to "pay atention" to the task for the duration of the session, earning their fifty reinforcements within the twenty minute period. This was accomplished by reinforcing only the task of concern and ignoring other incompatible behavior.

Some authors have suggested that subjects with a short attention span for a certain event or activity often invent activities with greater appeal to them (Goldstein and Seigle, 1961). Relevant to this suggestion are the observations taken during the test sessions. The disruption of the stable pattern of responding in the presence of the confederate was due to the occurrence of activities that are incompatible with lever pressing, such as staring, pointing, laughing at the other person, or tapping on the plexiglass partition. It might be suggested that the subjects invented these activties because of their greater appeal, since the only evidence ever offered for this explanation is the fact of their occurrence. However, such an explanation adds nothing in the way of correction procedures. By ignoring these activities and reinforcing only the lever pressing task, the subjects came to pay attention even in the face of the variety of visual and auditory stimuli provided by the confederate. A recent report indicates that even the occurrence of an earthquake in the middle of an experiment failed to disrupt the attending behavior of a retarded subject when that behavior was reinforced (Sloane and Harper, 1965).

Observations reported by other authors support this analysis. Kerr (1962) worked with two brain-injured girls who supposedly had short attention spans and were irresponsible and hyperactive in the classroom (the hospital staff had reported the girls to have such short attention spans that they could not attend to a particular task for longer than three to six minutes.) Kerr devised the task of folding 2 by 5 cards along a dotted line and placing each folded card in a container. During the first session the usual or traditional technique of urging the child to continue was used whenever a lag in productivity occurred, i.e. the experimenter would say such things as, "Come on, you can do better than that," and approximately ten minutes of productive behavior was obtained. During the next two sessions, experimenter attention was made contingent upon task performance, in the manner dictated by the empirical principles of reinforcement, and a full hour of work was obtained each time. Two more sessions of the traditional technique and two more reinforcement sessions replicated these effects. In discussing these results, Kerr reported

The significance of a demonstration that attention span of brain damaged children can be increased through manipulation of reinforcement variables is quite obvious. Procedures which induce a child to attend to a task facilitate education, therapies, and even physical examination. For example, a question about the eyesight of one of the children in this study had been raised by other staff members. An attempt to have her eyes examined was unsuccessful, "because of her short attention span." However, in the present experiment, it was easily determined that she could discriminate the fine printed line along which the paper was to be folded. Had the goal been to test her vision, other visual tasks could have been presented (1962, p. 118).

So far, emphasis has been placed upon the reinforcement of attending behavior. In addition, an operant analysis also stresses a concern for environmental variables that maintain behavior incompatible with a long attention span. For example, several staff members from the institution where the authors' research was conducted had commented upon the short attention spans of their students as a major barrier to their education. However, observation of these students in their respective classrooms revealed that they received attention from the teacher only when they left their desks, cried, or, in short, emitted behavior that was incompatible with a long attention span.

Evidence supporting the importance of reinforcement principles in eliminating behavior that is incompatible with attending to a task comes from two recent experiments. Zimmerman and Zimmerman (1962) eliminated unproductive classroom behavior in two emotionally disturbed boys by removing social consequences of the behavior. In both cases, the student would respond to a teacher's request by emitting behavior that was incompatible with the task of concern (such as having temper tantrums, emitting irrelevant verbal behavior, and talking baby talk). The experimenter initially responded to such behavior, giving the subject much atention and encouragement to respond appropriately. As this approach proved unsuccessful, the experimenter next proceeded to give attention (reinforcement) in the form of smiling, chatting, and physical proximity only after the emission of desired classroom behavior, or some approximation of it in the desired direction. As a result of this treatment, the students soon came to attend to the teacher's questions and classroom tasks.

Birnbrauer, Bijou, and Wolf (1963) selected eight boys from the youngest and educationally most naive educable children from the Rainier School for Retarded Children in an effort to teach them for a school year, using programmed instruction and reinforcement techniques exclusively. With these techniques, the investigators had a great deal of success in teaching primary academic subjects and related practical skills. Relevant to this discussion, they report

> Behavior problems did arise frequently and were handled almost exclusively with extinction; i.e., they were simply ignored. The physical arrangement of the room and the staggered schedules permitted temper tantrums, for example, to "wear themselves out" without overly affecting the other pupils. Shortly after the pupil stopped the inappropriate behavior, he received attention. In other words, adult attention was reserved for socially acceptable behavior (1963, p. 3).

Under these conditions, the retarded students came to read for twenty minutes at a time with the teacher, work quietly at their desks at various tasks, and even do homework.

An operant conditioning approach considers attention span only in terms of the time spent engaging in a task, and uses reinforcement variables in accounting for task persistence. This approach provides teachers with a powerful tool with which to strengthen good attending behavior.

References

Angell, J. R.: *Psychology.* New York, Holt, 1904.

Birnbrauer, J. S.; Bijou, S. W., and Wolf, M.: Programmed instruction in the classroom. In L. P. Ullman and L. Krasner, (Eds.): *Case Studies In Behavioral Modification.* New York, Holt, 1965, pp. 358-363.

Blodgett, Harriet E., and Warfield, Grace J.: *Understanding Mentally Retarded Children.* New York, Appleton, 1959.

Bott, H.: Observation of play activities in a nursery school. *Genet Psychol Monog, 4:* 44-88, 1928.

Bridges, K. M. B.: Occupational interests of three year old children. *J Genet Psychol, 34:* 415-423, 1927.

Cockrell, D. L.: A study of the play of children of preschool age by an unobserved observer. *Genet Psychol Monogr, 17:* 377-469, 1935.

Cromwell, R. L.; Baumeister, A., and Hawkins, W. F.: Research in activity level. In N. R. Ellis, (Ed.): *Handbook Of Mental Deficiency.* New York, McGraw, 1963, pp. 632-663.

Cushing, H. M.: A perseverative tendency in preschool children; a study in personality differences. *Arch Psychol, 108,* 1929.

English, H. B., and English, Ava C.: *A Comprehensive Dictionary Of Psychological And Psychoanalytic Terms.* New York, McGraw, 1963.

Garton, Malinda D.: *Teaching The Educable Mentally Retarded.* Springfield, Thomas, 1964.

Goldstein, H., and Seigle, Dorothy M.: Characteristics of educable mentally handicapped children. In J. H. Rothstein (Ed.): *Mental Retardation.* New York, Holt, 1961, pp. 204-230.

Gutteridge, M. V.: *The Duration Of Attention In Young Children.* Australian Council of Educational Research, Melbourne University Educational Research Series, Number 41, Oxford U.P., 1935.

Herring, A., and Koch, H. L.: A study of some factors influencing the interest span of preschool children. *J Genet Psychol, 38:* 249-279, 1930.

James, W.: *The Principles Of Psychology.* New York, Holt, 1890, vol. 1.

Kerr, Nancy: Applications of behavioristic techniques and field theoretical concepts in somatopsychology. Unpublished doctoral dissertation, U. of Houston, 1962.

Kuhlman, E.: Experimental studies in mental deficiency. *Amer J Psychol, 15:* 391-446, 1904.

Lewis, R. S.; Strauss, A. A., and Lehtinen, L. E.: *The Other Child.* New York, Grune, 1960.

Martin, G. L., and Powers, R. B.: Social disruption of an operant response in retardates. Paper presented at American Association for the Advancement of Science, Flagstaff, Arizona, 1965.

Michael, J. L.: The relevance of animal research. Paper presented at a symposium on language learning in the mentally retarded, University of Kansas, Lawrence, 1963.

Michael, J. L.: Guidance and counseling as the control of behavior. *In Guidance In American Education: Backgrounds And Prospects.* Cambridge, Harvard Graduate School of Education, 1964.

Moyer, K. E., and von Haller Gilmer, B.: Attention spans of children for experimentally designed toys. *J Genet Psychol, 87:* 187-201, 1955.

Schacter, H. S.: A method for measuring the sustained attention of preschool children. *J Genet Psychol, 43:* 339-371, 1933.

Sidman, M.: Operant techniques. In A. J. Bachrach (Ed.): *Experimental Foundations Of Clinical Psychology.* New York, Basic Books, 1962, pp. 170-210.

Sloane, H., and Harper, L. J.: Experimental control during an earthquake. *J Exp Anal Behav, 8:* 425-426, 1965.

Strauss, A. A., and Kephart, N.: *Psychopathology And Education Of The Brain-injured.* New York, Grune, 1947.

Van Alstyne, D.: *Play Behavior And Choice Of Play Materials Of Preschool Children.* Chicago, U. of Chicago, 1932.

Weber, E. W.: *Mentally Retarded Children And Their Education.* Springfield, Thomas, 1963.

Zimmerman, Elaine H., and Zimmerman, J.: The alteration of behavior in a special classroom situation. *J Exp Anal Behav, 5:* 59-60, 1962.

Chapter 32

An Example: Reinforcement Principles In A Classroom For Emotionally Disturbed Children

VENITA DYER

T HERE IS an ever increasing awareness of the problems created in attempting to educate the emotionally disturbed child. As a result, new methods and techniques are being developed. Demands for more effective techniques are being made by teachers who need methods to aid them in educating these children which, however, do not need to be rigidly applied to the whole group but may be adapted to take into account observable individual differences.

Behavioral modification techniques have proven extremely effective in this regard. For example, Whelan and Haring (1966) and Quay, Werry, McQueen, and Sprague (1966) have done research with emotionally disturbed children pointing to the utilization of these techniques to eliminate maladaptive behavior. Most studies use a structured and controlled environment with highly trained technicians who apply the behavioral modification techniques. Teachers who have had only minimal exposure to behavioral technology find it difficult to understand such concepts as reinforcement, contingencies, and scheduling; therefore they neglect to apply this method in the teaching of an individual child.

The example presented in this paper occurred as part of a special education and day treatment program at the Jane Wayland

This paper was prepared as part of NIMH Grant #1-R11 MHo1242-01A3. Reprinted from *Exceptional Children*, Vol. 34 (1968), pp. 597-599. By permission of the author and publisher.

Child Guidance Center, Phoenix, Arizona. This program, now community supported, began with a three year grant sponsored by the National Institute of Mental Health. It is designed to study and demonstrate methods of special education with emotionally disturbed children.

The example presented is the case of Virgie, a bright little twelve-year-old girl. It is concerned with her first encounter with academic learning in the day treatment classroom. Virgie is a very slender girl with medium length brown hair and very dark, deerlike brown eyes. When she first came to the Jane Wayland Child Guidance Center, she was most unconcerned with her appearance and was quite a tomboy. She was extremely shy and withdrawn and completely excluded herself from most group activities.

She had been referred by a local school because she had extreme difficulty with peer relationships, did not complete her school work, and was shy and depressed. Psychological testing indicated that she functioned in the bright intellectual range, that she was experiencing difficulty in interpersonal relations and was withdrawing. She also possessed a great deal of anger which was turned inward. It was felt that this was a deteriorating situation and if allowed to continue would confirm a psychotic potential.

Virgie entered the special education and day treatment program and her parents started in group therapy. In the first classroom, Virgie was given tokens which were paired with warm approval whenever her social behavior approximated appropriateness. She was particularly encouraged to mix in group activities and to express anger toward others in the outside world. After three and a half months of using this procedure, her behavior improved in that she was now able to express a mild amount of anger and a number of positive feelings toward peers and adults. She was also better able to enter into group activities. On entering the second class, however, she demonstrated a complete disinterest in academics and was lucky even to complete one lesson a week.

Since she had responded adequately to the token system in the first classroom, consideration was given to again initiating this procedure. The case was presented at staff conference and the following recommendations were made: (a) Time limits would be established during which time Virgie was expected to work on two subjects; (b) at first, she would be given tokens for merely attempting the work; and (c) the situation would be graduated—after a certain period in the program, she would be rewarded only for accomplishing any portion of the two assigned subjects. The goals were to eventually have her work in all subject areas to completion. This plan was in effect for two and a half months with little observable success.

It was then decided that the teacher should observe Virgie for several days to note which particular foods she seemed to favor in her lunchbox; the teacher concluded that Virgie had a sweet tooth. After discussion with the parents, who verified this, it was decided to reinforce Virgie by giving her candy immediately upon completing the behavior required. The parents were contacted and asked to cooperate by not sending any more candy or cookies in Virgie's lunch so as to make the reinforcers more meaningful. The operant technician might refer to this as increasing deprivation. The teacher discussed this idea with Virgie and asked her to select whatever candy she wanted. Virgie felt this was an excellent reward. The manner of reinforcement was that one candy would be given contingent on choosing the subject and three candies for completing the subjects. Gradually she was not rewarded for selecting the subject but merely for completion, and finally only for correct answers. The difference in her attention span and interest level became markedly observable within ten days. The number of subjects completed increased from less than one to more than three and the time limit for completing the subjects decreased from two hours for one area of work to one hour for three areas completed. In two months, Virgie had reached an output of five subjects a day, all at grade level, with at least one outside report a week.

It is generally the impression of most teachers that the utilization of the reinforcement principle is too complex, involves too much preliminary training, and that the removal of maladaptive behavior may compound the overall problem. In the example presented in this paper, it was found that the preparatory training of the teacher could be minimal and it was not necessary for her to interrupt the usual ongoing classroom procedure to work with the child. When Virgie's behavior in the academic area improved, her successful learning experiences generalized to the rest of her behavior.

One important aspect noted in this example is the importance of teacher observations and the teacher's awareness of an individual child. It was necessary for the teacher to observe Virgie's behavior, evaluate potential reinforcers, and then apply these reinforcers contingent upon approximations of the desired behavior. It is interesting that, although Virgie had responded adequately to the token system used in the first classroom when applied to reinforcing her social behavior, it was necessary to utilize a more meaningful, immediate, primary reinforcer when attempting to modify her maladaptive academic behavior. It is hoped that by the presentation of this example, of the use of the reinforcement principle in a classroom for emotionally disturbed children, teachers will be encouraged to take another look at their students and their methodology and not ignore a potentially successful technique because of its seeming complexity.

References

Quay, H.; Werry, J. S.; McQueen, Marjorie, and Sprague, R. L.: Remediation of the conduct problem in the special class setting. *Exceptional Child, 32:* 509-515, 1966.

Whelan, R., and Haring, N.: Modification and maintenance of behavior through systematic application of consequences. *Exceptional Child, 32:* 281-289, 1966.

SECTION I

TEACHERS OF DISTURBED CHILDREN

Chapter 33

A Hierarchy Of Competencies For Teachers Of Emotionally Handicapped Children

FRANK M. HEWETT

$\mathbf{T}$ ENDER WITHOUT being sentimental, tough but not callous, sensitive but not irritable, possessed by conviction, profoundly aware without loss of spontaneity, trusting in the intuitive humane responsiveness of one's self and one's colleagues, and self-actualized. While this description may seem an excerpt from the canonization of a saint, in actuality it is a statement of desirable characteristics for teachers of emotionally handicapped children compiled from writings of Rabinow (1955); Mackie, Kvaraceus, and Williams (1957); and Haring (1962). The implication is that teachers must possess a personal giftedness and an educational artistry in the tradition of Maria Montessori, Grace Fernald, and August Aichhorn in order to be effective with disturbed children.

Elsewhere, Rabinow (1960) has stated that "the artistry of the teacher is more significant than the trainable competencies" (p. 293). Such a statement may be valid, but it is of questionable usefulness if recruitment and training of teachers are to keep pace with the growing demand for special classes for disturbed children.

Mackie *et al.* (1957) have attempted to be more specific and objective in delineating necessary qualities for teachers of the socially and emotionally maladjusted. They had teachers of such children rank 88 competencies in order of importance, from

Reprinted from *Exceptional Children*, Vol. 33 (1966), pp. 7-11. By permission of the author and publisher.

understanding of techniques adaptable to the classroom situation for relieving tensions and promoting good mental health (rated number 1) to knowledge of the cultural patterns of other societies (rated number 88). Although this is an impressive and ambitious undertaking, the reader may not feel well informed after completing the study, due to the large number of competencies ranked and the wide scope of educational skills covered.

In an effort to be more concise while retaining the operational flavor of Mackie's work and reflecting some of the dynamic personal qualities suggested by Rabinow and others, the staff of the Neuropsychiatric Institute (NPI) School at the University of California, Los Angeles, has developed a hierarchy of competencies for the teacher of the emotionally handicapped. These competencies were selected after four years of offering a one semester training course to public school teachers in a psychiatric hospital school setting. Many of these competencies have been stated elsewhere (Mackie *et al.*, 1957; Lord, 1950; and Stullken, 1950) as desirable for all teachers of exceptional children. The purpose of this paper is to emphasize their order of importance and to attempt to define them objectively.

The hierarchy of teacher competencies roughly parallels a hierarchy of educational tasks for children with learning disorders developed earlier in the NPI School (Hewett, 1964). The hierarchy presupposes that teachers entering the field of education of the emotionally handicapped will possess the dedication and vitality necessary for all individuals who become effective teachers of exceptional children. In order of importance (from most basic to highest level), the hierarchy emphasizes that the teacher of the emotionally handicapped child should be objective, flexible, structured, resourceful, a social reinforcer, a curriculum expert, and an intellectual model.

Objectivity

The most important single requirement for the effective teacher of the emotionally handicapped is to be objective. He must be knowledgeable in the field of normal and deviant psychosocial development and familiar with professional literature relating to special education, particularly with the emotionally handicapped. More important than familiarity with theory and experimental findings, however, is the development of an objective, questioning, educational attitude toward teaching. It is not enough to rely on the cafeteria approach to special education, using this technique because it seems appropriate or that material because of its previous success. The teacher should make an objective assessment of why particular approaches are successes or failures and communicate his findings to others, particularly the student teacher. Educational artists often prefer to radiate inspiration and personal example, rather than to attempt to quantify successes and failures.

Also within the framework of an objective, educational approach is the need to relate professionally to other disciplines such as psychiatry, clinical psychology, and social work. The teacher must strive to define educational goals and practices so that they are understandable to members of these disciplines and relate to the broadest treatment plans for the child, whether in a hospital or day school setting.

Mackie et al. state that the teacher of the emotionally handicapped child must be emotionally stable and not "need to be loved by all, or given to achieving vicarious satisfaction through the antisocial feelings and behavior of others" (p. 17). Rabinow (1960) has described the "crackpots" who are drawn to the field and whose own needs are met through involvement with disturbed children. At the NPI School, some 10 percent of the teachers who enroll in the training course appear too unstable to work successfully with such children. A full discussion of this problem, including whether or not mildly neurotic teachers actually are more effective with disturbed students, is beyond the scope of this paper. Suffice it to say that the objective teacher has some recognition of his own emotional needs and attempts to separate these from the needs of his students.

Flexibility

Closely related to an objective approach to the education of the emotionally handicapped child is the need to be flexible. Perhaps in no other area of education is the teacher faced with such variability among students. What promotes a student's success today may result in a classroom catastrophe tomorrow, depending on the shifting needs and interests of the child. The flexible teacher is comfortable operating in such a state of flux. Continual assessment of students' available learning capacities and subsequent modification of educational goals are essential. As in all special education programs, success experience for the student is given primary focus. The flexible teacher communicates complete acceptance of all students as individuals, regardless of their manifest intellectual, perceptual motor, and social skills, or current emotional states.

Structure

While maintaining a flexible approach, the teacher of the emotionally handicapped child must be structured and must set consistent and reasonable behavioral and educational limits. If these two competencies seem incompatible, they are not. Some aspects of classroom routine and expectation will change on a day-to-day, minute-to-minute basis; but there must be a clearly defined substructure operating at all times. At the NPI School, allowance is made for the changing needs and interests of the children as long as they successfully fulfill the role of a student. This role is carefully defined for the child upon admission to class, and it assumes the ability to tolerate some restriction of space, noise level, and activity and to respect the working rights of others. When a child is too upset to function as a student, he is removed from the classroom immediately. Although school is taken away, schooling is not. The latter is provided on a one-to-one basis until the child can resume the student role.

In addition to maintaining predictable behavioral limits, the teacher must carefully structure student assignments. Units of work which are well defined and realistically attainable, rather than vague and open ended, are preferable. Immediate feedback is also an important adjunct to the structured approach. Assignments should be corrected at once and errors discussed. Daily behavioral rating scales have also been requested by several NPI School students as a means of providing feedback regarding their current class standing.

Resourcefulness

The objective, flexible, and structured teacher who is also resourceful is in an excellent position to teach the emotionally handicapped child. The resourceful teacher provides classroom experiences which emphasize maximum reality testing and multisensory stimulation. He also selects materials and activities that are meaningful and impactful and which draw the child into an exploratory relationship with his environment. Chronologically appropriate curriculum assignments are not utilized at the expense of student motivation and satisfaction. Not only must the teacher create entirely unique lessons for individual students, but he must be prepared to alter or replace these at a moment's notice. The resourceful teacher also assesses sensory and perceptual motor needs of the child and selects learning activities which provide development in these areas and promote readiness for more formal curriculum experience.

Social Reinforcement

In all contact with the emotionally handicapped child, the value of the teacher as a social reinforcer cannot be overemphasized. Most such children display seriously disturbed relationships with others, particularly with adults. At all times it is important to understand how the child perceives the teacher and what opportunities and limitations exist in the teacher-student relationship. Having assessed the child's capacity for relating to an adult authority figure, the teacher can use positive social reinforcement, such as praise and individual attention, in an appropriate manner to motivate and control the student. Negative reinforcements are also essential in maintaining a structured working relationship. For some children, a stern look, a shaking of the head, or a restraining touch may be meaningful and effective. For others, allowing inappropriate behavior to extinguish by ignoring it may be the most successful approach. Selecting successful reinforcement techniques and constantly evaluating their effectiveness are important tasks for the teacher who, as an adult model, can often aid in reshaping the child's social attitudes and behavior. At times, peer groupings may also be used to promote positive social experiences for the child.

Curriculum Expertise

Despite the fact that the competencies previously discussed tend to emphasize the teacher's clinical judgment and psychosocial awareness, skill as a curriculum expert cannot be overlooked. Regardless of the psychological sophistication of the teacher of the disturbed, his ultimate success will depend on a sound basic understanding of educational practices and techniques. As a result, in the selection of the best candidate for a teacher of the disturbed, the individual with an advanced psychology degree but no training in education is often less promising than the stable, flexible, and resourceful classroom teacher who is thoroughly knowledgeable in basic curriculum methods and materials. During the four years of teacher training experience in the NPI School, this has generally been the rule. There is a point in the special educational program for most emotionally handicapped children when the primary contribution of the teacher is good teaching. The ability to set realistic academic goals in keeping with the student's intellectual and achievement levels and to institute appropriate developmental and remedial procedures in reading, arithmetic, and other basic skills is an essential competency.

Intellectual Model

Finally, the teacher must be competent in functioning as an intellectual model with those emotionally handicapped students whose problems do not interfere with intellectual functioning and who are often best helped by an educational program of enrichment. Development of good study habits, pursuit of academic work in considerable depth, frequent discussion with the teacher on issues of importance to the student, and involvement in special projects of research may be important aspects of such a program.

An effort has been made to rank seven basic areas of competencies for teachers of the emotionally handicapped. The concept of a hierarchy immediately raises the question of priority of one competency over another. Since objectivity and flexibility are given the most important places in the model, would a teacher possessing these qualities but who is poor as a social reinforcer and curriculum expert be a better teacher of the emotionally handicapped than one possessing social reinforcement and curriculum skills but who is more subjective and rigid in his approach? No definitive answer to this or the other numerous possible comparisons can be given. The competencies within the hierarchy must be viewed collectively. Each is important. Certain teachers adequately compensate for limitations at a particular level and certain emotionally handicapped children respond best to teachers who are more competent in one area than in another.

The value of the concept of the hierarchy is in placing emphasis on the most basic competencies. Objectivity, flexibility, and structure are requisites for the resourceful teacher who functions effectively as a social reinforcer, curriculum expert, and intellectual model. In addition, the hierarchy attempts to aid recruiters, trainers, and prospective teachers in the field of education of the emotionally handicapped by replacing the vague and mystical notion of the gifted artist with a more objective concept of the trainable teacher.

References

Haring, N., and Phillips, E.: *Educating Emotionally Disturbed Children.* New York, McGraw, 1962.

Hewett, F.: A hierarchy of educational tasks for children with learning disorders. *Exceptional Child, 31:* 207-214, 1964.

Lord, F., and Kirk, S.: The education of teachers of special classes. In *Forty-ninth Yearbook Of The National Society For The Study Of Education.* Chicago, U. of Chicago, 1950, pp. 103-116.

Mackie, Romaine; Kvaraceus, W., and Williams, H.: *Teachers Of Children Who Are Socially And Emotionally Maladjusted.* Washington, D.C., U.S. Depart. of HEW, 1957.

Rabinow, B.: Role of the school in residential treatment. *Amer J Orthopsychiat, 25:* 685-691, 1955.

Rabinow, B.: A proposal for a training program for teachers of the emotionally disturbed and the socially maladjusted. *Exceptional Child, 26:* 287-293, 1960.

Stullken, E.: Special schools and classes for the socially maladjusted. In *Forty-ninth Yearbook Of The National Society For The Study Of Education.* Chicago, U. of Chicago, 1950, pp. 281-301.

Chapter 34

How To Alleviate The First-Year Shock Of Teaching Emotionally Disturbed Children

SHIRLEY COHEN

AMONG THE RESULTS of the Elementary and Secondary Education Act of 1965, with its encouragement of innovations to bring educational opportunities to "educationally deprived children," is a widespread interest in establishing special classes for emotionally disturbed children. In some States this interest has been augmented by State legislation, as in New York State where the establishment of such classes is now mandatory. Though under a 1963 act some Federal money has been made available to States for training teachers to conduct such classes, a great many schoolteachers with little or no special training will undoubtedly find themselves faced with classes for disturbed children in the near future.

While thousands of books, pamphlets, manuals, and articles are aimed at guiding the new teacher of a regular class, few shed light on the difficult task facing the experienced teacher who is working with a class of emotionally disturbed children for the first time. Therefore, it seems appropriate to describe some principles for approaching this task. Those that follow are derived from my own experience in just such a situation and from my subsequent work supervising other teachers in their first year of teaching classes for emotionally disturbed children.

Based on a paper presented at the First Conference of New York State Educators of the Emotionally Disturbed held in Hawthorne, N.Y., May 1966. Reprinted from *Children*, Vol. 13 (1966), pp. 232-236. By permission of the author and publisher.

The first year with emotionally disturbed children is often a year of crisis for the teacher—a year in which a teacher's beliefs, premises, values, and expectations are shaken. The approaches the teacher has come to have faith in do not bring the expected results, and the usually reliable methods for making things work better, more preparation and planning, prove not so reliable.

Whether a teacher's relationship to her class, her skill as a teacher, and her maturity as a person grow or wither depend on how she responds to the crisis of finding her "reliable" methods no longer working. She can respond to the shock of this new experience either by becoming more distant and more rigid, or by opening herself up to a kind of "culture" and a way of communication that are new to her, painful as this may be. Some persons who turn out to be the best teachers of classes for emotionally disturbed children have the most difficult time the first year. They are, so to speak, "shook up" the most, but the experience makes them more receptive to new ways of looking at events, new understanding, and new approaches. Take, for example, the following incident:

> One day a teacher in her first month of working with a special class of emotionally disturbed children put on a record by the Beatles, got out some colored chalk, and encouraged the children to draw on the chalkboard to the music. Having taught for several years in regular classes, this teacher had a rationale for what she was doing. She felt that most of these disturbed children were too inhibited and needed more opportunities for free and creative activities. She had used this kind of activity successfully with classes of young children before.
>
> For the first 10 minutes the result was beautiful. The children were interested and involved. They were communicating with one another and working cooperatively. The chalkboard was brilliant with color and design. But then the quality and tenor of the experience began to change. The children became wilder, less creative, and more destructive. The beauty of the cooperative production disappeared under a barrage of uncontrolled actions. The floor and the children themselves were covered with colored chalk. Some of the children became highly anxious.

When I described this incident to a group of teachers of disturbed children, each one was quick to point out the teacher's obvious errors: she had used the wrong music, at the wrong time of day, without having established clear aims and limits. These criticisms had some validity.

Yet the experience turned out to be a good one for most of the children. The next day I watched the teacher talk to the children about what had happened, and it was obvious from their faces and their voices that something good was happening to them. For the first time in the lives of many of them a disaster in which they had participated was not being blamed on them. The adult did not turn against them; on the contrary, she was taking a share of the blame for what had happened. She said to them: "I didn't plan that very well, did I? Next time we'll have to plan more carefully."

This woman will most likely turn out to be an excellent teacher for disturbed children.

Some Principles

The following are the principles that, I believe, if followed, could alleviate the shock of the first year with such children if understood by the teacher.

1. *The teacher will do much better if she understands that what disturbed children need is someone who can be stable and orderly in the midst of their disorder.*

When I first considered teaching seriously disturbed children, I was advised against it by another teacher on the grounds that such children need a teacher who can regress with them. Time and experience have led me to a different viewpoint. What these children need is not someone who can regress with them, but someone who can live with, accept, understand, and see the need for their regressions, without becoming threatened or disrupted by them herself. The teacher who is cut off from her own feelings may not be able to understand and communicate with such children, but the teacher who is herself chaotic will not be able to serve as a model of health and strength for emotionally ill children.

On the physical level, for example, the idea that the teacher, rather than the children, has to be orderly means that for a long time the teacher may have to be the one who takes major responsibility for "setting up" and "cleaning up." Cleaning up is often a center of conflict between teachers and disturbed children. Here teachers fall back upon the old expectation that if children are properly warned of the approach of clean-up time they will or should clean up. If these children could get ready and clean up when, and simply because, the teacher told them to, they would probably not be in a special class. Being willing to clean up implies a set of attitudes and a degree of strength that do not exist, or exist only in rudimentary form, in many disturbed children.

2. *The teacher of disturbed children will do much better if she comes to expect the unexpected.*

The teacher who is working with disturbed children for the first time, in a sense, is moving into a new "culture"; the language is different, the way of perceiving the environment is different, and the rules are different. It takes time to understand how the class differs from a group of normal children as well as to understand the idiosyncratic ways each child has of perceiving and relating to the world. Of course, it takes more than just time to understand disturbed children. Training and sensitivity are crucial. And some severely disturbed children will leave even the best teacher puzzled.

3. *The teacher will do better if she expects and accepts little progress in some of the children for the first few months.*

It takes many disturbed children months before they are willing to conclude that the teacher is really for them, that they can really trust her, that she will not turn against them when the going gets rough. Until they reach this point, they may not be able to really get to the learning task that is the purpose of their being at school (Bruner, 1966). They may not be willing or able to expose what they do not know or what they want to know. They may not be able to accept the position of one who knows less in relation to the teacher as one who knows more.

The teacher will also do better if she learns to recognize other kinds of growth besides academic achievement. If a child who was a habitual truant now comes to school regularly, growth has taken place. If a child who in the past rarely finished anything, or immediately destroyed anything he did finish, is now able to accept some of his work and allow the results to exist, growth has taken place. If a child who used to respond to teaching efforts with braggadocio is now willing to expose what he does not know or cannot do and ask for help, growth has taken place.

Time takes on a different meaning when one works with disturbed children. Something that a regular class may adapt to immediately may take a class of disturbed children weeks to accept. Here is where just the right amount of "flexibility" in the teacher counts. Some teachers rigidly cling to practices carried over from regular classes in spite of overwhelming evidence that these practices are not appropriate for the disturbed children now in their charge. On the other hand, some teachers, finding that nothing they try works immediately, shift about so much that the children cannot tell what is expected of them or what to expect.

4. *The teacher will do better if she learns to attend to and understand nonverbal communication, her own as well as the children's.*

Only a small fraction of what disturbed children feel or think is communicated through words (Hay, 1954). The teacher has to learn to read gestures, facial expressions, body movements, and actions. Doing so will help her not only to understand the children but also to anticipate their reactions. Anticipation is essential in working with disturbed children. The teacher also has to become sensitive to her own nonverbal messages because most disturbed children learn to "read" them very well (Cohen *et al.*, 1964).

In the following two examples, the teacher failed because of insensitivity to what the child was asking and how she was answering him.

> Robert was a seriously disturbed boy who had been discharged from regular class in the first grade and was now in a special class. One day early in the term he came up to the teacher, removed a bandage from his right hand, and told her that his hand hurt. The teacher looked at the hand and replied: "That cut looks almost healed to me. Besides, the nurse isn't in today, and there's really nothing I can do for it." Then she turned back to her desk. Within 5 minutes Robert had attacked three children and disrupted the entire class.

This teacher had answered Robert's words in a rational manner, but in response to his message, "I need some support; I need
to know that you care about how I feel," her response, unfortunately, was negative.

> Billy, another very disturbed child, had just returned to school,
> after having been excluded for 2 years in which he received intensive
> therapy and home instruction. The teacher was going around the
> room asking each pupil his name. When she came to Billy, he
> announced himself as Martin Luther King. The teacher became very
> angry and accused the boy of insolence and disrespect (Grant).

This teacher felt threatened, and in defending herself forgot
about the child. She might better have said: "Martin Luther
King is a good person to want to be like," or "Martin Luther
King is a man of peace, so I expect you to contribute to the peace
in this classroom."

Thus she would have been telling Billy and the rest of the
class that she was not being taken in, but that she recognized
that he may have felt like nothing and nobody that day; that his
response was a defense against his own feelings, and that she was
not going to try to rip it away.

Awareness of nonverbal communication is also important for
achieving *congruence* between words and actions and between
methods and aims, an aspect of teacher consistency not often
enough recognized.

5. *The teacher will do better if she reexamines everything she
does in the classroom in the light of the questions, Is this really
worthwhile? Is it really a good way to achieve what I intend?*

Probably most teachers who go about such a reexamination
seriously will find that much of what they have been doing does
not pass this test. Recently I watched a teacher who had had the
same class of disturbed children for almost two years spend a
half hour on the attendance, the calendar, the weather, the daily
"story," the patriotic song, and the seasonal poem, all standard
procedures in the primary grades of many schools. During the
process the children became more and more restless, bored, and
cut off from the teacher. Afterward I asked the teacher what
she expected to achieve by "doing the weather" every morning.
She replied that she "did the weather" (with the pictures of a

cloud, an umbrella, the sun, and a snowman) to make the children aware of the weather and of weather changes. Why had this teacher not considered that if, after nearly two years, this daily procedure had not achieved the goal of making children aware of weather changes, either it was an inappropriate method or her goal was inappropriate? If the goal had been achieved, why was she "beating a dead horse"? The elimination of such wasteful procedures will help eliminate some of the restlessness or apathy so often exhibited by disturbed children at school.

The teacher also needs to reexamine every aspect of classroom management, including selection and arrangement of furniture, use of bulletin boards, selection and storage of supplies, arrangement of activity centers. Which materials are kept in closed closets and which are left on open shelves? Where should the child who runs away be seated? Are "current events" only what one reads about in the newspaper, or do stories about events current in the lives of the children themselves also belong in this category and rate space on the bulletin board? Such questions are important in relation not only to classroom management but also to communicating the philosophy of this class to the children (Kornberg, 1955).

Seeing Individual Needs

The crux of what a new teacher has to learn is to see not only the goals which she wants children to reach, but also how well all the parts of a child's personality—attitudes, controls, and areas of strength and skill—must be functioning before these goals can be reached. She has to learn how to help malfunctioning children negotiate the quarter-steps toward these goals, small achievements which most other children do not need to work at consciously.

For this type of planning, preparation of the standard type based on curriculum guides, reference books, charts, and the like is not enough. Hand in hand with it must go another kind of planning based on knowledge about disturbed children in general and about each specific child in the class. This kind of planning cannot be done by the teacher alone. It requires the insight of persons well versed in the recent developments in psychology, neurology, sociology, psychiatry, and education; in other words, a team of persons from different professional disciplines working together.

Such planning is concerned not only with the standard questions about reading, writing, and arithmetic, but also with such questions as, When should the teacher keep out of something and when should she move in to confront the child with reality? What should she do about such group reactions as scapegoating? How much protection can she give a child without fostering unhealthy dependency? How can she tell when she is becoming overinvolved with a child and perhaps repeating an unhealthy parental pattern? How can she know when withdrawal signifies a marshalling of resources or when it is serving no healthy purpose? What avenues of expression are to be made available to a particular child and what ones are to be avoided? How much weight is to be given to general school standards and expectations in defining special class activities and procedures? How can a child be prepared for return to a regular class?

Behind the labels "emotionally disturbed children" or "maladjusted children" are children having widely varying symptoms, degrees of pathology, and etiology of pathology. Some are aggressive, destructive, and delinquent; others are self-destructive, picking at their skin, banging their heads, biting their hands. Some are far behind in academic achievement; others are academically advanced. Some are constantly fearful; others show an abnormal lack of fear. Some are hyperactive and impulsive; others are lethargic and withdrawn. Some are caught up in complex fantasies; others are extremely concrete. Some are only mildly troubled; others, deeply so. Some are responding to the stress of acute situations in their lives; others have shown abnormal behavior since birth and are extremely disoriented.

Thus, in working with a class of disturbed children, the teacher cannot address herself to "the group." She must study, plan for, and relate to each child as an individual. It is here that she needs the help of the mental health specialists—psychiatrists, psychologists, social workers—who work in or with the school.

Teams, of course, will vary according to the type of personnel available. For example, in one school I know of a team which consists of three teachers assigned to special classes, a psychiatrist, and a school guidance counselor, which meets regularly once a week. Additional school or outside agency personnel, including social workers and psychologists, are asked to attend the team conferences when their special skills are particularly needed. The guidance counselor also meets separately with each teacher weekly.

In this school, a few weeks after the beginning of a term, a team meeting was focused on planning for a 7-year-old boy, David. Even among his peers in the special class David's behavior appeared bizarre. He never said a word to anybody about anything going on in the class, but occasionally he would come out with a phrase which seemed to make little or no sense. Anxious about how to deal with him, his teacher described his behavior to the others at the conference. The psychiatrist who had been seeing David individually told about some of the factors in David's background which seemed to have a bearing on his behavior, and then the team members considered together how to help David in the classroom.

Since childhood David had been cared for by his father, a seriously disturbed person who regarded himself as a poet. He only attended to David when the boy said something "poetic"—something unrelated to everyday needs and expressions. Then, the father, who himself often spoke "poetically," wrote David's words down and showed him much affection. The father was now no longer in the home and David's mother had become very much worried about David's verbal behavior.

The psychiatrist explained that David's strange way of speaking was probably a normal reaction to his past environment. The team decided that the teacher should relate to the boy in the following ways: translate his bizarre statements into everyday language whenever possible; talk to him as much as possible in simple words about concrete, pleasurable activities—eating, blockbuilding, ballplaying, woodworking.

Feeling more confident, the teacher was able to carry out this plan. She and the guidance counselor continued to discuss David's behavior periodically. By the end of the term David's verbal behavior was greatly improved.

Because of the pressures of time and the inadequacy of funds, many teachers work with classes of disturbed children without the aid of a mental health team. This is unfortunate. No one person alone can understand the needs of all the children in a class for maladjusted children. Some teachers have been hurt by trying to do so; in some instances the special class has degenerated into chaotic destructiveness.

In brief, a working team that includes the teacher and mental health specialists can perform five essential functions to enlarge the potentialities of the special class for helping disturbed children:

1. *Supporting the teacher:* The knowledge that she is working with others toward a common goal can keep a teacher from becoming prey to discouragement, anxiety, and the feeling of being hopelessly overburdened. The team also provides her with an outlet for expressing the strong feelings that inevitably arise over the frustrations encountered in working with disturbed, and disturbing, children.

2. *Providing vital information:* Team members of different professions are equipped to gather and interpret special kinds of information relevant to working with a disturbed child. Psychiatric interviews, psychological tests, data from social casework histories, and medical records may be critical in shedding light on the meaning of a child's behavior and on possible approaches to helping him.

3. *Acting as a sounding board:* The team helps the teacher become more aware of her own attitudes, feelings, and behavior and how they influence individual and group dynamics, and gives her perspective for evaluating her ideas and plans and the occurrences in the classroom.

4. *Participating in the formulation of plans for individual children and for the group:* The team helps the teacher set realistic expectations and appropriate goals, and suggests approaches to specific problems.

5. *Providing, or arranging for, supportive services:* These may take the form of family counseling, individual psychotherapy for the child, or an after-school recreation program.

Summary

The standard kind of educational planning often fails in a classroom for the emotionally disturbed because it is based upon premises about children that do not always hold true for seriously disturbed children. What the teacher who is new to this type of class must do before, during, and after giving her attention to content, methods, and materials, is strengthen her insight into the personality dynamics, perceptions, beliefs, abilities, and disabilities of these children. The most difficult aspect of planning for disturbed children is the translation of such insight into appropriate goals, methods, materials, and educational content.

Many of the principles I have here outlined for teaching special classes of emotionally disturbed children are also relevant for teaching regular school classes. It would indeed be hard to find a classroom that did not house two or three "difficult" or "difficult to get to" children. Better insight into the effective communications between teachers and children, reexamination of the relevance of standardized teaching methods and content, and planning individually for troubled children by a team of mental health specialists and educators might lead to radical improvements in many schools in which behavior problems are rampant.

References

Bruner, Jerome: On coping and defending. In *Toward A Theory Of Instruction*. Cambridge, Harvard, 1966.

Cohen, Rosalyn, *et al.*: An inquiry into variations of teacher-child communication. In *Educational Programming For Emotionally Disturbed Children*, Peter Knoblock, ed., Syracuse, Syracuse, 1964.

Grant, Lestina M.: Clinical psychologist, Bureau of Child Guidance, New York City Board of Education, personal communication.

Hay, Louis: How the classroom teacher can help the troubled child. *Nervous Child, 10:*(No. 3), 1954.

Kornberg, Leonard: *A Class For Disturbed Children*. Bureau of Publications, Teachers College, New York, Columbia, 1955.

The Elementary and Secondary Education Act of 1965, Public Law 89-10. Title I, sec. 201.

The Mental Retardation Facilities and Community Mental Health Centers Construction Act of 1963, Public Law 88-164. Title III.

SECTION J

PREVENTION

Chapter 35

Primary Prevention Of Mental And Emotional Disorders: A Conceptual Framework And Action Possibilities

Eli M. Bower

M AGIC and science have had a curious and interesting alliance in the history of human societies. One specific
kind of science-magic which man has developed over the years
is that of word power. It is illustrated by fairy tales or folktales
in which discovering or using an appropriate word enables the
hero or heroine to gain power over a natural, supernatural, or
human enemy. *Ali Baba and the Forty Thieves* and *The Story
of Rumpelstiltskin*, for example, utilize such magic words to move
mountains and solve a complex personal problem. Folklore and
myths* also exemplify the solution of a problem by abstention
from or disuse of an appropriate word or name. In Grimm's
The Wild Swans, the sister's power to help her seven brothers is
gained by her ability not to utter a single word. Odysseus in his
adventure with the Cyclops gains power over the giant Polyphemus by telling him his name is "Noman." When Polyphemus
is attacked by Odysseus he cries out, "Noman is killing me by
craft and not by main force." His brother Cyclops, somewhat
dismayed, answers, "Well, if no man is using force and you are
alone, there's no help for a bit of sickness when heaven sends it."
Odysseus continues, "With these words away they went and my
heart laughed within me to think how a mere nobody had taken
them all in with my machinomanations" (Homer).

Presented at the 1961 Annual Meeting; accepted for publication, June 6, 1961.
Reprinted from the *American Journal of Orthopsychiatry*, Vol. 33 (1963), pp.
832-848. By permission of the author and publisher.

* Not surprisingly, myth is derived from the Greek, *mythos*, meaning *word*.

In the Twentieth Century our "open sesame" to the solution of problems has been the word "prevention," which has found some of its magical fruition in many of man's relationships to viruses, bacteria, and protozoans. The "magic bullet" and the newer "miracle drugs" are still part of the "abracadabra" of man's relationship to microbes. Dubos (1959) observes, "The common use of the word 'miracle' in referring to the effect of a new drug reveals that men still find it easier to believe in mysterious forces than to trust to rational processes. . . . Men want miracles as much today as in the past" (p. 132). Smallpox, however, *is* prevented by a nick on the arm and polio by several shots. The magic of prevention as a word, idea, or myth remains a Twentieth Century Rumpelstiltskin in all branches of man's activities except one. Little in the way of magic words, incantations, or mystical emanations exists for the prevention of the emotional and behavioral disorders of man. Indeed, one would be hard-pressed to divine the kinds of conjurations and "answers oracular" a contemporary John Wellington Wells might dream up to get the job done.

Thus it appears that the lack of creativity and action in the prevention of mental and behavioral disorders originates in forces too powerful for either magic or science. We do not need a Sherlock Holmes or an Arsène Lupin to perceive that there may be more to this conceptual and research abyss in prevention than a lack of imagination and interest. Indeed, one could make a good case for the existence of explicit and implicit cultural resistances to the prevention of emotional and behavioral disorders. Perhaps a necessary first step, then, in any preventive program is to examine the antagonism realistically, and plan strategies of action that take into account the probabilities of success in light of an understanding of the opposition (Cumming and Cumming, 1957).

Community Antagonisms Toward Prevention

A common conception of prevention often obfuscates thinking and action, namely, that little can be accomplished short of major social overhaul. Prevention of mental and emotional disorders is seen as the exclusive result of the abolition of injustice, discrimination, economic insecurity, poverty, slums and illness. To seek less is to attempt to fell a giant sequoia with a toy axe. Any effort, therefore, that is not aimed directly at major social change is viewed as an inadequate and inconsequential attack at the problem. A corollary of this notion is that prevention involves wheels within wheels within wheels. Thus, any possible action is perceived as if it were a combined luncheon check presented by an inexperienced waiter to a group of women at the end of an a la carte meal. The alleged magnitude of the complexities and the ungeared wheels within wheels perceived are also major deterrents to biological and social scientists who can, with little effort, find more digestible problems to define and solve. Other scientists who see some value in pursuing this kind of "elusive Pimpernel" search in vain for something akin to Archimedes' lever with which the whole of the problem can be moved. Many believe one should concentrate on immediate needs such as the care, treatment, and rehabilitation of mental patients. Such problems are real and specific. If one means to do anything in this field, "they" say, let's start with this problem. Small beginnings, however, need to be made on many fronts. Farnsworth (1961), for example, notes, "Both the treatment of mental illness and the promotion of mental health are necessary in any well-conceived community program designed to reduce crippling emotional conflict. To throw up our hands and stop promoting mental health programs because we cannot define mental health or can portray results only inexactly is to show both lack of common sense and lack of courage." There is a *need* and there is a *problem*. The need to care and treat the ill is our major concern, yet it is fairly obvious that all the king's horses and all the king's men will have little effect on the problem: how to reduce or curtail the development of the illness in the first place.

A second and related phenomenon that influences preventive efforts in the mental health field is the high, often impregnable, fortress of personal privacy: the right and privilege of each person, and family, in a free society to mind his own business and have others mind theirs. If prevention of any kind includes early effective intervention in the lives of persons in the population at large, then the intervention must take place prior to such time as the person is singled out for special help. Where it can be shown that such intervention is necessary, indeed, mandatory for the common good, as it is in automobile use, school attendance, and physical hygiene and sanitation, acceptance may be given. Yet, in polio inoculations and water fluoridation, invasion of personal privacy is still a major issue in families or communities that decide to accept or reject these preventive programs.

"At present," Bellak (1959) writes, "the governing of men and the raising of children seem to be among the very few occupations in civilized society for which no training or certified ability are required—and for fairly sound reasons. Imposition of laws on either activity could constitute a serious invasion of personal freedom. Laws providing sanctions for intervention by an agency or person in the private life of an individual are, therefore, clearly and with sound reason limited to situations that endanger the life or health of the person or his neighbors. In essence, one can only stop minding one's own business and become one's brother's keeper when "brother" is in pretty sad shape. Nevertheless, few persons would be prepared to sacrifice the values of a free society on any nebulous, preventive altar.

Yet, some primary institutions are actually mobilized and authorized to help the family in a positive and potenially preventive manner. For example, the well-baby clinic and the public school are given informal and official sanction to interfere and meddle; the former, in relation to the child's health, the latter, in terms of the child's educational progress or lack of it. However, these institutions must also be alert to the dangers inherent in such sanctions. The school must find its leverage in its assigned task of educating children and carefully define and demonstrate the role of auxiliary services such as health examination, psychological testing and mental health consultation as necessary in carrying out this assignment. The health and educational progress of children represent to most parents important and highly significant achievements; almost always, there is a strong motivation to do whatever is necessary to work with the school or well-baby clinic in enhancing their child's health or educational success.

Another major social resistance to prevention, pointed out by

Ruth Eissler (1955), lies in the realm of the reduction of criminal and antisocial behavior:

". . . modern society, with all its dazzling technological progress has not been able to protect itself from individual or mass aggression against property or life. Must we assume that this helplessness is accidental and has no psychological basis? If we take the standpoint that society needs its criminals in the same way as the mother of my delinquent patient needed his delinquency, then we understand the existence of two general tendencies. The first is the seduction of individuals into criminal acting-out. The second is the interference with or the prevention of anything which promises to prevent delinquency."

One explanation advanced for this phenomenon is related to cultural values in which success lies with virtue and failure with sin. In a free society each person has equal opportunity with his fellows to show his mettle as a conscientious, hard-working and, therefore, successful citizen. If he chooses not to be conscientious and hard-working, he has only himself to blame for the consequences. Such competition in games, school work, business, and life can only be perceived as successful for all when it is unsuccessful for some. As Don Alhambra sings it in *The Gondoliers*:

> In short, whoever you may be
> To this conclusion you'll agree
> When everyone is somebodee
> Then no one's anybodee.

To a great extent, the ritual of the TV-Western in which good wins over evil fair and square celebrates this notion at least once or twice each evening. On the other hand, increasing clinical and research evidence supports the notion that those individuals who find positive satisfactions and relationships in family, neighborhood, and school also find these satisfactions and relationships as adults; and that those who find frustration, failure, and defeat in these primary institutions also tend to be defeated in adulthood. This unconscious sponsorship and enhancement of defeat and alienation in and among groups of children and adolescents is often spelled out in terms of pseudo-Darwinian theory (Hofstadter, 1955). Yet the idea of equalitarianism is in our historical bones. How have we come to place equality for all and excellence for all as one-dimensional opposites? Gardner (1961) states the question more succinctly: "How can we provide opportunities and rewards for individuals of every degree of ability so that individuals at every level will realize their full potentialities, perform at their best and harbor no resentment toward any other level?"

Who Bells The Cat?

As a specific activity, prevention still has the major problem of interesting and involving members of the professions dealing with mental illness, most of whom are involved in individual relationships, with patients. Clinicians trained in treatment, rehabilitation, and adjunctive therapies in a one-to-one relationship naturally find this more rewarding than they find plunging into the misty arena of prevention. The physician is responsible for the health of his patient, particularly when such health is threatened. As Fox (1960) points out,

> Curative medicine has generally had precedence over preventive medicine: people come to the doctor to be healed, and most practicing physicians still think of prevention as subsidary to their main task—which is, to treat the sick. Though they subscribe, intellectually, to prevention, they really feel more at home when the disease has "got going."

Often, the mental health worker, be he psychiatric technician, nurse, psychologist, social worker or psychiatrist, is deeply impressed by the mountainous obstacles to effecting positive, healthful changes in mental patients and, consequently, finds it difficult to comprehend how other less intensive types of experiences might have prevented the illness.

Yet, one is often surprised by the range, variety, and quality of human experiences and human relationships that can and do produce significant changes in personality. Sanford's experience and research lead him to conclude that marked and profound changes do occur in students during the college years:

> Some students undergo in the normal course of events changes of the same order as those brought about by psychotherapy. Not only may there be expansion and reorganization in the ego, with increased sophistication, broader perspective, increased flexibility of control but, also, there may be changes in the relations among the

ego, the id, and the superego. The question is, what makes these changes occur and what can be done deliberately to bring them about. There is a common notion that changes so profound as to involve the relations of id, superego, and ego can be brought about after adolescence only by means as thoroughgoing as psychoanalysis or deep psychotherapy. I'm suggesting that changes of a pretty fundamental kind can be brought about by regular educational procedures or by events occurring in the normal course of events, provided we know enough about what makes changes occur (Sanford, 1959).

In bringing prevention into the ken of the psychiatrist, clinical psychologist, or social worker, one may need to recognize and deal with the minimization or depreciation of change processes other than a depth peeling of defenses. Stevenson (1959), in his study of direct instigation of behavioral changes in psychotherapy, finds that some patients often improve markedly when they have mastered a stressful situation or relationship and that by helping such patients manage a day-to-day problem, change is brought about. In the early relationships of the mental health professions and the parents of retarded children, it was often assumed that being a parent of a retarded child necessitated intensive psychological help or mental health counseling. Yet, many such parents were more puzzled and distressed by a lack of information and skill in basic home management of the child, and were often best helped by simple instruction in how to help retarded children learn to feed and dress themselves.

It is possible, as Sanford suggests, that our overemphasis on individual therapy as a major community resource retards to some degree our interest in or our giving priority to prevention. The fact is, primary prevention is the concern of all of the mental health professions, but the responsibility of no one group. Much preventive gold can be mined from clinicians and therapists by encouraging them to translate their clinical experiences and knowledge into programs with preventive possibilities. Such translations, however, must be within a framework of what is operationally feasible within one of the "key integrative systems" of our society. Gardner Murphy (1960) may well be right:

> The ultimate keys to the understanding of mental health will come, not through exclusive preoccupation with the pathological,

but with the broader understanding of the nature of life and of growth. Perhaps the understanding of resonant health and joyful adaptation to life will help us to understand and formulate the issues regarding the prevention of mental disorder.

Prevention Of What?

Lastly, there is the knotty problem of defining the goals of prevention. Do such goals include the development of individuals who can more easily be helped by community resources, a reduction in hospitalized schizophrenics, or making persons more amenable to psychotherapy? If our purpose is the promotion of emotional robustness, what exactly does this mean and how can this goal be translated into specific, positive and, hopefully, measurable objectives of health? Dubos (1959) notes, "Solving problems of disease is not the same thing as creating health. . . . This task demands a kind of wisdom and vision which transcends specialized knowledge of remedies and treatments and which apprehends in all their complexities and subtleties the relation between living things and their total environment" (p. 22). The lack of specificity as to what constitutes mental illness, plus the changing character of such illnesses, make this baseline difficult to define or use in evaluating programs. Yet, where living is equated with and therefore measured by degrees of illness rather than health, one can easily perceive the world as a giant hospital peopled by patients whose only health lies in discovering how sick they are. Nevertheless, reliable measures or indexes of health or illness of a community are the _sine qua non_ of any preventive program.

A Framework For Primary Prevention

No single problem in primary prevention has a solution deserving of greater priority than the development of a platform or position from which one can begin to organize and act. One cannot exert leverage on any field of forces except from some fixed position. Without such a theoretical framework little can be done in developing hypotheses, testing them and further developing or, if need be, abandoning them.

Primary prevention of mental and emotional disorders is any specific biological, social, or psychological intervention that promotes or enhances the mental and emotional robustness or reduces the incidence and prevalence of mental or emotional illnesses in the population at large. In this framework, primary preventive programs are aimed at persons not yet separated from the general population and, hopefully, at interventions specific enough to be operationally defined and measured.

Measured how? along what dimensions and by what value system? To be sure, some types of primary prevention can be specified in relation to specific diseases or impairments. In such illnesses as phenylketonuria or pellagra psychosis, an appropriate diet initiated at an appropriate time may prevent some of the serious complications of the illness. Other types of mental illness, however, may come about as the cumulative effect of a myriad of interacting social and biological causes and be relatively uninfluenced by any single intervention. Yet, if one assumes that emotional robustness is built on the interactive elements of a healthy organism with enhancing life experience, one must consider how one could increase those social forces in a community that helps the population at large to cope with normal problems, rather than to defend against them, to deal with stress effectively, and to be less vulnerable to illness, including the mental illnesses.

There is, of course, a basic assumption about human behavior and mental health in these propositions, namely, that those social, psychological and biological forces which tend to enhance the full development of the human characteristics of man are desirable and preventive of mental illness; those factors which tend to limit or block such development have greater illness-producing potential and are, therefore, undesirable. By human characteristics, the full development of which are sought, I mean the ability to love and to work productively (Freud's *Lieben und Arbeiten*). In this framework one might support those social and biological forces that tend to make man an effectively functioning organism with maximum ability to adapt to his own potential as well as to the potential of his environment. One can, therefore, hypothesize that forces which increase or enhance the degrees of freedom of man's individual and social behavior are mentally healthful, whereas, those which reduce such freedom are unhealthful.

What, specifically, is meant by degrees of behavioral freedom? Behavioral freedom may be regarded as the ability of the organism to develop and maintain a resiliency and flexibility in response to a changing environment and a changing self; operatioally, such freedom may be defined as the number of behavioral alternatives available in a personality under normal conditions. Such behavioral freedom is not unlike that of a sailboat that can take full advantage of changing winds and currents by changing sails and direction, but is bound by the nature of the craft and the strength and direction of the forces driving it.

> We say of a boat skimming the water with light foot, "How free she runs," when we mean how perfectly she obeys the great breath out of the heavens that fills her sails. Throw her head up into the wind and see how she will halt and stagger, how every sheet will shiver and her whole frame will be shaken, how instantly she is 'in irons' in the expressive phrase of the sea. She is free only when you have let her fall off again and she has recovered once more her nice adjustment to the forces she must obey and cannot defy (Wilson, 1926).

In thinking of preventive action as increasing or enhancing man's behavioral degrees of freedom, one must refer to Kubie's relentless pursuit of this notion in differentiating normal behavior from neurotic behavior. His contention is that socially positive behavior can be the consequence of either healthy or neurotic processes, but that there is a basic difference in organismic elasticity or homeostasis between the normal and neurotic. This elasticity manifests itself in the individual's freedom and flexibility to learn through experience, to change and to adapt to changing external circumstances.

> Thus, the essence of normality is flexibility, in contrast to the freezing of behavior into patterns of unalterability . . . that characterize every manifestation of the neurotic process whether in impulses, purposes, acts, thoughts, or feelings. No single psychological act can be looked upon as neurotic unless it is the product of processes that predetermine a tendency to its automatic repetition (Kubie, 1954).

In brief, the neurotic is like the magic broom in "The Sorcerer's Apprentice"; he cannot change or curtail actions and becomes overwhelmed by the consequences of repetitive behavior. In its beginnings repetitive behavior represents an economic and ecological solution to a problem or conflict faced by the organism. Because the essence of the solution is only dimly perceived by the individual, the pursuit becomes more and more relentless and recurring. Since such goals are basically symbolic and highly masked to the individual, the chances of crossing the goal line and moving on to new patterns of behavior are slim.

Considerable clinical evidence supports the view that fixed or rigid patterns of behavior are derived from the unconscious components of personality. Despite the possibility that behavior primarily motivated by unconscious forces may be useful and valuable in maintaining the health and personality integration of the individual, such behavior is relatively unresponsive to changing environmental conditions. On the other hand, behavior resulting from forces at a level of relative awareness is most often directed at goals that are reasonably attainable and, subsequently, reduces the need to continue the same pattern of behavior. The degrees of freedom or the number of behavioral alternatives available to an individual are therefore enhanced to the extent to which his behavior is the result of preconscious or conscious forces in the personality.

One might well question the assumption, as does Redlich (1952), that acts determined by conscious or preconscious forces move the individual in a more healthful direction than acts determined by unconscious forces. For example, are not unconscious defense mechanisms health-producing and health-oriented in their adaptive and ego-protective goals? To the extent to which the organism needs ego defense to maintain himself and mediate noxious forces in his environment, such defenses are health producing. Yet, the increased use of such unconscious defenses will, in the long run, render the organism less and less able to choose alternative modes of behaving and weave into the personality an inflexible and repetitive behavior pattern (Kubie, 1957). It is also true, however, that repetitive, inflexible types of behavior can produce benefits in some relationships, particularly in specific vocations or jobs. Neurotic processes in individuals can and do result in *culturally defined* successful behavior, just as one can be a blatant failure without benefit of personality defect or neurosis.

The concept of degrees of behavioral freedom as differentiating between health and illness is utilized by Murphy (1961) and by Bruner in their discussion of the differences between coping and defending. *In coping with problems,* one enhances and expands the resiliency and resources of the organism; *in defending against problems,* developmental blocks and distortions develop, reducing the resiliency and resources of the organism and depriving it of the freedom to act in new ways. Coping can be conceived of as integrative to personality, defending as disintegrative. Bruner points out that there is always a mixture of coping and defending in dealing with problems, but it is highly important that one distinguish sharply between the two processes which can best be made in terms of learning effectiveness.

> Let me suggest that effective cognitive learning in school—in contrast to the gratification-demanding, action-related, and affect-infused earlier learning—depends upon a denaturing process, if I may use such a fanciful expression. This involves at least three things. It requires, first, the development of a system of cognitive organization that detaches concepts from the modes of action that they evoke. A hole exists without the act of digging. Secondly, it requires the development of a capacity to detach concepts from these affective contexts. A father exists without reference to the thinker's feeling of ambivalence. It demands moreover, a capacity to delay gratification so that, figuratively, each act of acquiring knowledge is not self sufficiently brought to an end either by success or failure, and whatever happens can be taken as informative and not as simply frustrating or gratifying (Bruner, p. 8).

In a defensive, neurotic pattern of behavior, inflexibility or illness would reduce the effectiveness of the organism's functioning, especially as a constructive social being. Thus, one index of the health of a community or a society could be the ways people choose to spend their time, especially their uncommitted time. Meier (1959) sees the possibility of compiling an index representing the variety of life in a society—specifically, ways in which people *choose* to spend their time. He proposes that an increase in variety almost always reflects an enhancement in social integration and that

> human hours have allocation properties which are not dissimilar from those applied to land. Time, like land, can only be consumed or wasted. There are only trivial exceptions to this rule. Yet, intuitively, we have the general impression that time can be conserved. Like money income, it can be invested. Schooling and the acquisition of skills are examples of such investments of human hours. The return on the investment is not more time but an increase in the range of choice in gainful employment and in social activities. Thus, we arrive at a significant index for social progress: variety in the pattern of life (p. 29).

One could, therefore, conceive of *degrees of behavioral freedom* in terms of operational social indexes that would reflect changes in variety and patterns of life and could be used as a method of evaluating preventive programs. For example, one might examine the allocation of time of persons with personality disturbances or a mentally ill group in a hospital as compared to various other persons and communities.

A Framework For Prevention

The zonal classifications of people and services in Figure 1 presents a framework and a functioning methodology for prevention. Primary prevention can be considered medical, social, or psychological action within Zones I and II, which reduces the need for the services and institutions of Zones III or IV. The goals of such action, with respect to the institutions and services of Zone I and Zone II, are threefold:

1. To increase the biological robustness of human beings by strengthening those institutions and agencies directly involved in prenatal, pregnancy, and early infant care.

2. To increase the flexibility of the agencies serving persons of Zones I and II, so that such agencies may encompass and affect a greater variety and number of persons in the general population. For example, the extension of school services for retarded or emotionally disturbed children may make it possible for a child usually needing Zone III or IV services to remain in Zone

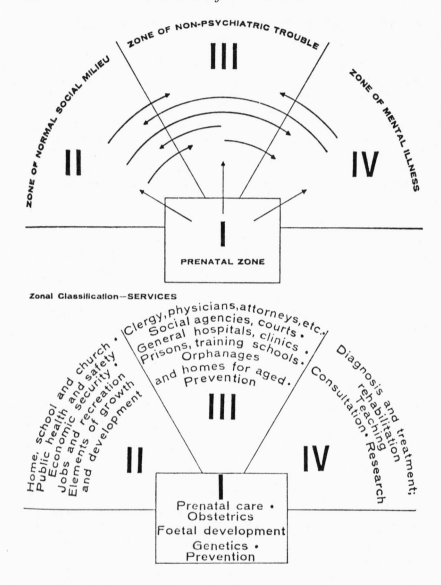

FIGURE 1. Zonal classifications of people and services. These are indicative, rather than inclusive. From Daniel Blain, M.D. Copyright, The American Psychiatric Association. Reproduced by permission.

II. The utilization of prenatal medical or nursing advisory services for lower-class pregnant mothers may be significantly influenced by placing such services close to neighborhood shopping or laundry centers. Or the presence of a counseling center for workers may make the difference for a number of individuals in maintaining employment and family economic support.

3. To assist primary institutions in planning individual and social techniques by which stress immunity or manageability can become a natural outcome of their relationship to children and their families.

It is evident that, in this scheme of primary prevention, the preventive forces will be those affecting the operation, accessibility, adaptability and modifiability of the institutions and agencies found in Zones I and II. Particularly, one needs to determine (a) which specific social and community forces tend to push Zone II persons into requiring Zone III or IV services; (b) how present medical, genetic and biological information can be translated into social action so as to reduce the number of Zone I infants entering Zones III or IV; and (c) how Zones I and II agencies and institutions can be reinforced, modified or developed to lessen the need for Zones III and IV services.

The institutions and agencies in Zones I and II can be denoted as the front-line defenses of a community. If such institutions and agencies cannot adequately serve individuals in their field, Zones III or IV services are required. Some of the forces moving people into Zones III or IV are the number and character of the emotionally hazardous situations and crises the individual has been required to mediate and manage, and how mediation and management were accomplished. The key, therefore, to movement from one zone to another lies in the quality of the mediation (coping or defending) of the emotionally hazardous situation or crisis. Klein and Lindemann (1961) define an emotionally hazardous situation as any sudden alteration in the field of social forces affecting an individual so that the individual's perception and expectation of self and others undergo change. In each instance an emotionally hazardous situation or crisis is a normal life occurrence that is temporarily upsetting, not always in an unpleasant sense, but one that necessitates rapid reorganization and mobilization of an individual's personality resources. Such life situations as birth of a sibling, death of a loved one, school entrance, school failure, marriage, job promotion, divorce, or inheritance of a large sum of money from a dead uncle's estate are examples of emotionally hazardous situations. The hazard in these situations is that the individual may find himself unable to manage the increased stress in a healthful way. Yet, such hazards and hurdles are part of the normal process of living and are, in large part, the cutting edges that sharpen and crystallize personality development and integration.

Whether for good or bad, emotionally hazardous crises have these aspects in common: (a) They cause a rise in inner tension and uneasiness; (b) they cause some disorganization in normal functioning; and (c) they necessitate some internal change in self to manage the situation. In baseball parlance, an individual in an emotionally hazardous situation is said to "stand loose at the plate," that is, the individual is lightly balanced to be able to move quickly in any direction. During this period of relative instability, minimal forces have their greatest effects, much like the effect of a one-gram weight at one end of a delicately balanced teeter-totter. Such a gram of weight would have little effect if the forces governing the organism were relatively stable.

The implications of the emotionally vulnerable situation or crisis as a fulcrum for preventive action is clear. To the extent to which such situations can be identified and the "crisis" institution or agency prepared and strengthened to make the most of this opportunity, to that extent can it place grams of force on the side of health and personality growth. In primary prevention one is focused on the emotionally hazardous situation that occurs in the context of the operation of each of the services or agencies in Zones I or II. Such institutions and agencies are often aware of some crises and do a great deal to help individuals deal effectively with them. Sometimes, however, the agency or service may fail to recognize relevant crises, or fail to take advantage of the health-producing potential of the situation. For example, the school may well be aware of the effect of the birth of a child on his siblings but, as an institution, it is seldom in a position to obtain and use this information systematically. Such an important and natural event in the lives of children may be sufficiently upsetting to the sibling to warrant some attention by the school. To capitalize on this emotionally hazardous situation, teachers may need to plan opportunities for the sibling to be recognized, to be helpful, to be successful—in short, to help the child, within the structure and role of the institution, to manage and mediate the crisis. In some cases, the child may need no more than an extra pat on the back from the teacher. In others, a planned conference with parents may be of some help. What is critical is the recognition by the institution of the emotionally vulnerable position of the child and a readiness to act positively upon it.

TABLE I lists some services and institutions of Zones I and II, along with some emotionally hazardous and enhancing situations or crises that occur in relation to each institution, with some possibilities for preventive action in each case. Neither the services, hazards, nor action possibilities listed are intended to be comprehensive or exhaustive. However, this conceptualization may help provide a fulcrum for the development of pilot and experimental studies and other preventive programs that can be delineated and evaluated. For example, the first emotional hazard under "family" is that of loss of father through death, divorce, or desertion. With few exceptions, the burden for breadwinning is thrust upon the mother who, in turn, finds it necessary to depend upon child-caring services for her children. In part, such services are provided by relatives, friends, nursery schools, foster homes and child care centers. In California, child care centers were initiated during World War II to increase the labor force, and have since continued in operation to serve one-parent families of modest incomes and some families of teachers and nurses. Such a child care facility usually serves preschool children all day and cares for school children part of the day.

There is sufficient evidence to support the hypothesis that one-parent families are more vulnerable to stress and emotional hazards than are intact families. The child care facility, properly staffed and oriented, would then be a potentially preventive force in developing and maintaining some type of assistance and

TABLE I

Zone II Service	Normal Emotional Hazard	Possibilities For Preventive Action
1. Family	Loss of father through death, divorce or desertion	Reinforcement of child-care services for working mothers
	Loss of mother	Reinforcement of foster-home services
	Adolescence	Increase in staff and professionalization of high school counselors, deans, and vice-principals
	Birth of sibling	Pediatric or well-baby clinic counseling
	Death	Management of grief—religious or community agency worker
2. Public health	Phenylketonuria	Detection and diet
	Childhood illnesses	Vaccination, immunization
	Stress caused by children—economic, housing, etc.	Reinforcement of well-baby clinic through mental health consultation to staff
	Pregnancy	Adequate prenatal care for mothers of lower socioeconomic status
3. School	Birth of sibling	Recognition of event by school and appropriate intervention
	School entrance of child	Screening vulnerable children
	Intellectual retardation	Special classes and assistance
	Teacher concern and anxiety about a child's behavior	Consultation by mental health specialists
	School failure	Early identification and prevention through appropriate school programs
4. Religion	Marriage	Counseling by clergy
5. Job or profession	Promotion or demotion	Opportunity to define role through services of a mental health counselor
6. Recreation	Appropriate and rewarding use of leisure time	Active community and city recreational programs
7. Housing	Lack of space—need for privacy	Working with architects and housing developers

support for the mothers and children utilizing this service. Such assistance could be provided by a psychiatric social worker or another professional person hired to work with the child care staff or families. In theory, the child care center as a primary institution would be reinforced as a preventive agency by enlisting trained personnel to work with parents or child care staff on the normal problems of people who are bringing up children but who are obliged to work at the same time.

Or, let us take the emotional hazard of pregnancy and birth. One of the points made by Wortis (1963), Pasamanick (1956), Freedman (1960) and others is that adequate prenatal and natal care is a significant and far-reaching measure in the prevention of neuropsychiatric disorders in children. In most cases, such care is available. Yet, significant numbers of mothers in lower socioeconomic neighborhoods are not normally motivated to seek medical care during pregnancy. Ordinarily they will use medical assistance only as a last resort. Many such mothers would take advantage of preventive medical services if such services were present somewhere along the paths they normally travel, or if they could be motivated to detour a few blocks for them. For example, space in empty stores near laundromats or markets could be rented for health department personnel and manned by nurses who could spend time with a mother while she was shopping or waiting for her load of wash. Such a program could be evaluated by comparing rates of premature births, birth injuries, or other birth difficulties before and after the service, or with rates in neighborhoods where no such service exists.

Fulcra For Prevention

It is increasingly evident that there are three basic interrelated ingredients in primary prevention: (1) a healthful birth experience, (2) a healthful family experience, and (3) a successful school experience. Healthful birth experiences are largely the result of early medical care and advice that help prospective mothers obtain and use preventive medical care. Although the evidence is far from complete, Bowlby (1951), Brody (1956) and Ribble (1943), to name only three, have emphasized the primacy of family relationships and their effect on the mental health of children. Bowlby summarized numerous studies from various countries that illustrated the emotional impact on children of early separation from their parents. Ribble and Brody studied the pivotal relationship of mothering and personality development, and Caplan (1951) pointed out how a neighborhood health center can be a preventive force in enhancing and strengthening family resources for the child. Goodrich (1961), at the Bio-Social Growth Center of the National Institute of Mental Health, studied the emotional hazard of early separation of the child from the mother in a nursery school setting. He found this crisis a potentially manageable staging area for research in primary prevention and suggested some areas of developmental influences that effect how a child or family manages a crisis. Early separation anxieties in a child often mean the possibility of greater problems later on with school entrance or bereavement.

The school has become increasingly primary to a child's personality growth. Consequently it can be the prime mover for alerting parents whose children need additional help or support within the school or, in some cases, additional services outside the school. In essence, the role of the school as a preventive force is realized to the extent to which it is able to make the educational experience a successful learning experience for all children. Two studies from widely disparate sources illustrate the intertwined threads of successful school experience and primary prevention. In a thirty-year follow-up study of children who had been referred to a municipal clinic because of problem behavior, the investigators included students from the files of the public schools who matched the patients in age, sex, I.Q., race, and residence. In addition, this group was selected on the basis of having no school record of behavior or discipline problems. Although the investigators were not studying the health of the control group, they were struck with the fact "that the simple criteria used to choose the control subjects—no excessive absences, no full grades repeated, no disciplinary action recorded and an I.Q. of 80 or better—have yielded a strikingly healthy group" (O'Neal and Robbins, 1958). This was particularly striking since the control group was drawn largely from disadvantaged classes and a history of broken homes was found in one-third of the cases.

The other link of evidence relating school success and primary prevention is found in Ginzberg and his associates' monumental study of the ineffective soldier of World War II. They found that, while poverty, racial discrimination, and lack of industrialization could help explain higher rates of emotional instability for individuals who came from certain sections of the country, each of these factors was also related to the differentially low educational achievement of the region. The study demonstrated that, although a higher level of educational attainment was no safeguard against emotional disorders, the lower the educational level, the higher the incidence of emotional disorders. As to cause, Ginzberg noted, "A disturbed childhood is likely to be reflected in learning difficulties; children who do poorly in school are likely to develop emotional problems (1959).

If the school is to become an effective preventive force, it must develop ways to identify early the children who are or are becoming learning problems, so that school and community resources can help such children most effectively and economically. The potential learning difficulty may be related to intellectual, emotional, or family-centered problems; even so, the problem may first manifest itself in the school, which can, if it recognizes the problem, pave the way for early help through parent conferences, counseling, or psychological or remedial service (Bower, 1960; 1961).

In job situations, the hazards seem to be just as numerous for going up the ladder as down. A person moving up in a large industrial or governmental agency may find it difficult to accept his new role or recast his loyalties with a particular group. He may have greater responsibility for men or production than he is able to manage. A staff-related mental health counselor in industry or work organization may provide some source of help for emotionally hazardous situations of this type.

Wilner and Walkley (1959) and others have mapped out preliminary steps for studying the interrelationships of housing and mental health. In studying the mental health of families in relation to their housing, including such things as the extent of plumbing leaks or the number of rats, the general impression of these investigators based on preliminary short-term evaluations is that moving from poor to good housing does not, on the average, result in measurable improvement in the mental health of the family. In the matter of housing and related social economic problems, one must be continually reminded of the large body of research describing the high, positive relationship between the indicators of social class and the many kinds of human illnesses. As Wilner and Walkley point out,

> The list of pathologies so related is long, beginning with early studies on crime and delinquency. Other examples are alcoholism, broken homes, and divorce (Beverly Hills notwithstanding) syphilis, tuberculosis, and childhood communicable diseases. New entries are being made as time goes by: Reading disability has entered the lists, as has the incidence of narcotics use among teenagers, as well as the incidence of mental illness.

Housing, by and large, shows a marked negative relationship with most illnesses so that, in general as housing deteriorates, illnesses rise. Psychoses have been found to increase with housing deterioration; neuroses, on the other hand, seem to increase with improved housing.

Whither Prevention?

Prevention is, at present, a high-status, magic word generally applicable to almost all professional endeavors in mental health. The term is applicable to newer and more effective treatment methods for schizophrenia, preventive hospitalization of suicidal patients or the use of drugs for quieting patients, or, in vague or general terms, to improved housing, better human relations, better schools, more staff, and so on. This lack of specificity in the term "prevention" is especially critical in a field that already has a large element of vagueness and expansiveness. If, as Freud noted, thinking is action in rehearsal, it behooves individuals interested in preventive action to get into rehearsal ideas that are primarily preventive, specific enough to be replicated in more than one locality and operational enough to be evaluated within one's lifetime. Also, it must be kept in mind that the preventive battlegrounds are the primary institutions or agencies of a society. We must determine the specific interventions or modifications these institutions can make to reduce the stress vulnerability or enhance the personality resources of the human organisms they serve.

Prevention has to do with the quality of the interactions and the degree of effectiveness of the primary institutions of a society in providing each person with increments of ego strength and personality robustness for coping with the "slings and arrows" of life. The nature of these interactions and experiences would be considered preventive to the extent to which such experiences enhance the degrees of psychological freedom of an individual to select behavioral alternatives and to act upon them. This preventive model and point of view was succinctly illustrated by an old Cornish test of insanity related by Woodward. The test situation comprised a sink, a tap of running water, a bucket, and a ladle. The bucket was placed under the tap of running water and the subject asked to bail the water out of the bucket with the ladle. If the subject continued to bail without paying some attention to reducing or preventing the flow of water into the pail, he was judged to be mentally incompetent. Similarly, any society that attempts to provide more and larger buckets to contain the problems of that society, without simultaneously attempting to reduce the flow, might be equally suspect. Treatment, rehabilitation, and incarceration are our necessary buckets to contain the flow. Prevention, however, deals with the tap, the sources of flow, and the leverages needed to turn the faucet down or off.

References

Bellak, L.: *Schizophrenia: A Review Of The Syndrome*. New York, Logos Press, p. viii, 1959.

Bower, E. M.: *Early Identification Of Emotionally Handicapped Children In School*. Springfield, Thomas, 1960.

Bower, E. M.: Primary prevention in a school setting. In *Prevention Of Mental Disorders In Children*, G. Caplan, ed. New York, Basic Books, 1961, pp. 353-377.

Bowlby, J.: *Maternal Care And Mental Health.* Geneva, Switzerland, WHO, 1951.

Brody, S.: *Patterns Of Mothering.* New York, Int. Univs., 1956.

Bruner, J. S.: On Coping and Defending. Mimeographed.

Caplan, G.: A public health approach to child psychiatry. *Ment Hyg,* 35: 235-249, 1951.

Cumming, E., and Cumming J.: *Closed Ranks.* Cambridge, Harvard, 1957.

Dubos, R.: *Mirage Of Health,* New York, Harper, 1959.

Eissler, R.: Scapegoats of society. In *Searchlights On Delinquency,* K. R. Eissler, ed. New York, Int. Univs., 1955, p. 228.

Farnsworth, D. L.: The provision of appropriate treatment: hospital and community collaboration. Ment Hosp, 12: 18, 1961.

Fox, T. F.: Priorities. In *Steps In The Development Of Integrated Psychiatric Services.* New York, Milbank Memorial Fund, 1960, p. 16.

Freedman, A., et al.: The influence of hyperbilirubinemia on the early development of the premature. *Psychiat Res Rep, 13:* 108-123, 1960.

Gardner, J.: *Excellence.* New York, Harper, 1961, p. 115.

Ginzberg, E., and Associates: *The Ineffective Soldier: Lessons For Management And The Nation.* New York, Columbia, 1959, p. 118.

Goodrich, D. W.: Possibilities for preventive intervention during initial personality formation. In *Prevention Of Mental Disorders In Children,* G. Caplan, ed. New York, Basic Books, 1961, pp. 249-264.

Hofstadter, R.: *Social Darwinism In American Thought.* Boston, Beacon, 1955.

Homer: *The Odyssey.* W. H. D. Rouse, Trans. New York, Mentor, 1949, p. 108.

Kawi, A. A., and Pasamanick, B.: *The Association Of Factors Of Pregnancy With The Development Of Reading Disorders In Childhood.* Yellow Springs, Ohio, Society for Research in Child Development, 1959.

Klein, D., and Lindemann, E.: Preventive intervention in individual and family crisis situations. In *Prevention Of Mental Disorders In Children,* G. Caplan, ed. New York, Basic Books, 1961, pp. 283-306.

Kubie, L. S.: The fundamental nature of the distinction between normality and neuroses. *Psychoanal Quart, 23:* 183, 1954.

Kubie, L. S.: Social forces and the neurotic process. In *Explorations In Social Psychiatry*, A. Lexington *et al.*, eds. New York, Basic Books, 1957.

Meier, R. L.: Human time allocation: A basis for social accounts. *J Amer Institute Planners*, 25(Nov.):27-33, 1959.

Murphy, G.: The prevention of mental disorder: Some research suggestions. *J Hillside Hosp*, 9: 146, 1960.

Murphy, L. B.: Preventive implications of development in the preschool years. In *Prevention Of Mental Disorders In Children*, G. Caplan, ed. New York, Basic Books, 1961, pp. 218-248.

O'Neal, P., and Robbins, L.: The relation of childhood behavior problems to adult psychiatric status. *Amer J Psychiat, 114:* 968, 1958.

Pasamanick, B.: The epidemiology of behavior disorders of childhood. In *Neurology And Psychiatry In Childhood*. Baltimore, William and Wilkins, 1956.

Redlich, F. C.: The concept of health in psychiatry. In *Explorations In Social Psychiatry*, A. Leighton *et al.*, eds. New York, Basic Books, 1957.

Ribble, M.: *The Rights Of Infants*. New York, Columbia, 1943.

Sanford, R. N.: The development of the healthy personality in the society of today. In *Modern Mental Health Concepts And Their Application In Public Health Education*. Berkeley, State Department of Public Health, 1959, p. 8.

Stevenson, I.: Direct instigation of behavioral changes in psychotherapy. AMA, *Arch Gen Psychiat, 1:* 99-107, 1959.

Wilner, D., and Walkley, R.: Housing environment and mental health. In *Epidemiology Of Mental Disorder*. Washington, D.C., American Association for the Advancement of Science, 1959, pp. 143-174.

Wilson, W.: The New Freedom. In *Essays Old And New*, Essie Chamberlain, ed. New York, Harcourt, 1926, p. 43.

Wortis, H.; Heimer, C. B.; Braine, M.; Redlo, M., and Rue, R.: Growing up in Brooklyn: An early history of the premature child. *Amer J Orthopsychiat, 33(3):*535-539, 1963.

Bibliography

Aaronson, Shirley: Changes in I.Q. and reading performance of a disturbed child. *Reading Teacher, 19:* 91, 1965.

Angrist, S. S.: Mental illness and deviant behavior. *Sociolog Quart, 7:* 446, 1966.

Arrill, Mildred, and Braun, Samuel: Programs for emotionally disturbed children. *Childhood Educ, 42:* 21, 1965.

Balow, Bruce: The emotionally and socially handicapped. *Rev Educ Res, 36:* 120-133, 1966.

Bentzen, Frances A.: Educational programming for disturbed children. *Amer J Orthopsychiat, 32:* 472-76, 1962.

Berkowitz, Pearl, and Rothman, Esther P.: *The Disturbed Child.* New York, N.Y., 1960.

Bernstein, Lewis, and Burris, B. Cullen (Eds.): *The Contribution Of The Social Sciences To Psychotherapy.* Springfield, Thomas, 1967.

Blackham, Garth: *The Deviant Child In The Classroom.* Belmont, California, Wadsworth, 1967.

Blinder, Martin: The pragmatic classification of depression. *Amer J Psychiat, 123:* 259, 1966.

Bower, Eli M.: *Early Identification Of Emotionally Handicapped Children In School.* Springfield, Thomas, 1960.

Brody, Elaine: The need for refinements in the techniques of interdisciplinary hostility for social workers and psychologists. *Amer J Orthopsychiat, 37:* 797, 1967.

Bromberg, Walter: History of the treatment of mental disorders. In *The Encyclopedia of Mental Health,* Albert Deutch, Ed. New York, Watts, 1963, vol. III, pp. 37-46.

Carroll, Lewis: *Alice In Wonderland.* New York, Random, 1946.

Clark, Donald H., and Lesser, Gerald: *Emotional Disturbance And School Learning: A Book Of Readings.* Chicago, Sci. Res. Assoc., 1965.

Clausen, John A.: *Sociology And The Field Of Mental Health.* New York, Russell Sage, 1956.

Dain, Norman: Concepts of insanity. In *The United States 1789-1865.* New Brunswick, N.J., Rutgers, 1964.

Denty, Ralph, and Yates, William: Empatherapy: Reaching the emotionally disturbed child," *Education, 85:* 425, 1965.

Reprinted from *"Emotionally Disturbed": A Terminological Inquiry.* Unpublished doctoral dissertation by Naomi W. Cohen, Arizona State University, Tempe, 1968. By permission of the author.

Despert, J. Louise: *The Emotionally Disturbed Child—Then and Now.* New York, Robert Brunner, 1965.

Dunham, H. Warren: *Sociological Theory And Mental Disorder.* Detroit, Wayne, 1959.

Emery, Louise: Diagnosis of childhood schizophrenia. *Exceptional Child, 33:* 265, 1966.

Emotionally disturbed children: Whose fault? Whose responsibility? *Instructor, 77:* 22, 1967.

Eron, Leonard D.: *The Classification Of Behavior Disorders.* Chicago, Aldine, 1966.

Farnsworth, Dana L.: *Psychiatry, Education And The Young Adult.* Springfield, Thomas, 1966.

Goldman, William, and May, Anne: Dynamics of classroom structure for emotionally disturbed children. *J School Health, 37:* 200, 1967.

Grossman, Herbert: *Teaching The Emotionally Disturbed.* New York, Holt, 1965.

Guttmacher, Manfred, and Weihoffen, Henry: *Psychiatry And The Law.* New York, Norton, 1952.

Haring, Norris, and Phillips, E. Lakin: *Educating Emotionally Disturbed Children.* New York, McGraw-Hill, 1962.

Hellmuth, Jerome: *Educational Therapy.* Seattle, Straub and Hellmuth, 1966, vol. I.

Hellmuth, Jerome: *Learning Disorders.* Seattle, Straub and Hellmuth, 1965, vol. I.

Hollingshead, August B., and Redlich, Frederick: *Social Class And Mental Illness.* New York, Wiley, 1958.

Hunter, Richard, and Macalpine, Ida: *Three Hundred Years Of Psychiatry, 1535-1860.* London, Oxford U. P., 1963.

Jenkins, Richard, and Cole, Jonathan: *Diagnostic Classification In Child Psychiatry.* Washington, Am. Psychiatric Asso., 1964.

Jones, Betty: Education of the emotionally disturbed child. *N.Y. State Education, 53:* 36, 1966.

Knoblock, Peter (Ed.): *Educational Programming For Emotionally Disturbed Children: The Decade Ahead.* New York, Syracuse, 1964.

Knoblock, Peter (Ed.): *Intervention Approaches In Educating Emotionally Disturbed Children.* New York, Syracuse, 1966.

Kraepelin, Emil: *One Hundred Years Of Psychiatry.* New York, Citadel, 1962.

Krim, S. (Ed.): The insanity bit. In *The Beats.* New York, Faucett, 1960, pp. 60-77.

Kubie, Laurence S.: Social forces and the neurotic process. In *Explorations In Social Psychiatry*, Leighton, Clausen, and Wilson, Eds. New York, Basic Books, 1957.

Kupferman, Saul C., and Ulmer, Raymond A.: An experimental total push program for emotionally disturbed adolescents. *Personnel Guidance J, 62:* 896, 1964.

Kupper, William: *Dictionary Of Psychiatry And Psychology.* Paterson, N.J., Colt Press, 1953.

Kvaraceus, William C.: Emotionally disturbed and socially inadequate. *Education, 85:* 91, 1964.

Lavietes, Ruth: The teacher's role in the education of the emotionally disturbed child. *Amer J Orthopsychiat, 32:* 854-56, 1962.

Levy, Jerome (Ed.): *Dialogues: Behavioral Science Research Approaches To Selected Mental Health Problems.* Boulder, Colorado, Western Interstate Commission for Higher Education, 1965.

Liebman, Samuel (Ed.): *Management Of Emotional Problems In Medical Practice.* Philadelphia, Lippincott, 1956.

Llorens, Lela, and Rubin, Eli: *Developing Ego Functions In Disturbed Children.* Detroit, Wayne, 1967.

Long, Nicholas; Morse, William, and Newman, Ruth (Eds.): *Conflict In The Classroom: The Education Of Emotionally Disturbed Children.* Belmont, California, Wadsworth, 1965.

Luszki, Margaret: *Interdisciplinary Team Research Methods And Problems.* Washington, National Training Laboratories, N.E.A., 1958.

MacKenzie, Norman (Ed.): *A Guide To The Social Sciences.* New York, New Am. Lib., 1966.

Manlove, Frances: Aggressive symptoms in emotionally disturbed adopted children. *Child Develop, 36:* 519, 1965.

Mateer, Florence: *The Unstable Child.* New York, Appleton, 1924.

Meiselman, Bernard: Helping the emotionally disturbed child. *Wisconsin J Educ, 97:* 12, 1965.

Merton, R. K.: *Social Theory And Social Structure.* Glencoe, Illinois, Glencoe Press, 1963.

Mesinger, John F.: Professional training to work with seriously socially and emotionally disturbed children. *Virginia J Educ, 59:* 14, 1965.

Mohr, George J., and Despres, Marian A.: *The Stormy Decade: Adolescence.* New York, Random House, 1958.

Noffsinger, Thomas: A survey of follow-up procedures in residential treatment facilities for emotionally disturbed children in the U.S. *Mind Or Matter, 12:* 1, 1967.

Pasamanick, B.: Epidemiologic investigation of some prenatal factors in the production of neuropsychiatric disorder. In *Comparative Epidemiology Of The Mental Disorders*, P. H. Hoch and J. Zubin, Eds. New York, Grune and Stratton, 1961, pp. 260-75.

Patrick, Sister Mary: Identifying the emotionally disturbed. *Catholic School J*, *115:* 47, 1965.

Pearson, Gerald: *Emotional Disorders Of Children*. New York, Norton, 1949.

Philips, Irving: Psychopathology and mental retardation. *Amer J Psychiat*, *124:* 43, 1967.

Potter, Howard W.: Schizophrenia in children. *Amer J Psychiat*, *139:* 1253-70, 1933.

Psychopathological Disorders In Childhood: Theoretical Considerations And A Proposed Classification. New York, Group for the Advancement of Psychiatry, 1966, vol. VI.

Quay, Herbert; Morse, William, and Cutler, Richard: Personality patterns of pupils in special classes for the emotionally disturbed. *Exceptional Child*, *32:* 297-301, 1966.

Rabkin, Leslie (Ed.): *Psychopathology And Literature*. San Francisco, Chandler Pub., 1966.

Radin, Sherwin: Orthopsychiatry and special services for emotionally disturbed children in a public school setting. *J School Health*, *36:* 246-47, 1966.

Reese, Frederick D.: School age suicide and the educational environment. *Theory Into Practice*, *7:* 10-13, 1968.

Reichenbach, H.: *Elements Of Symbolic Logic*. New York, Macmillan, 1947.

Rickard, Henry, and Deinoff, Michael: Behavior change in a therapeutic summer camp for emotionally disturbed boys. *J Genet Psychol*, *110:* 181, 1967.

Rothschild, Barbara: Incubator isolation as a possible contributing factor to the high incidence of emotional disturbance among prematurely born persons. *J Genet Psychol*, *110:* 287, 1967.

Rubin, Eli, *et al.*: *Emotionally Handicapped Children And The Elementary School*. Detroit, Wayne, 1966.

Rubin, Sol: *Psychiatry And Criminal Law: Illusions, Fictions And Myths*. Dobbs Ferry, New York, Oceana, 1965.

Russell, Bertrand: The cult of common usage. *Brit J Philosophy Sci*, *3:* 303, 1953.

Scheffler, Israel: *The Language Of Education*. Springfield, Thomas, 1960.

Siemens, Margaret: The emotionally disturbed—How much do they benefit from the regular classroom? *Ohio School, 42:* 28, 1964.

Silving, Helen: *Essays On Mental Incapacity And Criminal Conduct.* Springfield, Thomas, 1967.

Smith, B. Othaniel, and Ennis, Robert (Eds.): *Language And Concepts In Education.* Chicago, Rand McNally, 1961.

Smith, Edward; Krause, Stanley Jr., and Atkinson, Mark: *The Educator's Encyclopedia.* Englewood Cliffs, N.J., Prentice-Hall, 1961.

Spivack, George, and Levine, Murray: The Devereux child behavior rating scales. *Amer J Ment Defic, 68:* 700, 1964.

Stimpfig, A. T.: Ten troubled children. *School And Community, 53:* 8, 1967.

Sullivan, Ellen Blythe: Emotional disturbance among children. *J Juvenile Res, 16:* 56-65, 1932.

Szasz, Thomas S.: *Law, Liberty And Psychiatry: An Inquiry.* New York, Macmillan, 1963.

Szasz, Thomas S.: *The Myth Of Mental Illness.* London, Secker and Warburg, 1962.

Tesch, Robert: Study-work programs for emotionally disturbed students. *Wisconsin J Educ, 98:* 11, 1965.

Ullman, Leonard, and Krasner, Leonard: *Case Studies In Behavior Modification.* New York, Holt, 1965.

Wattenburg, William (Ed.): Social deviancy among youths. In *Sixty-fifth Yearbook Of The National Society For The Study Of Education,* Chicago, U. of Chicago, 1966, part I.

Webster, Thomas: Problems of emotional disturbance in young retarded children. *Amer J Psychiat, 120:* 37, 1963.

White, Mary Alice, and Charry, June: *School Disorder, Intelligence And Social Class.* New York, Teachers' College Press, 1966.

Williams, M. E. K.: Help for the teacher of disturbed children in the public schools. *Exceptional Child, 34:* 87, 1967.

Winton, Rebecca, and Fleiss, Bernice: Guidelines to teaching emotionally disturbed children. *Instructor, 75:* 39, 1965.

Index